The Mulligan Guide to
SPORTS
JOURNALISM
Careers

The Mulligan Guide to
SPORTS
JOURNALISM
Careers

Joseph F. Mulligan ◆ Kevin T. Mulligan

VGM Career Horizons
NTC/Contemporary Publishing Group

Library of Congress Cataloging-in-Publication Data

Mulligan, Joseph F., 1931–
    The Mulligan guide to sports journalism careers / Joseph F. Mulligan and
    Kevin T. Mulligan
       p.   cm.
    Includes index.
    ISBN 0-8442-4540-2
    1. Sports journalism—Vocational guidance.   I. Mulligan, Kevin T.
II. Title.
    PN4784.S6M85   1998
    070.4′49796′023—dc21
                                         98-8171
                                           CIP

Cover design by Amy Yu Ng
Cover photographs: top left, copyright © Tim DeFrisco/Allsport USA; top right,
copyright © Otto Greule/Allsport USA; bottom, copyright © Doug
Pensinger/Allsport USA
Interior design by City Desktop Productions, Inc.

Published by VGM Career Horizons
A division of NTC/Contemporary Publishing Group, Inc.
4255 West Touhy Avenue, Lincolnwood (Chicago), Illinois 60646-1975 U.S.A.
Copyright © 1999 by Joseph F. Mulligan and Kevin T. Mulligan
Manufactured in the United States of America
International Standard Book Number: 0-8442-4540-2

98 99 00 01 02 03 CU 19 18 17 16 15 14 13 12 11 10 9 8 7 6 5 4 3 2 1

I wish to dedicate this book to the Mulligan family, one and all, but especially to its heart and soul, Betty, quintessential wife and mother. As always, she provided encouragement, unfailing support, unselfishness, and her best gift—her love.

—Joseph Mulligan

To Dad and Mom, for a lifetime of support and encouragement as I pursued my sportswriting dream.

To my sisters Chris, Karen, Tricia, Nancy, and Kate; and brother Terry—the most loyal fans a sportswriter could ever ask for.

To Drs. Gerald Waite and Ed Walsh, who provided direction and polish to an aspiring college sportswriter many years ago.

To Art Wolfe, my first boss, for getting me started the right way.

Finally, congratulations, Dad, for pulling this off against incredible odds (and me on the disabled list). Your dedication is amazing.

—Kevin Mulligan

Contents

Acknowledgments

By Joseph Mulligan:

The development of this book required and received a classic team effort. My deep and warmest thanks are for the unbelievable efforts of my talented son Kevin, who played hurt through all these innings, and two Mulligan sisters, because we wouldn't have succeeded without their professional efforts:

- To Kate for her strong, well-written chapter on media relations, and for her excellent interviews and research for other sections.

- To Karen Mulligan Heiser, invaluable as our technical and production expert, our remote transcriptionist, and our unselfishly hardworking partner, especially under pressure. She was an inspiration; she made things happen.

By both of us:

- The editorial team of copy editor John Conceison (*Union-News*, Springfield, Mass.); and no-punches-pulled critic/reviewer, Betty Mulligan.

- To all of clan Mulligan, always volunteering to give aid, comfort, advice, and hard work.

- To two pros who provided early encouragement for this project when we needed it: Professor Ed Walsh of Slippery

Rock University (retired) and Mr. Robert Calvert of Garrett Park Press.

- To editor Betsy Lancefield (VGM), for her patience, guidance, and enthusiasm for this book.

- To this great group of sports journalism professionals, coaches, and players who helped us in many ways (in no particular order):

  - Craig Branson, American Society of Newspaper Editors (ASNE)

  - Joe Paterno, head football coach, Penn State University

  - Melvin Helitzer, author, and teacher, Ohio State University

  - Duke Little, career services coordinator, *Sports Careers*

  - Mike Sansone, sports copy desk chief, *Sacramento Bee*

  - Anne Glover, assistant managing editor, copy desk, *St. Petersburg Times*

  - Jay Beberman, sports editor, Bloomberg Wire Services

  - Diane Tomasik, ex–copy editor, *Cincinnati Post*

  - Jim DeStefano, sports copy editor, *Philadelphia Daily News*

  - Rick Gosselin, columnist, *Dallas Morning News*

  - Adam Schefter, sportswriter, the *Denver Post*

  - Kevin Monaghan, director of business development, NBC Sports

  - Jack Gibbons, assistant managing editor for sports, the *Baltimore Sun*

  - Donna Eyring, sports editor, the *Orlando Sentinel*

  - Mike Rathet, executive sports editor, *Philadelphia Daily News*

- Mike Emmett, managing editor, Total Sports on-line publications

- Stephanie Sawyer, intern, WCAU-TV (Philadelphia)

- Timothy S. McCarty, freelance television videographer

- David Bergman, sports photographer, *Miami Herald*

- Christine Brooks, teacher and author

- Josh Zeide, student journalism intern

- Gary Gach, author of writers.net

- Steve Outing, writer and president of Planetary News

- Michael Mercanti, executive photo editor, *Philadelphia Daily News*

- Scott Newman, sports business writer, Bloomberg Wire Services

- Andrew Brandt, sports attorney/agent

- Jeffrey Pollack, former editor, *The Sports Business Daily*

- Bill Carter, television/business writer, *New York Times*

- Will Wagner, editor, *Football Digest, Auto Racing Digest*

- Ray Didinger, NFL Films

- E. M. Swift, writer, *Sports Illustrated*

- David Scott, writer, *College Sports* magazine

- Mark Anderson, sports editor, *Gaston Gazette* (North Carolina)

- Todd Jones, reporter, *Columbus Dispatch*

- Mike Strom, sportswriter, *Times-Picayune* (New Orleans)

- John Rawlings, editor, *The Sporting News*

- Mark Kram, reporter, *Philadelphia Daily News*, and magazine freelance writer

- J. D. Lasica, copy chief, Microsoft's *San Francisco Sidewalk*

- Tom Watson, coeditor, *@NY* on-line publication

- Herman Holtz, consultant, and author

- Michael Perry, author

- Jon Hendershott, associate editor, *Track and Field News*

- Suzanne Halliburton, reporter, *Austin American Statesman*

- Howard Unger, freelance writer

- Tom Fuller, reporter, *Seattle Times*

- Steve Blust, sports editor, *Sacramento Bee*

- Ed Storin, secretary, Associated Press Sports Editors (APSE)

- Christian Ewell, reporter, *Baltimore Sun*

- Mike Krzyzewski, head basketball coach, Duke University

- Jane Allison Havsy, sports reporter for Gannett (New York) suburban newspapers

- Elliott Almond, investigative reporter, *Seattle Times*

- Armen Keteyian, sportswriter, CBS and HBO Sports

- Doug Looney, author and sports columnist, *The Christian Science Monitor.*

- Bobby Cremins, head basketball coach, Georgia Tech University

- Reggie White, Green Bay Packers

- Bobby Bowden, head football coach, Florida State University

- Bill Strickland, associate athletic director of external affairs, University of Massachusetts

- Larry Kimball, sports information director, Syracuse University

- John Calipari, head coach, New Jersey Nets

- Bill Little, associate athletic director for external operations, University of Texas

- Mike Tranghese, commissioner, Big East Conference

- Bob Kenworthy, sports information director, Gettysburg College (Pennsylvania)

- Charlie Bare, assistant sports information director, University of Virginia

- Leigh Torbin, media relations intern, University of Massachusetts

- Rick Brewer, assistant athletic director for sports information, University of North Carolina

- Sue Edson, sports information director, Syracuse University

- Larry Dougherty, assistant athletic director/sports media relations, St. Joseph's University

- Denise Gormley, assistant commissioner for public relations, Northeast Conference

- Harvey Greene, director of media relations, Miami Dolphins

- Jim Gallagher, former public relations director, Philadelphia Eagles

- Dave Coskey, vice president of marketing, Philadelphia 76ers

- Sandy Genelius, director of communications, CBS News

- Michael Humes, director of marketing, American Hockey League

- Kellee (Sparky) Harris, sports marketing specialist

- Jim Colony, radio sports broadcaster, WTAE (Pittsburgh)

- Harry Donahue, sportswriter, radio station KYW NewsRadio (Philadelphia)

- Richard C. Crepeau, radio sportswriter/professor

- Richard Johnson, anchor, ABC radio, and freelance writer, WNBC-TV (New York)

- Vernon Stone, professor, University of Missouri

- Fred Klein, sportswriter, *Wall Street Journal*

- Bill Fleischman, *Philadelphia Daily News*

The Mulligan Guide to
SPORTS
JOURNALISM
Careers

1 Welcome to the Wide, Wide World of Writing About Sports

Most Americans love sports. Millions of them love to play sports, watch sports, and read about sports. Many of them fantasize about playing professionally and then there are thousands of sports fans who dream of a career writing about the sports they love.

What a life. . . . Imagine getting the best seats at the prime sports events, press passes and special parking, interviews with sports heroes, complimentary meals—and then writing about all of it for magazines, newspapers, books, media guides, websites, and marketing brochures. Finally, imagine the satisfaction of seeing your words in print, to be read by tens of thousands or more, with your name in the byline and sometimes your picture.

What a job. But to get paid for it—that beats all!

As a result of the ever-increasing number of fans and the technological advances that popularize new and novel types of athletic competition, sports fever in America continues to grow and grow. There are more and more sports to enjoy, more and more teams to follow, and more and more fans to enjoy them. There are even more places to read about them. New sports publications hit the streets every month, while traditional sports media personnel work harder than ever to stay ahead of the competition. Newspapers program special pullout sections. Radio and television stations are continually expanding to keep pace with demand. And instantaneous coverage of all athletic competitions abounds in cyberspace for fans to access on their home and business PCs.

All of this portends tremendous opportunities for those who can write about sports and do it well.

Why We Wrote This Book

As a professional sportswriter, I (Kevin) am frequently called on to address young people who have an interest in the field of journalism. I enthusiastically accept and offer my time to schools and groups because I'm proud of my work and profession, and I'm certain that most of my colleagues also enjoy their speaking engagements and interaction with students. But one thing that surprises me in such exchanges is the apparent lack of knowledge students and teachers have about the business of writing about sports.

Although the questioners are usually bright high school juniors and seniors or young college students who are struggling with career decisions and beginning to plan their futures, they ask sports fan–type questions rather than what I'm expecting. I anticipate questions like "How can I become a sports journalist?" or "What's a writer's daily routine?" Instead they ask questions such as

- What's it like to be in the locker room?

- Do you get to go to away games?

- What's it like to interview John Elway?

These sessions usually begin that way, indicating to me that most 18- to 22-year-olds are totally unaware of the job. That's why my father and I felt that a comprehensive book on the subject would be helpful in informing students and interested novices about the wide world of sports journalism.

After those initial forays into "What's it like to . . . ," I ordinarily steer the talk toward when I was in a classroom, and the questions I thought they would ask if they were better acquainted with the business. Usually, I explain how I first became interested in sportswriting during my high school years and later, as an English major at Slippery Rock (Pa.) State College, pondered how I could combine my love of sports with my God-given talent for expressing myself via the written word. I related my experience as a member of the college paper, where my affection for the newspaper business grew more serious. I try to impress on students the importance and value of internships which helped me set newspaper sportswriting as my career goal. I think it's important for them to know how complete basic training is when you work on a suburban or small-town daily newspaper, as did thousands of established professionals like me.

Another point I try to stress with young people is that choosing a career should not be considered a 100-yard dash in college. Rather, it should be treated more like a marathon. There is no hurry. If it takes two years for you to begin focusing on a major, perhaps journalism, that's fine. Use that time wisely and test the waters. Set your sights on a broad-based education. Join the school paper, campus radio, and/or television station to help you identify your talents and give focus to your career interests.

That is what we want to result from your reading of this book— a piquing of your interest for certain jobs in the field so you'll be better able to inquire in depth about the work you might like to do.

Is This Book for You?

The audience for this book includes everyone who likes to write, enjoys the thrill of sports, and wants to experience the satisfaction and fulfillment of telling others about sports, in all of the many forms we'll be describing between these covers. But it's not only for newcomers. It's also for the writers and other professionals in broader communications and journalism fields who wish to explore career options in *sports* journalism. This book needs your attention if you're an undergraduate student enrolled in one of the following college programs:

- Journalism

- English

- Communications

- Sports journalism

- Photojournalism

- Sports management

- Radio and television

- Advertising and marketing

You will also be interested if you are a high school junior or senior with good writing skills or a reader of sports journalism who enjoys the inside stories of sports.

There are, of course, numerous books on the shelves covering the subject of journalism careers and sportswriting. They focus, however, almost exclusively on either general or nonsports journalism. Others focus on teaching writing mechanics in an instructional way.

That's why this book is unique. In these chapters, we explore the broad spectrum of writers' jobs in our sports-crazy society through the careers of respected professionals. Each describes the surprising number of exciting opportunities there are for talented writers who enjoy the excitement of organized athletic competition. We examine the pros and cons, the advantages and disadvantages of these interesting careers and provide a candid, no-punches-pulled analysis of what it takes to be successful.

In short, if you want to succeed in sports journalism, this book is definitely for you!

There are a few things you *won't* find in the chapters that follow. We haven't focused on

- Instructions on how to write. We examine how to capitalize on the skills you already possess.

- Stories only about the glamorous side of the journalist's life. We explain how this life can be both frustrating and enjoyable.

- The greatest sportswriters of our time—to the exclusion of the small-town journalists or those learning their trade at mid-size publications. We've examined professional life at all levels.

- The "big-four sports" (basketball, football, hockey, and baseball). We've interviewed journalists who write about all levels and types of amateur and professional sports.

What Is Sports Journalism?

There are those who say that sports journalism is an ancient profession, because Homer wrote about athletic events in *The Iliad*. Still others say that it dates back to the 19th century when Bat Masterson, of cowboy and western fame, was one of the earliest sports journalists. Masterson (1853–1921) was a scout, an Indian fighter, a buffalo hunter, and a deputy sheriff of Dodge City, Kansas. In 1902, he gave up his career as a gunslinger-lawman-gambler to work as a sportswriter in New York City. Masterson was named to the "Dream Team of Print Journalists" by the Associated Press Managing Editors (APME) in its "Eternal Journal" edition. (They also named John Steinbeck as the sports editor on their dream team.)

Our own working definition of sports journalism follows:

> Sports journalism is the research, compilation, and dissemination of sports information—whether it's in written, spoken, or visual form—for the benefit of readers, viewers, or listeners. It is usually factual, except when it's telling a fictional story. It is available to sports fans in newspapers, magazines, sportscasts, documentary films, on-line publications, advertising copy, marketing literature and plans, newsletters, news releases, books, and pictures.

We'll look at all of these forms of sports journalism in the pages ahead.

Whether you are a student of journalism, a recent graduate, an accomplished writer, or a grizzled veteran of the print or broadcast media, you know that to succeed in the business of sports journalism, you have to write well and you have to enjoy it. If you take pleasure in the process of envisioning an idea for a story, an advertisement, or a book and thrill at seeing the clarity, quality, and organization of the sentences you form to express your thoughts, then you can flourish as a sports journalist and you can have fun doing it.

We presume that you've already been honing writing talents with help from your creator, relatives, English teachers, university communications professor, editor, or associates, or by reading or listening to the best in the business. Writing is like that for many of us; we become better writers because we enjoy reading terrific prose (or poetry) written by someone else we would like to emulate. So, we become better writers by reading better writing and by thirsting for the joy of having our own material printed or spoken.

Now, having generalized a bit about the joy of writing good stuff and promising not to discuss the elements of composition or the importance of a robust vocabulary or detailed outlines, let's examine the real focus of this book. In order to become a sports journalist in any of the fine professions we'll discuss in this book, it's pretty obvious that you have to know the sports world well or have been an athlete, right? Wrong. Of course, it's an asset if you're a good writer and have played or enjoyed a number of the most popular sports. That background will allow you to work more confidently.

There are many of you who'll wonder whether there is a place in sportswriting for those who haven't been athletes or fans of a sport. Maybe you're a chess master, a poet, a mathematician, or (more predominant these days) a computer whiz. As you'll find in these pages, the sports world is big enough for all of us. There are exciting sports careers for lawyers, financial experts, photographers, advertising copywriters, teachers, marketers, editors, broadcasters, and others, even computer experts. But we need to emphasize this: You must be a good learner and a good writer capable of making even the most complicated or mundane aspect of a sport interesting to your readers. Your work has to make them come back for more.

The Scope of Journalism Careers

As you'll see within this book, newspaper reporting is only one of many exciting professions to consider within sports journalism. The American Society of Newspaper Editors offers this advice to students who are considering careers as journalists: "Most beginning journalists head into reporting, but the world of print and on-line media and the broadcast businesses also seek young talent as sports photojournalists, artists, copy editors, computer experts, librarians, and other specialists." We would add to those the professions of sports editing, investigative reporting, sports information (media relations), sports magazine writing, advertising and marketing, broadcasting, public relations, sports business, and freelance sportswriting. Jobs in any of these fields, especially at the entry level, are sometimes difficult to land. But the student who has writing ability, graphics or photo skills, curiosity, and determination, and who is well prepared by education and training, should have no difficulty finding an interesting and challenging position.

One expert on sports careers in general is Duke Little, career services coordinator of *Sports Careers*, a company that advertises jobs in the sports industry including sports teams, sponsorships, the media, racetracks, sports facilities, and college athletic departments. Job listings average about ninety jobs every two weeks throughout the industry of sports. "The majority of the positions we list," says Little, "are entry level to midmanagement, and 70 percent to 80 percent are for jobs that require writing skills, such as producing print materials for the media, proposals, contracts, and effective presentations. *Sports Careers* which can be accessed via the Internet, operates as a career services provider for a number of sports-oriented organizations, such as the National Sporting Goods Association, the Professional Golf Association (PGA), and health and fitness organizations.

Fundamental Definitions

In these chapters, we will discuss a variety of sports journalism careers and in so doing employ many terms new to the average reader. Let's examine them.

Columnists are at the top of the sportswriting newspaper ladder. They write columns rife with opinion or editorial comment on any subject, event, or athlete. *Feature writers* and columnists develop stories, articles, and series, including enterprise and investigative pieces.

Sports editors oversee the production of the daily sports sections and manage writing staffs of various sizes. They budget space and select stories.

> *Sportscasters* gather, research, and write the sports news and present it on radio or television.
>
> *Copy editors* are responsible for checking facts, correcting grammar, and rewriting reporters' stories, when needed.
>
> *Freelance sports reporters and writers* develop informative, publishable fiction and nonfiction articles and author sports books. They may write on a "for hire" basis and are usually self-employed. They sell their work for publication or broadcast.
>
> *New media sports writers* develop stories for on-line websites, "e-zines," and newspapers for Internet sports aficionados.

How New Media Affect Sports Journalism

As you search for the position that will best satisfy your writing skills in sports, don't be overly worried by the doomsayers who proclaim the "new media" (World Wide Web, Internet, cable television, etc.) means the death of conventional print journalism. There is a strong future for all forms of printed sports journalism as we now know it. The thirst for sports information of every kind seems unquenchable. The kinds of sports and their variations grow yearly, as do the numbers of sports-loving enthusiasts.

Even now, millions of Americans encounter the written word about sports in many ways. Their sports reading in a typical day may involve one or more of the following:

- Checking favorite sports websites for game action and stats

- Scanning the sports headlines on-line and downloading interesting articles

- Enjoying in-depth features, boxscores, and intimate game details in newspapers and magazines

- Exchanging faxes and regular mail with other sports enthusiasts

- Communicating with others about teams and favorite players via E-mail

- Reading themselves to sleep at night with popular sports books

There have been dire predictions about how soon computers and video will eliminate the enjoyment of reading, but there are more books and magazines now than ever; sports stories are still among the most popular of all.

Underlying Themes for Success

As we spoke to experts, practitioners, and newcomers in the field of sports journalism and prepared to combine their thoughts and ours, we found many ideas that repeated themselves in all of the professions. We thought it would be educational for you to examine them before we explored the details and experiences of each profession individually. The common threads throughout this book include:

- **Broad education.** Everyone we spoke to emphasized the importance of learning more than great literature and how to write. Writers, they chorused, must know the world around them—its history, geography, humanities, and the arts—in order to enjoy and share its fullness with readers. And make sure you attend some sports events along the way.

- **Reading.** This recurrent theme relates to "broad education," because it helps to enrich your vocabulary and phraseology. If you have a habit of reading a wide variety of material, your writing will take on a style and substance that will refresh your readers with its depth.

- **Internships.** Almost everyone praised the importance of internships in experiencing and choosing a career in these fields. There were many complaints about low pay or none at all, and of all the hard work entailed, but those who have reached the upper levels realize they started with an internship or similar entry-level training.

- **Volunteering.** The experts in most fields we covered recommended that during your high school and college years you get your foot in the door by offering to help in a press room or broadcast studio without pay (at least until they find they can't do without you).

- **Paying your dues.** The most common phrase used throughout our interviews was "paying your dues." Many applicants for jobs in sportswriting have the false impression that pay is good because they see the athletes and the high executives doing so well financially. But, for beginning writers, this is a low-paying industry and you need to know how to bide your time.

- **Great professions.** The amateurs and the pros in all of the fields covered in this book were almost unanimous that, despite the headaches and periodic frustrations, they wouldn't trade their careers for any other.

The Education of a Sports Journalist

Our survey of sports editors of the country's leading newspapers indicates that almost all sportswriters today are college graduates; only a small percentage have advanced degrees. The most common undergraduate degrees are English, journalism, liberal arts, communications, and education (history, political science, etc.).

After liberal arts and basic sciences, editors give some importance to skill courses that provide an understanding of multiculturalism, graphics and design, newsroom technology, and management. Of lesser importance are classes on journalism ethics, photography, the role of mass media in society, and media law. You'll see in other chapters, however, that many of the latter subjects are important in other fields of sports journalism.

Sports editors and journalists also agree that the years required to attain postgraduate degrees are better spent gaining valuable work experience in the field and putting to use what you've learned en route to your bachelor's degree. That's not to say that there aren't some great sportswriters out there who have advanced educations. But, the student deciding how to invest her or his time after attaining an undergraduate degree should understand that one learns the vital stuff of sportswriting by working ten to twelve hours a day, often in small towns, far from the maddening world of the big city sports market. During those hours, you'll perform almost every task possible either as an intern or as a cub reporter.

Sports Journalism Curricula

High school juniors and seniors and college students should explore all the educational opportunities offered to complement the standard journalism, English, and communications programs. A number of schools also provide sports writing and sports communications courses. It is not too late for even a college graduate to consider such options. This type of interdisciplinary program, typified by a sports communications minor at West Virginia University that prepares students for work in sports broadcasting, journalism, and sports information, requires course work in English, physical education, and communications.

Led by one of the most highly regarded schools of journalism in the country, Columbia University in New York, there has been a growing trend for schools to add sports journalism to their journalism curricula. Columbia even has an independent dean for its sports journalism program.

Schools of Journalism

Aspiring journalists frequently ask advisers, "Should I opt for a journalism school? If I do, must it be an accredited one?" Accredited journalism schools require students to take ninety semester course hours outside of journalism. At an unaccredited school, if you study journalism, it's still recommended that you earn three-fourths of the credits toward graduation outside the journalism curriculum. It bears repeating that editors are interested in young writers who have been educated in broad subjects such as those in the liberal arts and sciences, economics, history, and so on. This accounts for the high number of English majors turned sports journalists.

A recent survey by the American Society of Newspaper Editors (ASNE) indicates that fewer than half (43 percent) of the editors who consider candidates for employment care whether they've graduated from an accredited journalism program or not. Almost half of the editors surveyed didn't require that their writers have a degree in journalism, as opposed to other fields. But in the smaller circulation markets, where many journalists begin their careers, almost 75 percent of editors wanted graduates of journalism schools. For a list of accredited schools, write to: Accrediting Council on Education in

Journalism and Mass Communications, University of Kansas School of Journalism, Stauffer-Flint Hall, Lawrence, KS 66045.

Write, Write, and Write Some More

An important part of the educational process of an aspiring sportswriter is, of course, to continually work at the profession. Whether you're in high school or college, be a writer all the time. Write about anything. Don't just write for the school paper and the yearbook. Enter writing contests. Send letters to the editor. Write articles for local periodicals. If possible, contact the local newspaper sports editor in a determined effort to be a correspondent or work weekends. This is the recommended way to begin learning about the job you someday hope to perform as a professional.

If you are a high school senior, another point to remember as you begin the process of choosing a college is: it's not where you go that is most important. Rather, it is what opportunities you pursue and what you accomplish wherever you go. Join or organize a writer's club in your community or school. This is an effective and enjoyable way to test your writing skills on other writers and to gain valuable insights into the creative ideas of others. Check with local libraries, many of which are the focal point for writer's clubs. Ask professors and others to critique your efforts. It can only help.

Read, Read, and Read Some More

Writers and editors agree that to be an outstanding writer, you must read everything available. If you always read good writing, chances are you'll learn to excel as a writer. However, reading that includes low-quality literature, such as comics, pulp fiction, and cheap periodicals, can have a negative effect on your output.

Journalism Internships

The young journalist embarking on a career in sportswriting has many avenues to consider, but at this point we'll discuss internships, which very often occur before graduation (undergraduate internship) or soon after graduation (postgraduate internship). A reporter on the student newspaper or an intern at a city or suburban newspaper can learn enough about the specific job while performing it to determine, with little risk of time invested, whether it is the right career field or profession for him or her.

As with other career fields, budding sportswriters would do well to start paying their professional dues in internship programs, which are widely available. Formally, an intern is described as an "advanced student or recent graduate, gaining supervised practical experience." The most well-known internship for a career field is in medicine, where interns complement their schooling by practicing under the supervision of doctors and surgeons within a hospital or clinic. That's about the way newspaper sports internships function. You learn and practice by following an experienced mentor and performing a variety of jobs, some menial and some very important, but all intended to provide broad experience in the day-to-day operations of a paper.

Newspapers employ both undergraduates and graduates for internships. It's important to note that a few sports editors we surveyed in the small and midcirculation markets report that they often hire successful interns as staff reporters. Candidates for internships would be wise, therefore, to inquire about such prospects when they apply.

A common misconception is that sportswriters must know about every sport in order to report on any of them. Actually, it's at the school newspaper or small commercial papers that this knowledge is developed; you have to cover so much that you become a "jack of all sports." Even though you may never have been exposed to sports such as track and field or soccer, being force-fed through regular assignments to cover those competitions will soon make you a near expert.

Most undergraduate interns have already decided that they would like to explore writing as a career. In most cases, the internship experience is vital in cementing their decision. Postgraduate internships closely resemble full-time jobs, except that interns are not considered staff members.

Undergraduate Internships

You're an avid sports fan or a player. You've proven yourself as a writer with potential. You're a good student and now you wonder if you're ready to start realizing your dream of being a sportswriter. What's next? The place to find out is the undergraduate internship.

Some schools provide internship programs that help place students with newspapers, magazines, advertising and public relations agencies, on-line publications, etc., but at most schools the student must seek his or her own internship opportunities. Landing an internship is intensely competitive, not unlike the ultimate job hunt. Interviews with interns, sports editors, and college professors reveal that the number of colleges offering credits for internships are outnumbered by those that do not.

Interns not receiving college credits are often paid by the newspapers, ranging from hourly wages to weekly reporters' salaries. Internships can be worked during school semesters or in the summer. Students interested in such opportunities are advised to seek assistance in internship research from their faculty advisers. Professors in many English/journalism departments are also involved in screening applicants for sports publications. Organizations regularly publish their newspaper internship guides for postings at colleges. For example, the introduction to a recent ASNE *Newspaper Internship Guide* reads:

1998 Newspaper Internships: Great Places to Spend Your Summer—and Beyond

These ASNE-member newspapers are waiting for students to apply for 1998 summer internships and one- and two-year internships. They are looking for talented students to write stories, edit copy, lay out pages, design graphics, and take pictures.

This is a tantalizing prospect for a student who loves to write. Many of the internships specify whether the sports reporting position is full- or part-time. This year's ASNE posting listed almost 200 newspapers throughout the country where internships are being offered. The list showed that internships are available from many of the country's larger newspapers, including *USA Today* and the *New York Times,* as well as the smaller ones. Craig Branson, publications director for ASNE, advises you to consult the current Web version of this data—http:\\www.asne.org/kiosk/careers/interns.htm—because internship listings are sometimes updated on a weekly basis.

Internships for Minorities and Women

The newspaper industry actively seeks minority and women applicants. Both groups are widely underrepresented on newspaper sports desks. As a result, these students will find that they are very welcome candidates for internships, as indicated in the *Newspaper Internship Guide* described earlier. The 1997 ASNE guides listed three "Corporate Minority Internships" (for Cap Cities/ABC Newspapers, Gannett, and Landmark), as well as eleven "Minorities Job Fairs" held at newspapers and press associations throughout the nation to enable minorities to find journalism internships and entry-level jobs. As minority students approach graduation, in addition to their full-time job hunt which we will discuss later, they should plan to participate in programs and job fairs sponsored by journalism groups such as the ASNE, the Asian American Journalists Association, the National Association of Black Journalists (NABJ), the National Association of Hispanic Journalists, and the Native American Journalists Association. Refer to the Appendix for contact information.

All newspaper sports editors should note the following statistics from a recent "Annual Survey of Journalism and Mass Communication Enrollments" in U.S. colleges and universities, published by Ohio State University's School of Journalism:

- In 1995, women earned 60.5 percent of the bachelor's degrees in journalism programs.

- In 1995, minorities earned 18.4 percent of all national bachelor's degrees in journalism programs (African Americans, 10.1 percent; Hispanic Americans, 4.6 percent; Asian Americans, 3.3 percent; Native Americans, 0.4 percent).

Our survey of sports editors across the country indicates that despite this significant representation of minorities and women in university journalism programs, national newspapers have only token representation of these groups on sports department staffs. Notwithstanding the argument that large numbers of all journalism graduates, including minorities and women, take positions in other fields such as those described in this book and outside of journalism, newspaper sports editors should seriously consider the fairness of their hiring practices.

The NABJ offers internships for minority sophomores and juniors majoring in journalism or planning a journalism career. The annual application deadline is November 1.

Internship Salaries

The average undergraduate summer internship lasts for ten to fourteen weeks. The summer income from sports internships varies, of course, from publication to publication and city to city. Some have unpaid internship positions, at which you usually work for course credit. A few of those we surveyed allow course credits and hourly wages (e.g., $8 per hour).

As with most financial aspects of the business, circulation determines the salary level an undergraduate can expect if it is a salaried position. If your internship is close enough to home for commuting, then the average summer income is probably more than adequate. If it isn't close, the costs of relocating for two or three months can tax the financial management skills of any undergraduate. Costs of short-term apartment rentals, utility and telephone costs (especially for a home PC), transportation, food, and so on will consume much of the intern's salary. The burden is often lessened by sharing an apartment, enjoying the benefits of company cafeterias, and preparing inexpensive but good meals at home.

Landing an Internship

The ability to sell your talent via the quality of your resume and published clips (copies of articles you wrote that were published in various periodicals) is essential. Save clips of your pieces that have been published in community newspapers and student publications. Copy them carefully, and send only the best with your painstakingly written cover letter and resume. Don't send your generic resume for every opportunity; tailor it to the specific requirements of the position you're seeking. To repeat our earlier recommendation, students should take *every* opportunity to write and be published.

As you might expect, the newspapers that offer the most internships are those with the greatest circulation; those with over 200,000 readers. Of those, the number of internships for sportswriting often equal those of general news reporting. Many such internships combine the two. Conversely, smaller market papers, mostly those with under 50,000 circulation, with less sports activity occurring during the summer internship season, have fewer jobs to offer journalism undergraduates. Established internship programs are available for more than half of the best 100 newspapers in the country. Although several of the major papers conduct nationwide searches in order to find the best talent for internships, applicants should also consider markets near their homes because newspapers are loathe to pay expenses for travel to interviews or other relocation costs if they can avoid it.

Novices should understand that, as with most professional pursuits, it is the aggressive, well-motivated person that secures the better jobs. Don't assume that all journalism students are competing with you for those few internships. They're not. One undergraduate at the University of Southern California School of Journalism was amazed to learn that only about 10 percent of a recent graduating class of about ninety students opted to try for internships.

Presenting Yourself to an Employer

Even when dealing with graduates of acclaimed journalism schools, many sports editors and other potential employers find job applicants unprepared for a professional interview. Their letters of application are often amateurish. Their interpersonal skills are frequently lacking. The way they present themselves is often unsatisfactory. All of the high university grades and awards will be of little use to the job candidate who doesn't dress or act professionally at an interview.

The American Society of Newspaper Editors offers this advice to job seekers:

- **Accuracy is important.** For many students, the letter of application reveals carelessness. Make sure all of the information in the letter is accurate, including names, titles, and addresses. Misspellings, typos, inaccuracies, and awkward phrasing in a letter will end your chances of being considered. Edit, edit, edit.

- **Pick your most effective clips.** Samples of your work should show the range of what you can do, as well as your best work. A selection that includes breaking news, enterprise, profiles, features, columns, and backgrounders may make a stronger impression than a collection of spot news stories. Clips of five or six stories are sufficient.

- **Call ahead for interviews.** Try to arrange an interview at your hometown paper or a paper in a city you might be visiting during a school break. Call ahead or write to ask for an interview. Walk-in interviews rarely result in an opportunity to talk to the editors who do the hiring. A job fair also is a good place to meet recruiters.

- **Dress appropriately.** Personal appearance is important. Business attire is always appropriate. Follow up an interview with a thank-you note to the editor or recruiter. Keep in touch, even if there is no opening. Discuss what you are doing, what you are learning. Send a few clips from time to time.

- **Polish your resume.** Your resume should be concise and well organized. If possible, keep it to one page. Edit for meaning, clarity, grammar, and spelling.

The best source for names of editors is *Editor & Publisher Yearbook*. Also, *E&P* employment classified ads are a good source for job openings. Candidates who have no newspaper experience might try some freelance writing to demonstrate their ability. Of course, reading about journalism is a good idea. There are several basic texts that a nearby journalism school may have available. *Columbia Journalism Review* and *American Journalism Review* (as well as *The American Editor*, published by the ASNE) are good reading.

If, after you have read this book, you're not sure that you can make it in sports journalism, remember the humorous words of the late, great political satirist Robert Benchley, "By the time I realized I couldn't write, I was making too much money to quit."

2 Newspaper Sportswriting

I believe a quality sports reporter is someone who is industrious, fair, and accurate. The responsibility of the reporter, in my view, is to be sure he or she has done the necessary homework, is confident that the facts are correct and that the issues are presented in a balanced manner.

Joe Paterno
Head football coach, Penn State University

Many young writers believe that writing about sports for national and local newspapers is the loftiest of the sports journalism professions, that it is the most popular and glamorous field in which to work. Ever since it became an art form in the 1930s, sportswriting has been among the most fascinating and well-respected careers. Although other writing forms covered in this book have, in recent years, vied for prominence with it as *the* most exciting sports career field, there are legions of sportswriters who will tell you they enjoy the best of all careers. You be the judge.

More journalism and communications graduates go to work for newspapers and wire services than for any other type of employer. There are currently more than 54,000 professional journalists employed at daily newspapers throughout the country. More than 20,000 of them write about sports, making them the largest group of journalists by far. As a result, newspaper sports journalism is one of the most fertile places for a writer to ply his or her skills. As you will see, although it is a very competitive profession, those who excel at their craft and know how to market their abilities can be very successful. This chapter examines the preparation, attitudes, methods, and career journeys of successful sportswriters.

Dreaming the Dream

Most professional sportswriters will tell you that their dream of writing about sports developed from a seed planted at a very young age. Remember your youth, when you looked forward to reading your favorite sportswriters or quotes from your favorite star athletes in the newspaper after school or after your homework was finished? Or maybe you remember playing high school or community basketball, baseball, football, or soccer and, after a good game, being interviewed by a reporter from the local newspaper. Later you thought to yourself, "It must be a neat job to be a sportswriter."

The careers of many of America's most respected, award-winning sportswriters began with those very same thoughts. At a young age, these writers discovered that they not only enjoyed school subjects such as literature, composition, and writing, but that they were good at them. Many realized, after a couple years of high school or maybe early in their college education, that they could actually combine their love and knowledge of sports with their ability to write and communicate—and begin pursuit of that "neat job" of becoming a sportswriter. As we will see, there are several ways to set sail for that dream.

One of the best known and most revered journalists of our time, former CBS news anchor Walter Cronkite, began his writing dream as a sportswriter on his high school newspaper. He writes in his book, *A Reporter's Life*, about his first newspaper experience at San Jacinto High School in Texas:

> That same year, suffering the disabling shin splints that kept me off the track team and realizing that I'd never make the football team at 110 pounds (and with distinctly limited talent), I had wangled the job of sports editor of the *Campus Cub*, our semi-occasional school paper.

His inspiring book traces the assortment of journalistic enterprises that formed the foundation for his career as a world-famous reporter, author, and radio and television icon. Few will achieve such heights, but your goal must be to reach the summit. It is good to know, however, that fine careers can be carved from your earliest dreams if you persevere.

Although sportswriters begin their careers in varied circumstances, most of them started by enjoying reading and writing about everything they could find. Typically, they expanded their skills in a college English program and began to write in earnest for college newspapers, yearbooks, and other publications. During this process, they either competed in school sports or enjoyed them as fans and became familiar with the rules, skills, and personalities involved. At the same time, they were influenced by their hometown sportswriters.

Rick Gosselin, an NFL columnist for the *Dallas Morning News*, remembers being about nine years old when he decided that sportswriting was for him. "I used to make little 'sports books' of my own," he recalls, "mostly writing about hockey and football. I would cut pictures out of newspapers and magazines, type a story about each on the family's old Underwood typewriter, and then paste them into my sports book. I typed so much then with only two fingers that it was extremely difficult to break the habit, even after I took typing classes in high school and later worked as a writer for the student newspaper at Michigan State University." Gosselin earned his bachelor's degree in journalism and moved right into a steady sportswriting position after graduation with United Press International (UPI), formerly one of the nation's top news wire services. Some twenty-eight years later, Gosselin is making deadlines and captivating his readers—still as a two-fingered typist.

Adam Schefter, a sportswriter for the *Denver Post*, says that when he first started writing as a student at the University of Michigan for the *Michigan Daily*, he didn't think sportswriting was something at which one could actually make a living. "I learned quickly, however, from an experienced newsman who took me under his wing, that you definitely can," he says. "Now, after many years at it, I can't imagine being happier at any other line of work."

This is a common perception among many sportswriters. There are some demanding aspects of the profession as well as nuisances they sometimes complain about, but these come with the territory. Only sportswriters who learn to ignore such headaches or work around them will realize the full rewards of the business. One constant prevailed in our discussions with sportswriters throughout the country at every level. They love their work!

Paving the Way

Young, ambitious writers must realize that a sportswriting position is not gained without significant preparation and effort, which begins with education.

Rick Gosselin says, "In order to excite your readers with your description of sports business, competition, events, and teams, you'll need knowledge of history, geography, computers, and the arts to draw interesting comparisons, develop thoughts, and have an appealing frame of reference." The best writers employ a broad education and knowledge of subjects outside of sports to enrich the reader's experience. They create an enjoyable story by applying that knowledge in the form of rich analogies, similes, and metaphors within the sports story.

Fine writing, such as the following excerpt by veteran columnist Bill Conlin of the *Philadelphia Daily News*, can provide enjoyment not only from the story line and the writer's angle of attack but also from the richness of the language. Note the many references to a variety of elements outside the world of sports. The use of cutting metaphors and similes clearly express dissatisfaction with the low-budget approach of the Philadelphia Phillies' management toward building a contending baseball team for its fans. Consider Conlin's attack on the owner's philosophy of bringing in marginal, inexpensive talent to try to compete in the National League:

> Bill Giles [former Phillies owner] has mandated Thomas [former general manager] to continue applying Band-Aids to hemorrhaging wounds. He [Thomas] can continue to load the pickup truck with used refrigerators, worn ottomans and other household discards in search of some tender, loving care. . . . It turned out that Thomas could have fit what he got for the veterans he

railroaded to the American League pennant races into a lunch box, with room left for a cheesesteak and a double order of fries.

Readers wait every day to read Conlin's columns, and he seldom disappoints their appetites for management-slashing, fan-friendly eloquence. Newspaper management, too, has to be pleased with the positive effect his work has on circulation.

Pursuing a broad liberal arts education helps you rise above the average work by newspaper reporters who report only who scored the most field goals or who ran the fastest race. Such writers do little more than record the facts, much like a tape recorder or video camera could. Sample the sports section of the local paper for the bylines of the "stringers," whose reports about local athletic contests can sometimes be dull and lifeless. (A stringer is a part-time free-lancer paid by the story.) Many of these writers have only marginal writing skills or limited knowledge of the world around them. This becomes readily apparent to the discerning reader. The better writers *always* provide their best work to their readers and generally are compensated accordingly.

Newspaper Journalism Internships

To learn what internships are like, we interviewed Christian Ewell, an undergraduate from the University of Southern California (USC). His first internship was in his sophomore year, in the sports department at the *Topeka Capital Journal* in Kansas, near his home. In his junior year, he sent out approximately thirty-five mailings to medium and large circulation newspapers that advertised internship openings every summer. He accepted a position as a general reporter/intern at the *Philadelphia Daily News*, which is annually voted as having one of America's top ten sports sections. He felt that this general assignment would provide more variety for his overall newspaper experience and for his resume. He worked in all departments of the paper, including the sports department. Having already been "turned off" by previous internships in broadcast and public relations, he decided after his *Daily News* internship that sports journalism was where he wanted to begin his career.

As a member of the class of 1997, Christian accepted his final undergraduate internship position at the Washington, D.C., bureau of the **Knight Ridder** newspaper chain. At the same time he took eighteen credit hours at Howard University, which has an exchange program with USC.

Christian, now a reporter for the *Baltimore Sun*, has embarked on his chosen career as a sportswriter and is on the road to an enjoyable, rewarding professional life. As he found, internships are extremely helpful in resolving a number of early career issues. However, completion of successful internships can lead to a career-defining dilemma: Does the intern apply for a job at a small newspaper or explore other internships in hopes that one could lead to a better opportunity in the big city?

"In the newspaper business," Christian says, "like almost anything else—it seems that where you go depends not so much on what you can do, as on the opportunities you make for yourself. People have told me I can find those opportunities most easily by going out and getting a job at a small paper."

"There," he adds, "as conventional wisdom goes, you can shine, make a name for yourself and become a big fish in a small pond. Then you can move up to the big leagues if you wish."

This philosophy also has another side. In many cases, interns who begin their career path in a small town run the risk of becoming so comfortable there that they decide to stay. "You don't want to get into a situation where you're planning to stay for a cup of coffee and before you know it, your kids are burying you there," Christian advises.

A recent survey by the *Daily Beacon* of the University of Tennessee listed the schools that publish daily student newspapers (Table 2.1), as well as those that publish "almost daily" newspapers, which provide a comparable level of experience for young writers.

Soliciting Internship Positions

Applying and competing for internships and marketing your talents begins with some important questions. We have tried to answer the most common ones here.

Q: *What kind of cover letter do I write?*

A: Sports editors surveyed for this book expressed the desire to have the applicant's cover letter limited to one page, briefly introducing the applicant. The best cover letters convince the

Table 2.1 A Sample of U.S. University Daily Newspapers

Arizona Daily Wildcat (Arizona)	*Online O'Collegian* (Oklahoma State)
Iowa State Daily (Iowa State)	*Daily Pennsylvanian* (Pennsylvania)
Kentucky Kernel (Kentucky)	*Post* (Ohio University)
Northern Star (Northern Illinois)	*Princeton Spigot* (Princeton)
Oklahoma Daily (Oklahoma)	*Daily Reveille* (Louisiana State)
California Aggie (Davis, Cal.)	*Rocky Mountain Collegian* (Colorado)
Chronicle Online (Duke)	*Stanford Daily Online Edition* (Stanford)
Columbia Spectator (Columbia)	*State Press* (Arizona State)
Daily Aztec (San Diego State)	*Daily Tar Heel* (North Carolina)
Daily Beacon (Tennessee)	*Daily Targum* (Rutgers)
Daily Bruin (UCLA)	*Temple News* (Temple University)
Daily Egyptian (Southern Illinois)	*Daily Texan* (UT—Austin)
Daily Forty-Niner (Cal. State Long Beach)	*Daily Trojan* (USC)
Daily Free Press (Boston University)	*Yale Daily News* (Yale)
Daily Illini (Illinois)	*Online Daily* (Washington)
Daily Nebraskan (Nebraska)	*Daily University Star* (Southwest Texas)
Daily Nexus (Cal. Santa Barbara)	*Brown Daily Herald's Heraldsphere* (Brown)
Daily Northwestern (Northwestern)	*Michigan Daily* (Michigan)
Digital Kent State (Kent State)	*Digital Cardinal* (Wisconsin)
Independent Florida Alligator (Florida)	*Minnesota Daily* (Minnesota)
Kansas State Collegian (Kansas State)	*Indiana Daily Student* (IU)
Lantern (Ohio State)	*The Crimson* (Harvard)
The Collegian (UMass)	

Courtesy: *Daily Beacon*, University of Tennessee.

editor of your writing ability. A bit of humor, excellent vocabulary, and a show of style are recommended. It also doesn't hurt to flatter the editor with words of praise about the paper's sports section and demonstrate a knowledge of the sports staff you hope to join. Make sure it is clear how proud you would be to be associated with this sports staff.

Remember: Less is always more with an outstanding, well-structured cover letter.

Q: *To whom do I send it—managing editor, the sports editor, or both?*

A: Most sports editors said that all applications for either internships or staff openings should be addressed to them, by name. Be warned that cover letters addressed to "sports editor" more often than not immediately find their way to the nearest trash basket. Sports editors want sportswriters who do their homework. Find (call the paper) the editor's name and proper title. Send material to the executive sports editor if there is more than one sports editor.

Q: *Do I send out my resume and clips randomly or only when there's a vacancy to be filled?*

A: Sports editors prefer to receive application packages (cover letter, resume, current clips) primarily only when there is a vacancy to be filled. Soon-to-be college graduates, however, are the exception. They should begin moving as many rocks as possible early in their final semester. It is recommended that you follow any mailing with a phone call within two weeks. If you wait a month, you run the risk of being forgotten.

Q: *What are the people in charge of hiring looking for?*

A: First and foremost, talent, then versatility, then a team player. This is just like trying out for a team; the priorities are similar.

Q: *When they inquire about the variety of my background and I have experience in sports "news," games, features, columns, press conferences, festivals, business, and so on, how do I show all that variety in six to eight clips, which seems to be their limit? Which ones do I eliminate without weakening my self-marketing?*

A: This is a common dilemma that all applicants must resolve with editors' wishes in mind. Most sports editors we surveyed preferred to receive no more than five clips that display your versatility and talent. Ideally, the clips would include a "deadline" story, a human interest feature, a report with an investigative aspect or item, a game story, and an opinion piece. But don't sacrifice quality in a trade-off for diversity!

Getting Paid

The most important element of interning for an ambitious university student is not the pocket money gained from this summer "job" but the valuable experience, skills, and contacts gained from an adventure that greatly expands his or her career horizons. Nonetheless, income is important, so let us consider how much the newspapers understand the plight of young interns.

Christian Ewell, the USC graduate, feels that, based on his experience and the research he has done over three years, interns seem to be fairly well paid as a general rule. However, he suggests that "if you intern a good distance away from home, it's important to have good credit (i.e., the ability to rent an apartment and to borrow money)." He reports that gross weekly salaries at the newspapers where he worked and those of other newspapers he considered are as follows:

Topeka Capital Journal	$250 ($13,000 calculated on a yearly basis)
Philadelphia Daily News	$523 ($27,000 calculated on a yearly basis)
New York Post	$700 ($36,000 calculated on a yearly basis)
Washington Post	$775 ($40,300 calculated on a yearly basis)

Our own survey of the top newspaper sports editors in the country reasonably confirms these figures, indicating that an average starting salary for interns is calculated at approximately $22,000 per year, or $423 a week.

Postgraduate Internships

Unfortunately, there isn't a standard practice throughout the business for hiring interns and newspapers vary in their approach. Very few sportswriters in the major-market papers change jobs or professions, so only a few staff openings exist and interns are seldom hired after their specified term. As a result, after working the more rarefied atmosphere of the higher profile newspapers, an estimated 90 percent of internship graduates must move to small and medium-sized papers to start their full-time careers. Although this can be unfortunate for sportswriting candidates, it is also proof that this career usually provides professionals with a long and very satisfying career.

On the other hand, national newspaper chains such as Knight Ridder, Times Mirror, and Cap Cities/ABC have programs in which interns work and learn at their flagship papers or regional/national bureaus for a period, usually one year. There also are more popular two-year programs, such as those at the *Baltimore Sun* and the *San Francisco Examiner & Chronicle*, which in many cases catapult an impressive intern to a full-time staff position.

Some metropolitan newspapers hire as interns writers who have graduated from college and have two to three years experience at a suburban daily where they've learned the fundamentals of the business, covering numerous types and levels of sports.

Intern Status in the Workplace

At newspapers, the intern can usually expect to be treated with a satisfactory level of respect by staff writers who seem to be genuinely interested in helping and giving advice. Most experienced writers seem to remember their own entry into sportswriting and are surprisingly helpful as mentors. In journalism school, students are led to believe that as interns they will perform mostly mundane chores as they learn the business, so Christian Ewell was pleasantly surprised with some of the writing assignments he received.

"When I was on the 'city side' at the *Daily News*," he explains with a bit of sarcasm, "I hoped to be involved with reporting on stories such as those in the courts and on the police blotter, but more often than not I was assigned to report on store openings and exciting stuff like that. So, when I went to the sports desk, I expected similarly low-level work. But I was pleasantly surprised when, on my first day, I was assigned to cover the story of Tommy Lasorda's retirement as manager of the Los Angeles Dodgers . . . on my own."

For that story, he spent long hours on the phone and fax and as a result enjoyed something of a baptism by fire. He was pleased to find, too, that he wasn't expected to perform purely clerical or "gofer" tasks such as photocopying. All of the city and sports desk's staff members tried to be helpful and always treated him with respect.

Like their more experienced colleagues, interns can expect some significant pressure to do well and to work long, hard schedules, often for ten to twelve hours a day.

How the Experts Got Started

It is helpful to young journalists embarking on a career to know how others started. We asked some of the best sportswriters in the business how their careers began.

"When I started, I took on all assignments that would give me experience and expand my resume," says Adam Schefter of the *Denver Post*. "I covered high school sports for the *Ann Arbor News*. I was a stringer for the *Detroit Free Press*. I did research for another writer on a book about Bo Schembechler, and did freelance pieces for national magazines about Michigan players. But after receiving a few hundred rejections and with no full-time job in sight, I decided on a year in graduate school at the Medill School of Journalism (at Northwestern University). I interned in Washington, D.C., while I was at Medill. It was my first nonsports assignment that convinced me that newspaper sportswriting was the right career path for me. After the tedium of covering the subject of campaign financing for three months, I made my decision to focus my career on writing solely about sports, and I've never regretted it."

Veteran *Columbus* (Ohio) *Dispatch* reporter Todd Jones spent his last two undergraduate years at the University of Kentucky writing for the student newspaper, the *Kernel*, published five days a week. He, too, sings the praises of the college daily as a great learning ground, and one which places students close to sports journalism professionals. "Covering Kentucky sports for the *Kernel*, I traveled with and worked close to 'real' reporters at the *Lexington Herald-Leader* newspaper, and I was able to work part-time there for two years, doing mostly standard copy desk chores. In my junior year, I interned at the *Kentucky Post* in Covington. When their sportswriting staff was combined with the *Cincinnati Post* reporters, I was able to do a lot more on pro sports. After another summer of internship at the *Los Angeles Times*, where I wrote sports features, I returned home to write as a freelancer at the *Cincinnati Post*. Soon, they hired me as a reporter, and I was there for eight and a half years, covering NCAA basketball and the Bengals and handling general assignments." More recently, Jones moved to the *Columbus Dispatch*, where he is an enterprise writer for a weekly insert in the sports section called "The Ticket."

Mike Strom is a sportswriter for the *Times-Picayune*, a major daily newspaper in New Orleans. On his graduation from Louisiana State University, he took his first job with the *West Bank Guide,* one of a chain of free weekly newspapers in the New Orleans area, with a circulation of less than 50,000. For a brief time, he became a stringer there, covering prep sports, and then went to the *Lake Charles American Press* (circulation of more than 50,000). There, he did layout, copy editing, and coverage of mostly college and high school sports. As a result of networking his contacts, he joined the *Times-Picayune* full time. Seven years after returning, Strom became the paper's New Orleans Saints' beat writer, a job he enjoys "immensely."

Rick Gosselin of the *Dallas Morning News* strongly advises journalism students to select a college or university with a complete journalism curriculum, especially one that produces a student newspaper on a daily or almost daily basis. "It's a great learning experience," he says, "for a student writer to learn the ropes by following and emulating experienced newspaper writers at their job, day in and day out. You learn their techniques of finding leads and sources, interviewing, covering stories, the language of the business, and how to handle yourself."

The Career Choices

The writer who has chosen newspaper sportswriting for a career can opt to work in one or more of these four major categories:

- Wire services

- National daily newspapers

- Metropolitan (major-market) newspapers

- Suburban newspapers, including major-market suburban dailies and dailies in medium or smaller cities and towns

A postgraduate internship at a newspaper is, of course, an option we have already considered. Many sports journalists, graduating with a bachelor's degree, have opted to work as interns for a considerable period before they accept a full-time staff position on these types of publications.

Wire Services

"While it's rare for a young journalist right out of college to hook on as a writer with one of the major wire services such as the Associated Press (AP), Bloomberg, Scripps Howard, or the Los Angeles Times–Washington Post News Service, it is well worth attempting," says Rick Gosselin. "Working for a wire service gives a broad range of experience and newspaper discipline." Although he has enjoyed his current position as a sportswriter for seven years in Dallas, as well as his eight years on UPI's sports desk and a few years at the *Kansas City Star* covering the pro football Chiefs and the St. Louis Blues hockey beat, he regards his early years working at UPI on the "city side" as great seasoning for his career: "Writing about city hall, politics, and everyday news hardens you for the tough newspaper schedules ahead."

National Dailies and Weeklies

The newspapers with the greatest circulation are, of course, the national dailies, such as the *Wall Street Journal, USA Today,* and the *New York Times.* With large circulations, their quality level must be outstanding, so national publications pay sportswriters very well, better than most major metropolitan dailies. Because of the wide variations in readership, these publications' writing styles differ from those of regional papers. *USA Today* is published in a telegraphic style with plenty of graphics, concise writing, and less detail than most other newspaper forms.

The Sporting News, a national sports weekly

The *Wall Street Journal* sports section presents its more upscale readers with an unusual writing style. Fred Klein, a veteran *Journal* sportswriter, is proud of the special presentation of his stories. "*Journal* editors require meticulous, distinctive writing quality in every section of the paper, including the sports section," he says.

Complete, in-depth reporting is a hallmark of *The Sporting News,* a national weekly. This newspaper is a giant in the sports publishing profession, considered by many to be the model for thoroughness and accuracy in sports reporting. It should be read by all aspiring journalists who wish to become outstanding writers.

Although some of the national publications have internship programs that young student writers should monitor, very few newcomers can expect to start their sports journalism careers at this level. However, national publications provide a wide variety of styles and uniquely professional writing techniques. Students will be well served if they study these periodicals regularly and emulate their styles.

Metropolitan Newspapers

Metropolitan newspapers are usually those that are published in major-market or metropolitan cities with circulations of more than 175,000 readers. Simply put, there is very little chance for an inexperienced writer to become part of the sportswriting staff for such a newspaper. There is very little turnover in big-city papers, so openings are not usually available to newcomers. It is almost unheard of to get a job on a metropolitan paper directly from school. That being said, we should hasten to add that there are numerous opportunities for a budding sportswriter to eventually enter the rarefied atmosphere of the "majors," either from a postgraduate internship on a suburban daily or as a reporter with fine credentials from a small or mid-market daily.

Suburban or Small-Town Dailies

Suburban and small-town papers have provided ideal training grounds for most sportswriters. Also, despite the presence of major metropolitan papers, popular and profitable newspapers with circulations much smaller than 175,000 are published within or extremely close to some major markets. These suburban and small-town newspapers are perfect starting places for a young sports reporter to cultivate his or her skills and learn about sports reporting. They provide a journalist new to the business with a full learning program, including plenty of practice at all phases of newspaper work. Much of the educational process on small papers is on-the-job self-teaching because there is neither time nor expertise available for any formal training. Therefore, readers must cope with marginal writing and mistakes while young writers learn their craft. The new writer must read and appreciate the best sportswriting in his or her market area and try to adopt a distinctive personal style.

Experience at this level comes with working the high school and local college beat and writing game-day stories on a tight deadline. Some of the larger suburban papers also afford young writers the opportunity to cover the local pro teams. The learning process includes handling the multitude of interesting and mundane tasks necessary to put a complete sports section "to bed" each day. These daily tasks hone the skills necessary for an aspiring sportswriter to move up to larger circulation newspapers.

Many of the veteran reporters currently writing for major-city dailies paid their dues working at smaller papers. They spent a year or two learning to write publishable newspaper stories; learning about sports they may never have been familiar with; and learning fundamentals such as editing, caption writing, and headline writing. They were initiated in covering nearby professional teams without the pressures of the big-city beat. Writers learn the business and become capable journalists at smaller papers.

The Upside of Smaller Markets

Life can be good on the smaller newspaper, and thousands of very good sportswriters, who constantly turn out excellent copy, find that they can be happy at that level permanently. Although the salary may not compare with that of the major papers, there are compensating factors that often make a smaller market a good career choice. To make such a decision, you need both the pros and the cons for complete analysis. Let's look at the best parts of working in this market level:

- *Developing a personal writing style in relative obscurity.* This is where you have the freedom and time to establish your own writing identity. A young journalist can learn how to gather information, editorialize, and work toward his or her level of excellence.

- *Admiring readers.* The better sportswriters can become important personalities in their local communities. Many become well regarded and enjoy the perks that go with such popularity.

- *Limited negative reporting.* There is frequently little pressure for the beat writer or columnist to write reports critical of local teams, athletes, or organizations.

- *Better hours.* The daily work schedule, although it is seldom a nine-to-five job, is predictable and manageable, taking less time away from family and lifestyle pursuits.

- *Less travel.* Reporting on local teams usually involves driving to local competitions fairly close to home, so airline flights and hotel stays are infrequent—or enjoyable changes of pace.

- *Less commuting time.* Reporters usually don't experience the tough commute that big-city traffic causes for writers at larger papers.

- *Lower cost of living.* Housing and other living costs are often less burdensome in smaller communities.

- *Lifestyle.* Family or single life is often less hectic and more tranquil than life in the big city.

The Downside of Smaller Markets

When making your career decision, the following disadvantages of small markets should also be considered:

- *Lower income.* On the average, suburban dailies pay less, some as much as 50 percent less than larger papers. However, lower living costs and opportunities for freelance income or other financial perks can offset some of this difference.

- *Hard work.* A small staff means overloaded schedules. If a reporter has little support and much to accomplish for each deadline, there can be lots of work and late hours, unless you learn to be extra efficient.

- *Antiquated equipment.* When you work without modern publishing tools, such as state-of-the-art computers, but with tough schedules, your workload and the quality of your product can suffer.

- *A heavy workload during overlapping sports seasons, especially on weekends.* For example, a suburban sportswriter may cover a baseball playoff game and then have to travel some distance to cover a state track meet, with little time to come up for air.

- *Anonymity.* Reporters who cover a professional sports team for suburban or small-town newspapers, may become anonymous among a pack of media personnel because: (1) they may not cover the team every day, and (2) their papers and reports may not be read often enough by organizations and players to enable the writers to build the necessary relationships.

- *Minimal impact.* It can be frustrating for reporters to write for a small, local readership. There's a sense, often mistaken, that their stories may not have much impact.

If you're not just starting out, remember that when the newspaper staff is small, demands on young reporters are large. For example, it's not unusual for a cub reporter to cover a game, follow with an interview or two, return to the office to write the game story and its headline, and do the page layout. Then, when his or her own story is finished, there's more to be done. The reporter may have to read and comment on other writers' stories and help put the paper to bed. Journalists are required to pay such dues at most smaller papers. Remember, it is this kind of commitment that makes the paper successful and your salary possible. At the same time, you are cultivating your talent for the long haul.

The Job of Getting Hired

One of the hardest jobs in sports journalism is getting hired. We've discussed most of the preparation you need for the profession: desire, talent, education, ambition, internships, and so on. But getting on the payroll of a sports department, large or small, requires varying measures of patience, self-confidence, marketing skill, networking, humility, moxie, and salesmanship, as well as a great resume, outstanding clips, and a large stroke of luck.

Sports editors around the country confided that they favor the following traits when they are filling openings on their staffs:

- Talent (including reporting and editing skills)

- Ambition and strong work ethic

- Versatility (and a willingness to handle a variety of issues)

- Personality (outgoing)

- Ability to listen

- Loyalty

• Exemplary character

If you have prepared yourself well for a sports journalism position and can demonstrate these seven characteristics when applying, you may be on your way (and Lois Lane will probably be your constant companion). Seriously, we all have had acquaintances who lacked some of these virtues and, in many jobs, the shortcomings are not all that obvious. But experienced journalists agree that in this field, all these traits must be present and operating constantly from the day you accept a position on the newspaper. No matter what size paper you apply to, it's more than likely that it was your reputation, your impressive cover letter and resume, and your captivating writing clips that attracted the managing or sports editor to you. Next, and probably more important, is the face-to-face meeting you will have with the editor. On the rare occasion of an opening on a large newspaper staff, it is not unusual for a candidate to be interviewed by two or more persons, often over lunch or dinner. Be well prepared for it. Dress and act professionally.

Your best chance of being hired for your first job is at a small newspaper. Your hometown paper may be the best possibility. Alternatively, you can study out-of-town newspapers in your school library or take out a mail subscription for a few weeks or months to acquaint yourself with the sportswriting situation in other areas.

What resources are available to help you get a job once you have worked so hard and earned the degree you coveted? Now that you have educated yourself and honed the skills and traits we listed earlier, assemble all of your self-confidence for the next step. Most colleges and universities offer guidance on internships and job hunting, and journalism schools post openings. Some state press associations have job banks, as do the minority journalism associations we described earlier. Check out the associations in the states you have targeted; they will welcome you.

Focusing Your Job Hunt

It's important for you as an applicant to have clear and definite reasons for wanting to work at a specific newspaper. The reasons should be any or all of the following:

• To get your feet wet. You know that there will be a short learning curve and that you can contribute immediately.

- To develop a local identity. It's very important when applying to a small-market paper to know the local market, especially for sports reporting. Knowing the area, the teams, the personalities, the leagues, the caliber of play, rivalries, and the history of the local sports scene can greatly assist in the writer's job hunt.

- To become a part of a highly respected newspaper sports section, regardless of your specific role. Once you get your foot in the door of the place you really want to be, you can prepare yourself for the job to which you really aspire.

If you are going to be in the geographic area where your target newspaper is located and will be available for an interview, be sure to include that information in your application letter.

Moving Up in the Pack

When the call finally comes from that editor or staff writer and you're asked to interview at a higher-level newspaper, don't be surprised when the position offered entails assignments similar to what you have been doing. More dues to pay! That, however, is the usual progression and it is not peculiar to the sports journalism business.

Almost every newspaper has a path that new writers must follow. Young sportswriters who join a paper usually begin as general assignment or high school or college writers. Despite their bachelor's degrees, many are actually called clerks and must perform a wide range of tasks, such as writing or rewriting wire shorts, inputting copy, and compiling statistical information and roundups of major amateur and professional league game action into a packaged story. Sometimes there are opportunities to write sports articles, but, by and large, most new hires at big-market papers are destined for lesser duties until their work quality, attitude, and experience qualify them for a special staff assignment. Once again, your daily work, even the mundane assignments, must always be your best because it is the evidence on which you will constantly be judged.

Staying the Course

To be successful, writers must be willing to commit to learning the ropes and working hard. They should look forward to some of the positive rewards of the profession and learn to ignore the negative issues. Some young writers become frustrated with waiting and do all they can to secure a position at major-market papers, sometimes prematurely. They want to start running in the fast lane, moving up to a larger paper with greater circulation, more interesting assignments, and, of course, the big bucks.

But the move they contemplate is really a quantum leap not easily achieved. Most transitions from small to large newspapers are the result of a writer's work being seen and read by editors and fellow writers in the larger, nearby markets. It's important for the young reporter to remember each working day that *you never know if your work is being read by someone who can positively influence your career goals*. Even though they may work in a metropolitan area, sports editors and writers from big-city papers read the local newspapers in the communities in which they live or to which they travel for personal or business reasons. Quality writing has a way of jumping out at sports editors when they read clips from smaller papers. When the time comes to fill an opening, they know where to turn. Sports editors are constantly updating their personnel files or looking for recommendations from their staff and colleagues so they are prepared when a vacancy occurs. Therefore, every article you write should always be your best because you may be judged solely by that one effort.

You also have to be able to deal with rejection—or just a lack of response. Adam Schefter tells a humorous story about one application and a waiting process he endured that is more than most young writers will ever have to suffer. While interning, he sent out a great number of resumes with clips. He aimed some of these at the desk of Kathy Henkle, sports editor of the *Seattle Times*, where he was then anxious to work. "She never got back to me," he recalls with amusement, "even though I kept calling and calling. Eventually, I went off to other professional pursuits and, in March 1996, while I was working on a football free agency story, a call came in from Kathy who was at that time interested in hiring someone to cover the NFL for her paper. 'Kathy,' I said, 'Thanks very much for returning my call. . . !'"

Although the return call was years in coming, they laughed together at the vagaries of their business, and all was forgiven. He turned down her offer because at that time, he had a position he liked very much at the *Rocky Mountain News* in Denver. Ordinarily, you won't have to wait that long for connections, but it is important to know that patience is an important trait in the sportswriter's makeup.

Finding Your Niche

So far, we have discussed the most common ways for a newcomer to become part of a big newspaper sports staff and find his or her niche with a specific, full-time beat to cover. The raw truth, however, is that editors usually hire only experienced sportswriters to fill a specific vacancy. For example, when there is an opening for a sports columnist, the editor recruits and finds the columnist he or she wants to hire, usually from another paper.

There is often a pecking order within each paper's sports department. Figure 2.1 illustrates the various positions normally found in this order for a typical, major-market newspaper sports department and, with smaller numbers, on many medium and smaller sized ones. The sports journalism positions on the diagram are explained here; the editorial positions (sports editor, assistant editor, copy desk or night editor, rewrite clerk) are covered in Chapters 3 and 4.

Not all movement in this pecking order is upward and, to a great extent your salary is not determined by your position on the ladder. Much of the movement among professionals on a sports staff is lateral: reporters become editors, pro beat writers move to a college beat, reporters begin writing columns, or vice versa. Some veteran writers or columnists may sometimes make a higher salary than the sports editor, and some high school reporters may make as much as professional beat reporters. So, you cannot discern too much from a sports department organizational chart other than the various jobs that are involved.

Figure 2.1 is not a true organizational chart, in the sense that a writer advances upward through the ranks as in other organizations. Instead, it shows how staff members interrelate functionally. For example, many fine journalists stay at their positions (reporter, columnist, etc.) throughout significant parts of their careers by personal choice. Their income advances within that position depending on the quality of their work, rather than on any supervisory talent. Experienced sports journalists, to a large extent, become

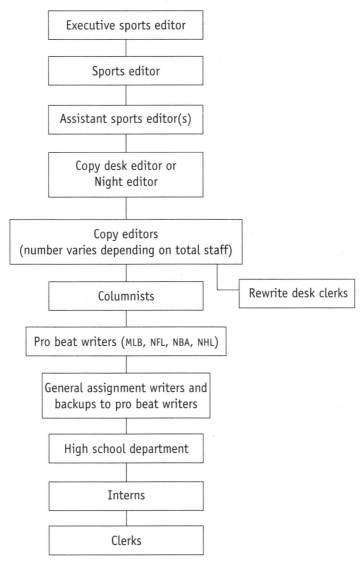

Figure 2.1 Typical hierarchy of a major city newspaper sports department

almost independent of the department organization, except for those functions with which they frequently interact. The many types of sportswriters are described here.

Feature Writers

These writers develop stories about the human side of sports, apart from the competition on the field. They write, for example, the story of a coach who counsels children afflicted with brain tumors or a running back showing his compassion to a seriously ill young fan. They may on occasion write a game story when needed, but they are paid primarily to develop human interest profiles.

Reporters

You should understand that every sportswriter is, first and foremost, a reporter. Reporters research and write descriptions of athletic contests (professional, college, semiprofessional, and high school). The job of the reporter/sportswriter is primarily to describe the detailed facts of the sports business, athletes, or events. Reporters who regularly cover the same team or organization on a daily basis are referred to as *beat writers*. All of the activities of each of your city's major league teams are covered by a beat writer. Although he or she may often take other major assignments, especially during the team's off-season, that beat is the reporter's prime responsibility. There are also beats for which a reporter covers a number of local teams, such as the major-market college basketball beat.

There is usually a beat writer for each of the major professional sports (hockey, baseball, football, and basketball). A pro sport like lacrosse or stadium soccer may also justify its own beat writer, depending on circulation and the team's popularity in the city. At large papers, where there are a number of colleges and many high schools in the area, reporters are regularly assigned as high school and college writers.

General Assignment Writers

These people are the handymen of the sports department, with assignments changing daily. For example, a general assignment writer may report on a college track meet one day, on a golf tournament the next, and a major tennis match on the next.

Columnists

Columnists are at the pinnacle of their sports journalism careers. They write stories that reflect their opinions about the players, coaches, and organizations. Not everyone can do this well, and most sports journalists never become columnists.

Clerks

Clerks perform a variety of general duties in the sports departments of most newspapers. Their daily tasks include compiling and assembling facts. Although they are usually college graduates and sometimes are assigned to substitute for a reporter, such as at a high school game, they are the office workers on the paper. Sports editors often hire clerks who they feel have the potential to learn the business and someday become reporters, but their primary role is to support the sports staff as required.

Interns

Interns are temporary sports department employees who perform a variety of jobs, including some writing as they learn the business. See the earlier section on journalism internships.

Stringers

These freelance writers are paid by the article to report, on the spot, at local sports competitions—frequently those for which the paper did not want to (or could not) invest the time of a staff reporter. Chapter 15 discusses freelance journalism more thoroughly.

Life as a Sportswriter

The life of a sportswriter is not nearly as glamorous as the average fan may think it is, nor is it as tedious as the average sportswriter would have you believe. Remember that most spend their entire careers as sportswriters. So it is, in fact, a good way of life; one that challenges the intellect and is almost always exciting, especially if you are a sports fanatic, as most sportswriters are.

Sports journalism yields great rewards for those who love sports and who wish to use their skills to tell others about it. It also has its frustrations. Let's examine both sides of the coin.

Rewards of the Sportswriter's Life

The American Society of Newspaper Editors (ASNE) asked a representative sample of newspaper journalists, "If you had to do it over again, would you choose newspapering as a career?" An amazing 84 percent said they would. Also, 78 percent said their present job had met or exceeded their expectations when they took the position. The most satisfying aspects of their work were:

- Creativity and meeting the daily challenge of my job (58 percent)

- Dealing with significant matters and having an impact (32 percent)

These formal survey answers directly correlate with the interviews we conducted throughout the industry.

On the subject of the most rewarding aspects of his job, Adam Schefter says: "I feel that although I have an obligation to my newspaper, I also know that I am my own boss. I pick and choose the stories. If I get beaten on a story, no one has to tell me; I know. I also know what I need to do to be effective in my job. I enjoy the occasional travel on the pro football beat, which requires far less travel than other major sports. I often look forward to those out-of-town game weekends (where I can somewhat escape the daily grind)."

Todd Jones of the *Columbus-Dispatch* offers: "Camaraderie and the opportunity to travel are among the aspects of our business that are most satisfying to me. Many fine people seem to flock to this trade, and you meet a lot of good friends in this work. I have enjoyed the continuing opportunity to travel throughout the country, and it has helped me to grow as a person."

Mike Strom of the *Times-Picayune* agrees: "Friendships you make along the way are the best part of the business, including those I made all the way back to the folks I met covering high school sports. I also enjoy the satisfaction you get from finding and reporting on a good story."

Creative Freedom

Despite different opinions about what they like most about their professional lives, most sportswriters ranked creative freedom first, second, or third. That's because one of the substantial parts of this career field is "being your own boss," deciding what is best for the story line and how best to present it to the readers. Unlike newswriting, where story lines are largely dictated by immediate happenings, veteran writers usually have no requirements to meet other than the substantive quality of their story and their deadline. Work hours are dictated by circumstances of the event, interviews after it, or travel. The reporter can choose his or her own story line, select who to interview, and decide how to structure the report.

More Pluses

Although the sports journalists we interviewed didn't always agree on how to rank the advantages of their profession, most agreed on what those advantages were:

- *Having an impact.* The mark of a good sportswriter is to know his or her audience and what material the readers will be most interested in. He or she must be able to project what the obvious story angles will be on radio and television before the newspaper comes out. Because readers will know from the broadcast media basic information such as how the scores were made, who starred, and who was injured, the writer must develop a story. A report about the game plan, the play calls, the defensive adjustments, or trouble in the locker room will be much more interesting to the sports fan than a rehash of game details. During the postgame press conference, for example, the reporter represents the fans by anticipating the questions he or she knows readers want answered.

- *Getting the scoop.* You uncover a piece of news that no one knows about and then make it the "talk of the town." Breaking a big or exciting story that becomes fans' topic of conversation for days or weeks is one of the most rewarding parts of the sportswriter's job. Disclosing such hard news results in writer recognition, but it does not happen by accident. It requires constant cultivation of sources that will enable the reporter to be alert to rumors and then investigate a possible story. One of the sports journalist's biggest thrills is to see or hear a media reference to his or her breaking story (e.g., when a televised sports report quotes the paper or the writer: "as reported by the *Daily Herald*" or "as reported by Jane Doe of the *Daily Bugle*").

- *Being able to travel all over the country and, for a lucky few, overseas.* Travel opportunities vary depending on the journalist's beat and place in the hierarchy, but most sportswriters enjoy getting away from the office. Travel, except maybe on the NBA or NHL beats, affords the writer time to catch his or her breath, to see the sights of a new city or visit different parts of familiar towns, to catch up on the golf game, or to visit friends.

- *Enjoying the excitement of the contests.* A journalist who doesn't enjoy or thrill to the spontaneous excitement of "the game" is probably in the wrong career. One of the most rewarding and challenging jobs for the sportswriter is to see and appreciate the great double play, the game-deciding jump shot, or the breaking of a world record, and then to capture that thrill in words for the reader.

- *Having opportunities for outside income.* Writers can supplement their salaries with freelance writing for magazines and doing commentaries on radio and TV shows (see Chapter 15).

- *Advising young people on the profession.* Writers may volunteer to speak at school career days assemblies, job fairs, and so on. It is flattering for sports journalists to be requested by their alma maters, local high schools, or community organizations to relate their experiences and help others in deciding about a career in journalism. Sportswriters are often invisible and stay behind the scenes, so these opportunities give them a chance to be seen and understood.

- *Building relationships with coaches, players, and others.* Aside from the events and competitions, the reporter's job revolves around personalities: coaches, athletes, and, of course, the fans. They provide the highs and lows of the sports journalist's life. The most likable ones make the job a pleasure. The job is made even more enjoyable by the colorful sports personalities. The fact that not all athletes perceive the reporter as the enemy and genuinely enjoy their time with the media is a big plus in the business.

Fortunately for the sportswriter, for every negative story about athletes like baseball's Albert Belle or Roberto Alomar (who is remembered for spitting at an umpire) or basketball's Dennis Rodman, there are legions of first-class men and women in the sports world who go out of their way to be respected as professionals and who try to make the reporter's job easier. Maybe it's those people we hope will win the contests.

Rick Gosselin named Dallas Cowboys quarterback Troy Aikman and Kansas City Royals third baseman George Brett as his favorite people to interview. When we asked Gosselin why he chose them, he said, "Those two are first-class people, not only when they've had a good day or won, but when they struggled." If only the sports world were populated with more Bretts and Aikmans . . .

Frustrations of the Sportswriter's Life

Although the sportswriter's life is for the most part exciting, rewarding, and even fun, it is not all golf tournaments, World Series, bylines, and expense-paid trips to San Diego or the Orange Bowl. There are obstacles for journalists, and you should consider each one seriously before you try to leap headlong into the profession.

- *Travel demands.* Pro basketball, hockey, and baseball beat writers must travel the most of any sportswriters by far. The long seasons of these sports involve the best and worst of being on the road. Baseball teams have 162 games a season—81 on the road—but at least you're in one city for two or three nights a week, on average. The NBA writer often finds himself or herself in four or five cities in a given week, sometimes with little sleep. If you like travel or if you are young and fancy-free, you may love the excitement of this lifestyle. With all expenses paid, life on the road costs a reporter very little. But if you have a family or other responsibilities at home, the road life can be tedious, even though you (and the team) are home for half the games. Donna Eyring, the sports editor of the *Orlando Sentinel* warns that "a professional sports beat writer's time is often not his own. For example, I don't think our NBA reporter has had a day off in three months. We were trying to figure out when he last had a day off. A major beat like an NBA team is an incredible commitment."

- *Structuring your workday.* Work schedules can vary significantly from day to day and week to week as sports seasons ebb and flow. As a result, some writers become frustrated that they do not have enough time to really flesh out a story and must turn it over for deadline long before they are satisfied with it. A common complaint about daily reporters' schedules, especially at the larger newspapers, is that they often put in much more than the typical ten- or twelve-hour days, intruding deeply into personal and family life.

  Although the unusual hours are often cited as one of the tougher aspects of the job, we were surprised to find that most families make the necessary lifestyle adjustments and have a happy home life. The schedule of the experienced writer, although it often requires a greater personal time commitment for certain parts of the job, is compensated by greater freedom of movement on days not so critical to the beat.

- *Being held hostage by a story.* The pressure of some stories takes writers captive, to the extent that for days or even weeks their time is not their own. Even when they're not researching or writing, they're thinking about it. Then, when the story finally runs its course, its importance is totally forgotten.

- *Facing the daily grind, especially early in your career.* There are times when a sportswriter must spend up to fifteen hours a day getting and writing the full story, and others when just a few hours are required to keep up with the beat. The average workday for a major-city beat writer during the season is ten hours, but that can stretch longer if he or she needs to get a story ready for the next day's newspaper.

Adam Schefter says that young sports journalists pay dues in different ways. "When I was a young writer at twenty-three and others my age were going to parties, I was often covering a high school game. That's not really a complaint because, frankly, I loved every minute of it."

- *Dealing with the prima donnas and jerks of the sports world.* The onset of free agency and the greed of the owners and athletes of the 1990s has brought a dissatisfying aspect to the job because the reporter must interact with the worst of them. Mike Strom agrees that interviewing or confronting the more unsavory sports characters is one of the least enjoyable parts of his job, ranking close to people who change their stories for what seem like frivolous reasons.

  Other reporters cited the persistent headache of trying to interview athletes and managers who couldn't be approached after they or their teams had a bad day. One writer described former Los Angeles Dodgers manager Tommy Lasorda as "often surly and unapproachable after a bad loss."

- *Run-ins with coaches and athletes.* Rub a coach or an athlete the wrong way with what may be an innocent question after a game, and you may suffer his or her wrath for a long time. Such occurrences often require lots of relationship rebuilding and, in the meantime, the writer must seek stories from other sources.

- *The modern trend away from in-depth coverage.* Almost every journalist we spoke with thoroughly enjoys writing and being able to express his or her own thoughts about issues. However, a number said they wish for an environment that would allow them to do more thorough stories. They feel that writing has changed in recent years and that much of sports journalism has focused on writing two or three short stories consisting of thirteen to fifteen lines, when one in-depth piece seems to be more appropriate.

The most successful and satisfied of America's sports journalists learned early in their careers to take the negatives in stride and instead focus their professional lives on the parts of the business they love. People in all professions experience a level of dissatisfaction with certain aspects of their work, and sports journalism is no different. Most of the 20,000 newspaper journalists who labor in and around our sports arenas and stadiums wouldn't trade in their notebooks and tape recorders for the tools of any other profession—and you probably won't either.

The Award-Winning Sportswriters

There are many associations for journalists, but the one that focuses on sports is the National Association of Sportscasters and Sportswriters, with a membership of 800. Edwin Pope of the *Miami Herald* currently chairs the association, which annually selects the National Sportscaster of the Year and the National Sportswriter of the Year. In its April 1998 awards, Frank Deford of *Newsweek*/HBO/CNN was inducted into the Association's 1997 Sportswriter Hall of Fame and Dave Kindred of *The Sporting News* was named National Sportswriter of 1997. The winners of State Sportswriter Awards are listed here. (Some state associations did not submit the names of their nominees.)

Alabama—Tommy Hicks, *Mobile Register*
Alaska—Tim Mowrey, *Fairbank's Daily News-Miner*
Arizona—Bob Moran, *Mesa Tribune*
Arkansas—Bob Wisener, *Sentinel-Record*, Hot Springs
California—Scott Ostler, *San Francisco Chronicle*
Colorado—Mike Monroe, *Denver Post*
Connecticut—Greg Garber, *Hartford Courant*
Florida—Gary Shaw, *St. Petersburg Times*
Georgia—Tom Stinson, *Journal & Constitution*, Atlanta
Illinois—Gene Wojciechowski, *Chicago Tribune*
Iowa—Marc Hansen, *Des Moines Register*
Kansas—Rick Peterson, *Topeka Capitol-Journal*
Kentucky—Chuck Culpepper, *Lexington Herald-Leader*

Louisiana—Peter Finney, *Times-Picayune*, New Orleans
Maine—John Holyoke, *Bangor Daily News*
Maryland—John Steadman, the *Sun*, Baltimore
Massachusetts—Bob Ryan, *Boston Globe*
Michigan—Jack Ebling, *Lansing State Journal*
Minnesota—Bruce Bennett, *Duluth News-Tribune*
Mississippi—Mike Knobler, *Clarion-Ledger*, Jackson
Missouri—Jim Thomas, *St. Louis Post Dispatch*
Montana—Mike Towne, *Great Falls Tribune*
Nebraska—Lee Barfknecht, *Omaha World Herald*
New Hampshire—Andrew Leibb, *Union Leader*, Manchester
New Jersey—Dave Weinberg, the *Press* of Atlantic City
New Mexico—Phill Casaus, *Albuquerque Tribune*
New York—Phil Mushnick, *New York Post*
North Carolina—Tom Sorensen, *Charlotte Observer*
North Dakota—Mike Scherting, *Minot Daily News*
Ohio—Sheldon Ocker, *Akron Beacon Journal*
Oklahoma—John Rohde, *Daily Oklahoman*
Oregon—Kerry Eggers, *Oregonian*, Portland
Pennsylvania—Rich Hofmann, *Philadelphia Daily News*
Rhode Island—Rick McGowan, *Newport Daily News*
South Carolina—Rick Scoppe, *Greenville News*
South Dakota—Dean Minder, *Daily Republic*, Mitchell
Tennessee—Joe Biddle, *Nashville Banner*
Texas—Frank Luksa, *Dallas Morning Post*
Utah—Doug Robinson, *Deseret News*, Salt Lake City
Vermont—Pat Garrity, *Burlington Free Press*
Virginia—Doug Doughty, *Roanoke Times*
Washington—Bud Withers, *Seattle Post-Intelligencer*
West Virginia—Doug Huff, the *Intelligencer*, Wheeling
Wisconsin—Bob Wolfley, *Milwaukee Journal Sentinel*
Wyoming—Ron Gulberg, *Star-Tribune*, Casper

What the Pros Most Like to Cover . . .

Writers are divided on the types of stories they like most to write. Most seem to enjoy the hard news piece as opposed to the feature story. Adam Schefter told us that he "writes for a *news*paper, not a *feature* paper! Hard news stories are what draws the most attention."

Schefter defines his favorite stories this way: "I remember when I was a young boy, I would wait for the daily paper and read it front to back, focusing heavily on the sports section. I would interrupt my reading to tell my father about especially interesting stories with, 'Hey, Dad, you've got to read this!' Now, those are the kinds of stories I like to write, the ones that young fans are out there reading with their Dads."

Todd Jones likes to write "people" stories best: "I like writing about individuals. I find it very challenging to get behind the perceived personalities and perspectives of some of the major sports celebrities. Some are seen by the public as cartoon caricatures (e.g., NBA stars like Sir Charles Barkley and The Admiral David Robinson) instead of real living and breathing people."

Many writers love to cover and report on the excitement of contests such as college basketball's Final Four or pro hockey's Stanley Cup finals. Mike Strom prefers writing about these kinds of major events. "But even better than my Super Bowl experience," he says, "was when I covered the Tournament of the Americas with the original NBA Dream Team (with Michael Jordan, Magic Johnson, Larry Bird, et al.). I sat twenty feet from courtside and the most famous basketball players of our time, and then tried to describe that excitement to readers."

. . . and What They Like the Least

A survey of sportswriters produced a variety of answers to the question "Which assignments or stories do you regard as the toughest?" Most popular answers were these:

- The past-midnight game story on deadline

- The running copy game story for the A.M. edition ("Running copy" refers to filing game details as they happen.)

- Having to criticize management, coaches, or players whom the writer genuinely likes and respects (It is sometimes an unavoidable part of the job.)

- Being assigned to cover an event about which the writer has little expertise

- Stories heavily involving unnamed sources alleging rules violations or criminal wrongdoing

One of the toughest stories for some writers to cover is the firing of a personality for whom they have great respect. It is depressing, for example, when you must describe the demise of a head coach of a team that has failed, especially if she or he is someone you like. There is usually great tension at those times. You have a job to do, asking many questions that affect the person's life and livelihood. There is little thrill in asking questions such as what caused the team's or coach's downfall, but it is what the job of reporting requires.

Mike Strom finds it toughest to write stories about the off-the-field behavior of some of today's sports personalities who bring their moral transgressions out in the open. "Having to write interesting, factual stories about the ugliness and distastefulness of a rape case involving pro football players is not something I enjoy," he says.

Sometimes interviewing can be the worst part of the business. Jane Allison Havsy of Yonkers, New York, is a part-time sports reporter for Gannett Suburban Newspapers (New York), "Part time because there isn't a choice!" she says. She works five nights a week, covering high school sports and is also the paper's professional soccer beat reporter. She writes biweekly columns on cyber-sports and women in sports. She remembers that Roberto Donadoni, the veteran Italian midfielder of the MetroStars (the New York/New Jersey Major League Soccer franchise) "tried to have me thrown out of the team locker room after the MetroStars were knocked out of the 1996 playoffs. He screamed at me in three languages. I understood Donadoni might be upset—it's natural when your season ends, particularly because of a teammate's mistake—but so was I. It was sort of funny afterward, particularly when the other reporters and a couple of players stuck up for me. But at the time, I was utterly humiliated, especially since I'd been there through the whole season."

The Financial Side of Newspaper Sportswriting

Stories of satisfaction with sportswriting income are as varied and numerous as the angles writers employ for their stories. One writer explained that when he was hired for his first job, he enjoyed writing so much and was so thrilled just to be working in the business, he forgot to ask what he would be making. When it soon occurred to him to ask, and he was told by the sports editor that he would be making $24,000 to start, he said, "Wow, I'm rich!" That story, however, really does not reflect the typical feeling writers have about the adequacy of their compensation.

Another sportswriter said that his salary permitted him to live comfortably and that he attained top-scale wages after only a few years, at about age twenty-eight. On the other hand, some of the sports reporters we interviewed at major papers felt that they were underpaid, although they were making what seemed to us to be a fine income. It's hard to believe they feel so underpaid, especially when you realize that sportswriters rarely leave their profession for other, seemingly more lucrative jobs.

Writers generally theorize that they are very well qualified to work in several related professions, such as public relations, advertising, and radio or television fields, all of which are discussed in other chapters of this book. Often, these fields offer high salaries, but the better writers tend to stay in the newspaper profession. It seems obvious that they relish their work and that they're well satisfied with the compensation and perquisites it offers, despite their protestations. Conversely, others admit that they are making more money than they ever thought possible.

Writers are often surprised to hear that sports editors on other newspapers pay their writers overtime and/or give compensatory ("comp") time for excessive time worked. Experienced writers who read this section will probably be shocked because they never heard of such a practice. One reporter said that usually he receives such compensation when he asks and shows justification for it. Young sports journalists should consider making such a plea when they have been overworked, but if the request results in a stiff "kick in the butt," don't say you read it here!

National Salary Survey

The salary data in Table 2.2 is excerpted from a report that was prepared by the Illinois-based Inland Press Association. Nationally, 509 daily newspapers reported salaries in eleven circulation categories ranging from less than 10,000 to more than 500,000. (Salaries in individual locales are almost bound to differ from these national averages.)

Table 2.2 National Salary Survey of Sports Departments

Job Title	Low	Average	High
Senior reporter (with substantial experience)	$16,246	$34,394	$109,405
Reporter (experienced)	$11,184	$27,055	$118,111
Reporter (entry level)	$10,816	$21,983	$ 43,604

Source: Inland Press Association

Newspaper Guild Salaries

Salaries at many metropolitan-area papers throughout the country are determined by local agreements or contracts such as those governed by the Newspaper Guild collective bargaining manual. Table 2.3 shows a minimum salary structure for Guild member newspapers across the country as listed in the manual. The Guild contract made no distinction among the various levels of journalists, such as those depicted in Table 2.2. Salaries of other professional positions on the newspaper such as photographers and some editors are also included in these salary tables.

Marion Needham, executive secretary of the Newspaper Guild Contracts Committee, explains that the average Guild contract runs for four years and that many are five- and six-year agreements. The salaries listed in the Guild contract tables are incrementally increased each year beyond 2000. Most Guild member newpapers and wire services member organizations are free to exceed these salaries based on merit. For all newspapers covered by Guild bargaining agreements, the average starting salary for reporters (as of October 1, 1997) is $481.99.

Table 2.3 Reporter and Photographer Starting Minimums in 101 Contracts (as of October 1, 1997)

New York Times	$1279.89	Seattle Times	571.29
Honolulu Advertiser	786.59	Seattle Post-Intelligencer	558.22
Honolulu Star-Bulletin	786.59	Denver Rocky Mountain News	543.00
Washington Post	784.70	Minneapolis Star Tribune	542.00
Victoria Times-Colonist	755.27	Portland (Maine) Press Herald	533.57
Philadelphia Inquirer, Philadelphia Daily News	734.70	Indianapolis Star	530.50
Pittsburgh Post-Gazette	728.00	Detroit News	529.84
Chicago Sun-Times	722.61	Detroit Free Press	529.14
Ottawa Citizen	718.90	Providence Journal-Bulletin	528.20
Boston Herald	715.31	Eugene (Ore.) Register Guard	527.89
Montreal Gazette	713.00	El Diario-La Prensa (N.Y.)	527.15
Maui (Hawaii) News	690.30	St. Paul Pioneer Press	518.11
Hilo (Hawaii) Tribune-Herald	663.29	Jersey City Jersey Journal	516.61
Boston Globe	648.33	Buffalo News	515.84
St. Louis Post-Dispatch	643.00	Denver Post	510.68
Toledo Blade	624.18	Chester Delaware County (Pa.) Times	502.43
Manchester (N.H.) Union Leader	620.10	Santa Rosa (Calif.) Press Democrat	500.94
Cleveland Plain Dealer	609.31	Modesto (Calif.) Bee	500.00
San Francisco Chronicle, Examiner (2)	598.57	Mt. Clemens (Mich.) Macomb Daily, Daily Tribune (2)	496.04
San Jose Mercury-News	577.45	Los Angeles Daily News	491.76
Milwaukee Journal-Sentinel	577.00	North Bay (Ontario) Nugget	483.51
San Mateo (Calif.) Times	572.81	Memphis Commercial Appeal	480.93

Monterey (Calif.) Herald	476.00
San Juan Star	475.18
Knoxville News-Sentinel	469.88
Allentown Call	469.51
Pottstown (Pa.) Mercury	461.02
Joliet (Ill.) Herald-News	459.79
Fall River (Mass.) Herald-News	453.71
Sheboygan (Wis.) Press	448.44
York (Pa.) Daily Record	445.50
Woonsocket (R.I.) Call	443.63
Noticias del Mundo	442.00
Erie News, Times (2)	438.65
Waukegan (Ill.) News-Sun	435.05
San Diego Union-Tribune	433.95
Long Beach (Calif.) Press-Telegram	432.81
Canton (Ohio) Repository	427.51
Sioux City (Iowa) Journal	426.43
Bakersfield (Calif.) Californian	425.00
York (Pa.) Dispatch	419.00
Kingston (N.Y.) Daily Freeman	418.65
Lynn (Mass.) Item	417.31
Peoria (Ill.) Journal Star	414.45
Pueblo (Colo.) Chieftain	413.85
Pawtucket (R.I.) Times	412.83
Kenosha (Wis.) News	411.96

Sudbury (Ontario) Star	409.81
Sacramento Bee	400.18
Akron Beacon Journal	400.00
Fresno Bee	398.79
San Juan El Vocero	395.00
Youngstown Vindicator	392.00
Bellevue (Wash.) Journal-American	392.00
Harrisburg (Pa.) Patriot, News (2)	388.28
Cincinnati, Kentucky Post (2)	385.00
Norristown (Pa.) Times Herald	385.00
Brockton (Mass.) Enterprise	380.76
Duluth (Minn.) News-Tribune	379.09
Baltimore Sun	370.00
Yakima (Wash.) Herald-Republic	366.76
Norwalk (Conn.) Hour	366.00
Waterville (Maine) Sentinel	364.00
Rochester (N.Y.) Democrat & Chronicle, Times-Union (2)	362.00
Scranton Times, Tribune (2)	360.91
Gary Post-Tribune	357.07
Terre Haute Tribune-Star	354.58
Wilkes-Barre Citizens' Voice	352.24
Dayton Daily News	351.00
Albany Times-Union	346.29

Table 2.3 continued

Hazleton (Pa.) *Standard-Speaker*	341.54	Lansing (Mich.) *State Journal*	308.53
Lexington *Herald-Leader*	330.00	Massillon (Ohio) *Independent*	278.05
Monessen (Pa.) *Valley Independent*	328.57	Utica *Observer-Dispatch*	245.00
Chattanooga *Times*	325.00	Battle Creek *Enquirer*	184.00

Comparing Wire Service and Newspaper Salaries

Table 2.4 compares salaries (as of October 1, 1997) of wire service professionals covered by the Guild with those of newspaper reporters for cities with Guild contracts.

Freelancing

We discuss freelancing in more detail in Chapter 15, but the subject has an obvious impact on the financial considerations of the newspaper sports business, especially for writers with some experience. In our survey of sports editors, they told us they regularly use freelancers to augment their staff functions.

Experienced beat writers for most major metropolitan papers can pick and choose the amount of freelancing they take on. Some are so busy on their beats, that they turn down most or all requests. Others are happy with the income and prestige it affords them. One typical sports journalist told us that he averages more than 100 pieces per year. A conservative estimate of his freelancing compensation each year is between $15,000 and $20,000. Another major city beat writer makes from $350 to $500 per story, depending on its scope, and is happy to get the extra work. Popular beat writers work for periodicals on a regular basis, adding significantly to their salaries and making up to $300 or $400 a week, during their particular sport's season.

Typical freelance assignments for established sports writers are:

- Daily notes about team activities for *USA Today*

- Articles for major city magazines

Table 2.4 Wire Service Newsperson and Reporter Top Minimums

United States	AP	Reuters, U.S.	UPI	Newspaper Reporter
Albany	$882.00			$750.20
Baltimore	887.00			979.00
Boston	925.00	$1367.73		1179.18/887.68
Buffalo	882.00			962.97
Chattanooga	877.00		$664.49	351.52
Chicago	925.00	1367.73	664.49	1081.08
Cincinnati	882.00			842.50
Cleveland	882.00			1001.76
Dayton	877.00			660.50
Denver	887.00	1367.73		925.00
Detroit	887.00			750.00
Fresno	877.00			675.00
Harrisburg	882.00			631.90
Honolulu	887.00			1000.00
Indianapolis	882.00			816.25
Knoxville	877.00			672.00
Lexington	877.00			525.00
Los Angeles	925.00	1367.73	664.49	672.95
Memphis	877.00			792.69
Milwaukee	887.00			752.00
Minneapolis	887.00			1019.75
New York	962.00	1367.73	664.49	1308.89
Peoria	877.00			721.00

Table 2.4 continued

Philadelphia	887.00		664.49	1110.00
Pittsburgh	887.00		664.49	985.00
Portland, Me.	877.00			772.75
Providence	877.00			922.03
Puerto Rico	489.00		664.49	470.00/484.00
Rochester	877.00		664.49	419.00
Sacramento	887.00		664.49	649.00
St. Louis	882.00			1028.00
St. Paul	887.00			979.08
San Diego	887.00			832.76
San Francisco	925.00	1367.73	664.49	944.35
San Jose	877.00			946.76
Seattle	887.00		664.49	816.00
Toledo	877.00			944.03
Washington, D.C.	962.00	1367.73		968.00
Yakima	877.00			574.80

Canada	Canadian Press	Reuters, Canada	Newspaper Reporter
Montreal	$1013.13	$1217.42	$1129.00
Ottawa	1013.13	1217.42	1044.11
Victoria	1013.13		1139.55

- *Sports Illustrated*

- *Pro Football Weekly*

- *The Sporting News*

- *Football Digest* magazine

Learning to say no to freelance requests becomes important for several writers because their time away from the beat or the column becomes more valuable than the income derived. It seems that the more experience a journalist gains, the more in demand her or his work is at other periodicals. Paradoxically, at that point in their careers, writers want more time to spend with their families or personal pursuits, or they need less extra income because they are well satisfied with their salaries.

Summing Up

To sum up this chapter on newspaper journalism, we examine the words of two of the great coaches in modern collegiate sports, who shared their ideas of a first-class sportswriter.

Joe Paterno, head football coach at Penn State, says "I believe a quality sports reporter is someone who is industrious, fair, and accurate. The responsibility of the reporter, in my view, is to be sure he or she has done the necessary homework, is confident that the facts are correct and that the issues are presented in a balanced manner. There will be honest disagreements between journalists and coaches/players/athletic administrators. Like those of us involved in the game, reporters make mistakes, and the good ones acknowledge theirs without reservation. We've dealt with a lot of quality journalists in 48 seasons at Penn State and found that, on balance, sports reporters have a genuine interest in what they do and a desire to be factual and objective in meeting their responsibilities to the reading/listening/viewing public."

Mike Krzyzewski, head basketball coach of Duke University, had this to say: "A quality journalist is someone who will write the truth and understand that he or she is actually accountable for what they write. Too many journalists hear a rumor and write a sensational story concerning that rumor without doing the work necessary to find out the complete story. One of my pet peeves is answering questions that indicate the reporter already has the story written and is just trying to get quotes to substantiate the article he is going to submit."

The ideas and recommendations in this chapter should answer most of the questions students and writers ask when they consider the exciting profession of newspaper sportswriting. This career field provides a level of challenge and reward found in few other vocations, especially for those who love to write about the roar of the crowd and the thrill of the athletic contest.

Although it is rare that sportswriters begin their careers as writers in other fields such as public relations, sports information, or marketing, it's not uncommon for a newspaper sportswriter to be attracted to and do well in the other professions described throughout this book. That is because they are, by definition, proficient writers who possess the talent necessary for many of the sports journalism careers. Remember that newspaper sports journalism can provide all of the professional challenge and enjoyment you need for one life, as it has for countless others. Or, as we said at the beginning of this chapter, it can lead, as it did for Walter Cronkite, to other satisfying journalistic rewards.

3 Sports Copy Editing

While copy editing is not usually the stuff of childhood dreams, with the right newspaper it can be a fine profession.

Craig Branson
American Society of Newspaper Editors (ASNE)

If on-the-field action and lively encounters with sports people are your journalistic forte, this field may *not* be perfect for you. But copy editing experts convinced us that, as Branson said, "it can be a fine profession," especially if you enjoy the camaraderie of the copy desk, the predictable hours, a steadier home life, and the opportunity to put your expertise to work to improve your publication's stories. If you are a capable copy editor with good sports awareness, you can enjoy the work of editing sports news, columns, and stories. Unlike some other chapters of this book, which are punctuated with journalists' entertaining tales of sports personalities, travel to exciting places, and exposure of behind-the-scenes secrets, this one is more like the typical copy editor: matter-of-fact, hardworking, and dedicated to making a top-quality production.

Defining the Role of the Copy Editor

In *The Journalist's Road to Success*, published by the Dow Jones Newspaper Fund, the copy editor is described as "an entry-level position that involves great attention to detail, accuracy and possible libel, as well as an advanced command of the language." Later, the description reads, "With some experience editing news stories and writing headlines, copy editors can quickly advance to positions such as layout/design editors and production editors."

Although much of that may fit at some publications, it is also true that very many well-educated and dedicated people proudly spend their careers as editors and contribute heavily to the image and quality of their newspapers, magazines, and other forms of communications. At many medium and large newspapers, editors concentrate their expertise on the special language of sports as "sports copy editors," whereas at smaller papers they may double as reporters and editors of the sports section.

Some of the best sports reporters and columnists depend on the skills of editors on the copy desk to check for accuracy, correct mistakes, and improve the readability of their stories. Other sportswriters may moan about or resist the editorial function, but if the checks and balances resulting from it did not exist, their work would take much longer and/or would produce subpar stories.

Craig Branson says, "Good copy editors are worth their weight in gold." The best edit copy, fix errors, correct grammatical mistakes, protect against libel, and convey the meaning of the writer. Many others, however, are alleged to be guilty of copy editor sins such as mass rewriting, obfuscation of a writer's meaning, and making stories muddier rather than clearer.

Generally, the copy desks throughout the newspaper business have recently achieved a higher profile and an enhanced degree of respect within the newsroom. Most copy editors enforce their paper's writing and editing standards via its editorial policy and guidelines. Most reporters and columnists know and respect the role of the copy editor in meeting those guidelines. When editors provide clear reasons for their recommended changes, management and most writers support them. Arguments and disagreements are common, however, when a reporter's work is targeted.

Some of the copy editors with whom we spoke are of the opinion that too many graduates of journalism courses are not great at grammar skills. "They go into journalism because they want to report, which is different from being skilled at sentence structure,"

Branson says. We agree that publishers should continue to elevate the status of the sports copy desk and ensure that young people realize how important the job is to the newspaper's quality. Then, talented journalists might be attracted to it.

Guardians of Editorial Policy

Copy editors, especially senior copy desk pros, are responsible for reflecting editorial policy in their publications. Sometimes the policy is well advertised; often it is only in the minds of a few editors. Whether it is conservative, liberal, or radical, the editor must reflect it consistently. When Jim DeStefano, now a sports copy editor for the *Philadelphia Daily News*, left the *Philadelphia Journal* for a new position at the *Arizona Republic*, he went from a "high-stepping paper" to a very conservative one whose editorial policy was diametric to the one to which he was accustomed. "At the *Journal*," he says, "the idea was the crazier the better; almost anything went. You could write a one-sided story and get away with it, but at the *Republic*, there was a strict and heavy emphasis on balanced reporting, the cautious side. If there was a press release that said there was going to be groundbreaking for a new facility—you'd have to attribute it (i.e., 'said the athletic director')."

The Arizona job provided excellent training for DeStefano because he had to question more things and be more selective about story material. He left the restrained copy desk of the *Republic* to join the *Daily News* fourteen years ago. In his new position, he found a blend of liberal and conservative policies and a large group of talented writers with a license to opinionize. This is one aspect that has made the paper so popular with its readership.

It's Not Just Spelling and Grammar

For those unfamiliar with the scope of sports copy editing, it is much more than spelling, punctuation, and grammar (although these are attended to in the process). To develop a story that readers enjoy requires the thoroughly researched and well-written input of the reporter. The editor analyzes the story for a host of elements such as readability, completeness, attribution, and legal concerns. Some reporters write so well that only a few of these elements require more than surface editing. However, the pressure of writer deadlines frequently necessitates a thorough evaluation and edit. DeStefano cites the following stories as testimonials to the need for good copy editors. "As I reviewed a recent story, I found it to be well written, except that the reader wouldn't find the compelling part of the story until three-quarters of the way through it," he says. "I suggested that the writer move those paragraphs closer to the beginning. The writer agreed, and the story was considerably improved."

In another case, DeStefano argued to keep a story *out* of the paper. "When I first read it," he says, "it told of suspicions that a local university was running its athletic program illegally, but the writer never got to the point of spelling out the infractions. I alerted our editor to my concern, telling him I didn't think we should print it. He was reluctant to hold it, because he had budgeted a page and a half for it, and something else would be needed to fill the space on short notice. I convinced him, however, to hold it, and we were glad we did because no documentation could be found to substantiate the allegations. Thankfully, our faces were egg free."

A copy editor must also be a research specialist. As long as there are careless writers, editors are the paper's last line of defense against inaccuracy. If you do not like researching sports details, finding just the right word, or questioning every statement, this field is not a good choice because such attention is needed in all newsrooms.

This work also requires an editor to have a background in sports, so that he or she knows what makes a story interesting to sports fans and can evaluate the facts and credibility of the piece. "It's difficult," says DeStefano, "to do a thorough job without familiarity with the specific sport, especially those that could involve a potential lawsuit and where people's rights are involved."

Instant News Judgment

One of the important talents of a successful sports copy editor is the ability to make instantaneous news decisions, sometimes minutes before the paper goes to press. This talent often displays itself when the "late" editor, the one in charge of the copy desk, has to decide what to do with an unusually late-breaking story. John Conceison, an editor at the *Union News* in Springfield, Massachusetts, cites an example when he was the late man on the night of the Orange Bowl game, which had implications for the college football national championship. The wire services were advising that the bowl results would hold up the Associated Press (AP) polling for the nation's number one team until the morning. But, at 2:10 A.M., when all the scores were in and he was about to leave for home, the wire suddenly advised that the AP's final Top 25—and the national champion—would be available at 2:30 A.M.

Conceison had to decide immediately whether to hold the presses (incurring printers' overtime and distribution delay) in order to get the "number one" story into some morning editions, so that fans would have the scoop with their morning coffee. He decided to go for it. He held the press run for the valuable story that Michigan was AP's national champion. "I had to change three stories related to the game and the poll within ten minutes," Conceison says, "But we were able to run the story in 18,000 papers. It was the first news many fans would have of the selection. Readers appreciate such efforts by their daily newspaper."

The Appeal of the Copy Desk

Expert editors in the business frequently come from the ranks of sportswriters. They enjoy their work and, because of advantages such as the following, recommend the copy desk to other journalists in search of a satisfying profession.

- *The excitement of deadline pressure.* "Especially," says Mike Sansone, sports copy desk chief of the *Sacramento Bee,* "when there's a big story to be worked on."

- *Stability and predictability.* Unlike reporters, whose frequently long workdays are determined by events and personalities beyond their control, an editor goes to work and leaves around the same time every day (or night).

- *Good income.* Copy editors at all but the smallest papers make a good living and are paid very well at the larger ones. Frequently, there are opportunities to make extra income with overtime.

- *Team atmosphere.* Sansone enjoys "the good feeling of the copy desk group working as a team with a common goal. Writing, on the other hand, is a solitary pursuit."

- *Satisfaction of rebuilding a story to make it better.* DeStefano says that he "gets more gratification from having helped a story as an editor. I get the same enjoyment from producing a polished sports section or doing an especially good edit as when I used to see my bylined story on the main sports page each morning."

- *Never a dull moment.* Copy editors agree that there's always something going on in their part of the sports world.

- *Regular sense of accomplishment.* "Every day you have that sense of accomplishment of having a good product on the street," Sansone says. "You don't have to wait for days or weeks to feel that satisfaction."

Walking the Talk

At most newspapers, the sports copy desk is involved in more breaking stories than in general news. There is also more updating and rewriting between editions because so many sports stories occur at night. A typical work shift runs from 4 P.M. until about 1 A.M. At papers with more than one edition, copy editors are always updating some story and sometimes there are as many as four versions of a story filed. Jim DeStefano likes knowing that he will go to work at 7 P.M., he will work hard, and with the help of six others he will produce a good sports section. He walks out the back door around 3 A.M. and does not have to worry about the job until the next day. "I really like that," he says, "Having that separation in my life of job and home . . . and seeing the fruits of our labor (when a quality section hits the streets). Let's face it, we make a pretty good living."

John Conceison describes some of the roles performed each night by four editors at his paper's copy desk:

- The *anchor* is in charge of assigning work; doing the major layout for each section; and specifying the story length, headline size, and other requirements.

- The two copy *readers* edit and place headlines on the stories.

- The *paginator* acts as a proofreader who takes the readers' output and sets it in place on the page using computer software.

Bylines for Copy Editors

Most journalists perceive the copy editor's job as consisting mainly of the conventional functions of correcting grammar, checking facts, and layout, but there are times at many papers when the copy editor jumps into the role of reporter. It is a versatile talent that sports editors appreciate; they can depend on the copy desk to take on an important, developing story when a beat writer is in transit or unavailable.

While at the *Boston Globe*, John Conceison filled in as a reporter from the copy desk during a late-breaking NHL trade between the Boston Bruins and the Philadelphia Flyers. "Our hockey beat writer, Kevin Paul Dupont, was in transit," he says, "when negotiations for the trade of Dave Poulin (then of the Flyers) were being finalized. I was assigned to find and interview the player and pin down the story. Despite Poulin's stressful situation, he was a class guy, providing the information I needed to help develop the story for Kevin, who finally arrived to compile the story."

At small-circulation papers, bylines for copy editors who double as reporters are commonplace, but they are somewhat unusual at larger newspapers. In another peek inside the copy editor's world, Conceison describes a byline opportunity that came his way on the "night watch." As a part-time editor at the *Boston Globe,* one of his duties was to monitor the wires and television for possible breaking stories. Filling that role on the desk one night during the early 1990s, he "learned that the University of Massachusetts football coach had been told that his promised player scholarships were being reduced by the school administration." Conceison recalls, "As the story was breaking, we received a tip about the probable resignation of the coach because of the cutbacks." As the editor on night watch, Conceison was assigned to track down the coach, who willingly provided the details of his planned departure. The resulting story was a lead-page scoop, with a byline for Conceison.

Finances

Few copy editors become wealthy from their profession, but many make a very good living. Salaries for editors/readers on a sports desk seldom differ from those at the same paper's news desks, according to our experts. At small newspapers with circulations of more than 50,000, editors told us they were well satisfied with their income.

We found that typical West Coast and Midwest salaries were similar to East Coast figures, ranging from $800 to $1,200 weekly for mid- to large circulation papers, especially those under union or guild contracts. Nonunion copy editor income is often considerably less. For example, in a given metropolitan area, unionized copy desk personnel with five years' experience might make close to $1,200 weekly, but a nonunion counterpart may earn $200 less.

English and journalism graduates should note that in some situations starting copy editors enjoy higher starting salaries than their reporter colleagues. *The Journalist's Road to Success* lists the following averages for intern and entry-level editing income in its "Beginning Weekly Salaries for Newspaper Jobs" section as follows:

Intern copy editing—$329.28
Intern reporting—$272.50
Copy editor—$426.49
Reporter—$368.96

Newspaper salaries in individual localities are almost bound to differ from national averages. Salaries at many metropolitan area papers throughout the country are determined by local agreements or contracts such as those governed by the newspaper guilds. Table 3.1 shows the recent editorial salary structure for the two major papers and smaller suburban papers in southeastern Pennsylvania near Philadelphia. In this area, copy editors reach their maximum salary level ($1,107) after only three years, whereas reporters take four years to reach their maximum pay (see Chapter 2).

Editors' Associations

The major organizations dedicated to sports editing and copy editing are the American Society of Newspaper Editors, the Associated Press Sports Editors (APSE), and the American Copy Editors

Table 3.1 Typical Metropolitan Newspaper Editorial Salary Scales

	Year 1	*Year 2*	*Year 3*	*Year 4**
Editorial Assistant				
Inexperienced	$ 492.30	$ 522.30	$ 552.30	$ 577.15
After 1 year	$ 502.62	$ 532.62	$ 562.62	$ 587.94
After 2 years	$ 519.94	$ 549.94	$ 579.94	$ 606.04
After 3 years	$ 581.43	$ 611.43	$ 641.43	$ 670.29
Copy Editor				
Inexperienced	$ 603.71	$ 633.71	$ 663.71	$ 693.58
After 1 year	$ 698.95	$ 728.95	$ 758.95	$ 793.10
After 2 years	$ 764.59	$ 794.59	$ 824.95	$ 861.70
After 3 years	$1,000.00	$1,030.00	$1,060.00	$1,107.70

Source: Contract between Philadelphia Newspapers, Inc. (the *Philadelphia Inquirer* and the *Philadelphia Daily News*) and the Newspaper Guild of Greater Philadelphia.

*This contract was in effect through September 1997.

Society (ACES). The American Society of Newspaper Editors (www.asne.org/index.htm) is an organization of editors of daily newspapers in the United States and Canada. Its principal purpose is to serve as a medium for exchange of ideas and the professional growth and development of its members. Associated Press Sports Editors (www.detnews.com/metro/apse) states that its purposes are to improve professional standards of newspaper sports departments, to discuss and attempt to resolve problems of newspaper sports departments, to improve communication between sports departments, other newspaper departments, and management, and to recognize professional excellence among its members. The American Copy Editors Society (www.copydesk.org) is a professional organization of copy editors "dedicated to improving the quality of journalism and the working lives of journalists." Its primary focus is on copy editing for newspapers and other types of publications. Each organization welcomes students and new journalists.

Top Ten Copy Editor Complaints

Every profession has its downside. According to our survey, copy editors' daily lives would be significantly improved and the copy desk more effective if managing editors would consider these almost universal problems:

1. The lack of a clear corporate statement about the direction and quality that management wants for the paper. Guidelines on story types, editorial standards, and personnel policy are frequently unavailable, leaving copy editors to make up editorial policy on a case-by-case basis.

2. A lack of interest in ensuring that writers and editors interact regularly and that reporters are encouraged to work closely with the copy desk.

3. Too many overlong meetings. The time lost is inordinate and frustrating. The duration of important meetings should be carefully controlled by a supervisor.

4. The need for training. Copy editors, especially those who are new and untrained, are frequently thrust into their assignments without adequate technical and professional training that would ensure quality output.

5. Unrelieved, day-to-day tedium. Many copy editors would benefit greatly from temporary assignments that would enable them to refresh their journalistic juices and assist the sports editor in other ways.

6. Too many interruptions to answer phone calls. Such interruptions, which could be handled by interns or clerks, affect the orderly flow of editing with a significant reduction in schedule efficiency.

7. Antiquated equipment and editing tools. Management should listen to and try to follow staff recommendations for hardware, software, and tools that make the editing task more efficient and enjoyable.

8. The lack of management interaction with the copy desk. Supervisors should become involved in the concerns and attitudes of their copy editors.

9. A lack of incentives. Management should advertise and reward examples of outstanding work to set standards of excellence.

10. The lack of a career ladder. Management should alert copy editors to open or planned positions and promotions. A copy editor should be aware of where advancement is possible, such as to assistant features editor and/or reporter.

Interacting with Writers

For many copy editors, confrontations with writers is one of the toughest parts of the job. When an editor attacks a story that needs a lot of work with little time to fix it, that's trouble enough. But if the writer is also obstinate and defensive about his or her work, the editor can become especially stressed in dealing with them, usually over the phone and often on deadline. Obviously, reporters react in different ways: some are receptive to the criticism and understanding of improvements made; some are not. But what would an editor do without challenges like that to punctuate the night?

Another problem distressing to "desk people" is that some writers do not learn from their mistakes and constantly repeat them. Although many are very diligent, according to Jim DeStefano, "too many writers are careless about facts, even though 175,000 to 200,000 readers may read their story. When they are reckless with facts, I have to sift through reference books to make it correct. I want it to be right."

Educational Paths of the Pros

Although a broad education is essential, the following section attests to the fact that success doesn't always follow a straight line from college to career.

Jim DeStefano took an uncertain route on the way to his job as sports copy editor at the *Daily News*. As a sociology major at La Salle University in Philadelphia, he wasn't really certain what career he would pursue after graduation. His early plan was to be a teacher. In his sophomore year, to become more involved in school activities, he became interested in sportswriting for the school newspaper, the *La Salle Collegian*. "After a few articles, I found that I met people I wouldn't have otherwise encountered," he says. In his junior year, he became the sports editor.

After graduation, he went to night school at Temple University to pursue a master's degree in elementary education, while teaching during the day. However, journalism was pulling him in another direction and he followed it—into newspaper work at the *Germantown Courier*.

Diane Tomasik, formerly a copy editor at the *Cincinnati Post*, graduated from Florida Atlantic University in Boca Raton with a bachelor of arts degree in communication and a concentration in print journalism.

Mike Sansone began his career by earning a degree in mass communications at Illinois State University. Most of the copy editors on his sports desk are also college graduates, with various degrees. Some schools (such as the University of Chicago and the University of California at Berkeley) offer a certificate program in publishing, under which a certificate in copy editing can be earned. Many other university programs offer courses, if not certificates, in publishing, editing, or both. A reference librarian can offer valuable—and free—advice on researching and applying to these programs.

Job Hunting

In looking for job-hunting resources for sports copy editors, we found that *Editor and Publisher* (*E&P*) magazine and the Internet's "J-JOBS" ("J" for journalism) site have a variety of listings for entry-level and experienced positions in the business. You can find regular on-line offerings of journalism jobs and internships on-line at journet-l@american.edu. A typical recent posting (all of which can usually be answered by fax or E-mail) read like this (we have changed names):

The *Tribune,* an award-winning daily, is searching for a sports-writer and sports copy editor. The positions require strong reporting and technical skills in writing and editing and some experience with layout, design, and pagination. Knowledge of QuarkXPress preferred. The copy editor position is about half editing/design and half writing, and the writer position is mostly writing with spot layout for three-person sports staff that covers twelve high schools and two colleges. Send resume, cover letter, and clips to the *Tribune* Sports Editor Scott Long. The *Tribune* is an Equal Opportunity Employer that encourages diversity in the workplace. Women and minorities are encouraged to apply.

The Career Kickoff

As Craig Branson's chapter-opening quotation says, copy editing is not usually the stuff of childhood dreams. Young writers are not too knowledgeable about the role of these copy desk journalists who make certain that the stories sports fans enjoy are accurate and easy to read. Copy editors usually select their profession, not as a primary goal in high school or early college, but rather after working at jobs such as newspaper reporting and public relations.

John Conceison tried many journalistic endeavors after graduating from Boston College with a degree in political science. After four years as a reporter and sports editor on the college paper and working in the college sports information office, Conceison opted for a full-time position the college offered him as the sports publicity assistant. He did not become interested in the copy desk until, after toiling full time in sports information for nearly four years, he began writing at the *Worcester* (Massachusetts) *Telegram* (now the *Telegram and Gazette*). He enjoyed the work there, then moved on to the *Boston Globe* copy desk.

If it were not for small-town and neighborhood papers, where would sports journalists begin their careers? Most editors and writers we surveyed found smaller publications to be a great place to learn. During a summer of reporting at the *Germantown Courier,* in suburban Philadelphia, Jim DeStefano earned the princely sum of $2 an hour for twenty hours a week before returning to complete his graduate-school education at Temple University. Eventually, however, he withdrew from Temple and a teaching position to stay at the *Courier* because he enjoyed sportswriting more.

He soon found a better opportunity at the suburban Montgomery Newspapers chain, which needed a full-time sportswriter for a newly launched daily, *Today's Spirit*. DeStefano covered the Philadelphia Flyers for most of the five years he worked for the *Spirit*, and they were the glory years for the NHL hockey team. He covered the Flyers through their play-off runs in 1974 and 1975 and in their Stanley Cup victory.

When the opportunity arose to join the fledgling city paper, *The Journal*, DeStefano saw it as a golden opportunity. "I was going to work for a paper with a much larger circulation," he says. "I was going to make more money and have more exposure. But during my interview, they laid it out in no uncertain terms: we would have to work six days (for six to twelve months), but they were offering $100 more a week than I was making. The paper was looking for a hockey writer, and my Flyer clips must have helped. The new owners were French Canadian, and the paper had a big hockey following."

Although he traveled regularly, got to know the players and writers from all over North America, attended fancy restaurants and lots of games, he really didn't enjoy it. "To management, my job was the most important one at the paper and the pressure was too much," DeStefano says. His decision that he was much more suited to the sports copy desk was of great benefit to the *Daily News,* where he has enjoyed working for the last 14 years.

Finding Your Way into Copy Editing

At many newspapers and periodicals, hiring good copy editors is not an easy task. To help in the process of creating qualified candidates, Anne Glover, assistant managing editor of the copy desk at the *St. Petersburg Times,* produced a handout for a Poynter Institute seminar for journalism educators. In it, she offers some inside tips on how to get a good copy desk job:

1. *Passion for the work.* We have a motto at the *St. Petersburg Times*: We hire *journalists*. Whatever you want to call yourself beyond that—copy editor, designer, visual journalist, reporter—is fine. But our experience has been

that if you have the journalism part down, your success is virtually guaranteed. If you work for a newspaper, you must care about news. You must be conversant in what the news of the day is. It's not enough to work at a newspaper. You must immerse yourself in it. Because we expect you to immerse yourself in ours.

2. *A solid education in the basics.* By basics, I mean copy editing, reporting, grammar, style, spelling, headline writing, and news decision making. It will help if you have some design or computer skills, or at least know some design concepts.

   Try not to be too discouraged by want ads that ask for Quark skills. There are still plenty of newspapers out there—small to major—that don't require such skills. While it's great to find technically inclined copy editors, it's important to remember that this technology is merely a tool with which to practice our craft.

3. *Experience.* Whether it's an internship or a stint on your college paper, there is no substitute. I rarely look at grade point averages on resumes. I look for experience that's going to help that person make a smooth transition into the pressure-filled world of a major daily newspaper.

4. *Creativity.* Your cover letter and your resume will tell a lot about you. If you have written to the human resources department, that makes me wonder how well you'll be able to use our research library to find information. After all, how hard is it to call the switchboard of a newspaper and ask them who is in charge of hiring copy editors? If you are applying for a job with a focus on design, ditch the standard resume form and show me what kind of flair you have. If it's a standard copy editing job, make sure your cover letter says something other than that you would enjoy talking with me about opportunities at the *Times*. Show me in that letter what sort of person you would be for the newspaper. Show me some passion for what you're seeking.

   Creativity, whether in headlines, cutlines, art ideas, or design, is an extremely attractive trait in copy editors.

Along those same lines, try to send your very best, most creative work. Don't just send clips. Make sure they are special clips.

5. *Knowledge of the newspaper.* We are available at most major newsstands. So, it puzzles me when people apply and have no knowledge of our newspaper.

    If you absolutely don't have any knowledge, ask me about all the things I have just described. If you don't ask these types of questions, I don't get a sense that you really want to work at the *Times,* you just want to work. Yes, flattery and a show of interest will get you everywhere. But please, be sincere.

6. *Convictions.* This is not a business for the wishy-washy. When you make a decision, you have to be able to defend it. So tell me how you feel about our news decisions, or the lead story that was in the *New York Times* that day, or the graphic photo that everyone ran of the bombing in Oklahoma City. Tell me about your newspaper's reputation in the community and whether that reputation is deserved.

    Talk to me about what you think a newspaper's role in the community should be. Tell me what you think a copy editor's role should be at a newspaper.

7. *Flexibility and a sense of reality.* Not everyone can start at a major newspaper, or start as the designer at a major newspaper. Use that entry-level position to find out how things work at your newspaper. Absorb as much knowledge as you can and be willing to work on just about anything your editors ask you to. The more you show your flexibility, the more valuable you become. You also show everyone that you can be trusted to do a variety of jobs.

8. *Attention to detail.* I scan cover letters and resumes for style and grammar errors. If you have an error, it's a good bet you won't get hired. I know people get in a hurry, but first impressions are extremely important, so

check, check, and check again. If you do send in clips, I'll be looking at headlines, cutlines, weird indents, cropping, teases, and just about anything else on the page that involves detail work. As the saying goes, "God is in the details," and so it is with journalism.

9. *Curiosity.* Do you know what's going on in the world, in your community? Do you know about trends in the journalism world? Can you put things into historical context? If you work on a local desk, do you still read about the latest congressional actions? Do you know about the extensive use of public records in today's newsrooms? Are you curious enough about design to investigate trends and advances in that area? In other words, do you have curiosity about things around you, or things that you know will help you in your career?

10. *Common sense.* This is the tricky little trait that usually separates the leaders from the followers in the copy desk world. Common sense is having peripheral vision, so that you can make informed decisions. Common sense is being able to make decisions on the fly that are the right decisions. Common sense is having an intuitive sense that something needs to be done and then *doing it.*

"To be a copy editor," Glover says "is to tackle one of the toughest and sometimes most thankless jobs in the newsroom. To get hired or to move ahead in the business is even tougher—in many newsrooms, it's 'sink or swim' for the copy editor, with very little help or advice along the way."

One final thought: anticipation and preparation are two things that can turn average copy editors into brilliant copy editors. Keep your ear to the ground, your eyes open, and your brain busy thinking ahead, and you will wow your fellow editors.

What It Takes to Be the Best

Many sports editors told us they look first for good editorial skills, not necessarily sports experience. Others said they do not hire editors who are not knowledgeable sports fans because doing so would present an unnecessary learning curve they cannot afford. Diane Tomasik states that enthusiasm for the subject matter certainly helps, but a sports editor wants someone sharp and creative, a problem solver. A good news editor is usually a generalist whose broad knowledge should include an awareness of what is happening on the sports pages and in world and national news.

In addition to designing layouts and writing headlines as a copy editor, Tomasik was also the *Cincinnati Post*'s website editor: "I enjoyed doing the total package," she says, "which meant picking the stories, editing them, writing the headlines, and laying out the pages." After graduating from college, she worked as news and sports copy editor at smaller Florida papers such as the *Sun-Tattler* in Hollywood and the *Boca Raton News*. She also has been a member of the Women in Communications Association and the Women's Sports Foundation.

"You have to be a stickler for detail." Tomasik explains, "If your general knowledge nags you that something's not quite right, you should be spurred to look it up. In this profession, you're being asked to be creative while working under severe time and space constraints. Sometimes that's a volatile mix. Those who can harness that best do well." She enjoys sports so much that she created a popular personal website, a tribute to George Seifert, former San Francisco 49ers coach.

All copy editors strive to be perfect, but everyone is human. To be the perfect copy editor, take note of the following "deadly sins" as enumerated by veteran copy editor, desk supervisor, and newsroom manager Anne Glover of the *St. Petersburg Times*. Avoid them and you will be a shining star on the copy desk.

The Seven Deadly Copy Editing Sins

1. *Arrogance.* This could also be described as selfishness: Your layout, your efforts to be clever in your headline at the expense of clarity, the choices you make about using space in your section say to the reader, "I don't care about you. This was more convenient for me to do." There are many

variations on this: grouped cutlines that make it unclear which photos they accompany, type that the reader can't read, photos played too small, a story that's hard to follow because of the layout, art heads that don't say anything.

2. *Assumptions*. You assume that the reporter did the math, or that the photographer got the name wrong, not the reporter. Or you assume that the reporter meant something that he or she did not. Or you assumed that someone else would take care of the weekend planning because you were about to go on vacation. Or you assumed that you could use a certain typographic style on your front because that's what you saw the designer do.

3. *Sloppiness*. There are so many ways this manifests itself, but here are a few: widows [stray characters at the end of a paragraph] left scattered throughout the page; no page number in a tease [a line referencing a story to an inside page]; a jump line that refers readers to the wrong page; a cutline that says someone is in the photo when they clearly are not; a cutline caption name that is different from the name in the story; a bad break in a headline that makes it difficult to understand.

4. *Indifference*. You treat a great story as if it is just another daily feature by giving it a small headline or playing it in a 15-pica-wide hole down the side of the page. Or you play a piece of great art in a mediocre way because you can't see its need to run large or with a great crop.

   Its cousin is *sameness*. Every page is predictable, from the headlines to the size of the art to the basic layout of the page. Give your readers something to take away with that day's page: an interesting headline, a tease, a great crop on a photo, a helpful info box.

5. *Ignorance*. You run a photo of the wrong congressman from your district because you haven't been paying attention. Or you decide that World War II ended on June 6 because you didn't bother reading the package we had on page 1A about V-E Day. Or you thought you would be clever by using

another language in a headline, but you used the wrong tense in the verb. Or you thought a television show was coming on that night when it had changed nights a month ago. Readers always know these things, and you damage the newspaper's credibility when you show that you don't.

6. *Laziness*. You didn't bother to check to see if we had file art to go with a profile because it wasn't your job and someone should have put it on the budget. Or you didn't bother teasing something because you couldn't find out what page it was on. Or you didn't finish up that advance page because your shift was up and you thought someone else could finish it for you the next day. Or you didn't bother looking up something in the style book because you're pretty sure it was right. Or you didn't want to check out the background of a story in the electronic library because you thought the copy chief would catch it.

7. *Inflexibility*. You can't possibly change that front page because it's late, and just how important could a downed helicopter in the bay be? Or, you have that page all done, why are they asking for another information graphic on it now? Or you resent having to work a later shift when someone is out. Or you don't feel comfortable working in sports.

Finding Your Way Out of Copy Editing

Do copy editors aspire to be *sports editors*? The experts were, of course, divided on this question. A typical response from one group was: "I don't want any part of that! I have no desire to be a sports editor. I wouldn't want to spend my day going to meetings, writing memos, and managing people." The other group was less vocal because they did not want their boss, the sports editor, to know they were after his or her job. But to many ambitious, talented, and experienced copy editors, the "top job" is a realizable goal.

A good copy editor can move from the copy desk to other positions, such as reporting. Many have had early training as writers at smaller papers and decide to return. They may be better writers than before because they have learned the difference between good and mediocre journalism.

Although he will not take credit for the fact that very few of his copy personnel leave the sports desk at the *Sacramento Bee,* Mark Sansone says that most of his staff has stayed put, several for ten to twenty years. "The main reason that anyone leaves the sports desk is to avoid weekend and night work," he says.

Mike Rathet, sports editor at the *Philadelphia Daily News* for almost twenty-five years, tells ambitious editors with an eye on a sports editor's job: "First, make sure you want to be in this business, which is a very tough one. It's much more bottom-line oriented now than when I started, and it's a little tougher to run through the mine fields. It was much more writer-oriented, writer-friendly years ago. There's a lot of emphasis now on profit, economy, and shared content.

"It was a glamorous business back then, and I always considered it fun. It's harder now, more of a job. Nonetheless, I think sports is still one of the joys, because we work in a field where life and death are not at stake. It's still fun and games—at least it's supposed to be."

Final Words of Advice from the Editors

The experts say that if you're going into sports you can't be a clock-watcher. There's so much to keep track of, and it doesn't all happen between 9 A.M. and 5 P.M. If you get bored with the nine-to-five routine, copy editing will allow you to see the opposite side of life, with hours very different from those everyone else works.

We have heard this advice offered to young writer/editors before, but it needs constant emphasis: "Read. Read everything. Read sports. Read news. Read entertainment. Read books, magazines, the Internet. Read!" says Diane Tomasik. Reading helps to build your knowledge and it also provides examples of different writing styles. Reading different authors and reporters can help you build a style of your own. Borrow what you like. "Develop a sense of rhythm in your writing and editing," she adds. "Help your vocabulary grow."

John Conceison recommends that editors and writers go back to their grammar textbooks to refresh themselves on the fundamentals of good writing. It is also important for editors to ensure objectivity in sports news stories. "There are some writers," he says, "who, despite their skill, sometimes allow themselves to slant a story toward a personal like or dislike." That is not good journalism, and budding sportswriters should pride themselves on the important trait of impartiality.

One of the best ways for writers to enjoy their profession is to appreciate the role of the editor—*without an attitude*. Some young journalists need to understand that they have limited experience, and, despite all of their education and their background, a good copy editor can be their best friend.

4 Careers as Sports Editors

The very best are separated from the rest in sports editing by their level of creativity. Even when there is a raft of daily details to work through, good sports editors are always looking for a different and better way to do things, and that always sets high standards.

John Rawlings
Editor, *The Sporting News*

Profile of a Sports Editor

The typical sports editor

- Ranges in age from thirty-two at small-town newspapers to forty-nine or older at big-city newspapers

- Averages a minimum of ten years' experience as a reporter, an editor, or both

- Earns an average of $53,000 in the smaller markets to $90,000 in the mid-size and larger markets, but goes well over $100,000 in the largest

- Is well satisfied with the job

- Is a white male

And he or she has the following roles and responsibilities: managing production, supervising the reporting and editing staff including copy editors), selecting the stories to be printed, and determining the space budget for the sports section.

From our sports editor survey, we found that there is a lot of individual variation among sports editors, but what they have in common is their dedication to the quality and integrity of the material published under their "watch." The next most common trait they share is their race (Caucasian) and their gender (male), although there are some signs of change. We discovered that only a few sports editors are from ethnic minorities, and only about twenty are women. Sports editors earn the lowest salaries at the smaller newspapers, of course, with some as low as $29,000. But, on the other end of the scale, they usually draw the highest incomes of all newspaper journalists.

Before we go on, let's clear up the important distinction between *sports editors* and *sports copy editors*. This chapter discusses the roles and responsibilities of sports editors, the men and women who plan and manage the resources, personnel, and production of sports publications. Although sports editors are best known as part of the daily newspaper industry, they also manage many other types of periodicals, including sports-oriented magazines, and on-line sports publications. Remember that sports editors and sports copy editors (see Chapter 3) are discrete types of journalists, with different jobs and usually distinctly different salary levels.

Because there are relatively few sports editor positions available (all of which are highly coveted), your chances of becoming a sports editor are much lower than landing other jobs in sports journalism.

Where Do Sports Editors Work?

Let's look at the publications that employ sports editors.

- *Newspapers.* In its 1998 compilation, the *Gale Directory of Publications and Broadcast Media* lists 1,518 daily newspapers in the United States, the majority of which have a sports editor. A few of the largest employ more than one (*USA Today,* for example, has many sports editors, each in charge of a department).

- *Magazines.* In his book *The Dream Job: $port$ Publicity, Promotion and Marketing,* Melvin Helitzer lists twenty-two sports publications among the top-ranked 200 magazines in national circulation. According to Helitzer, "An average of forty-one new sports magazines are launched every year, so a new media outlet for sports news opens almost every week." Sports editors manage these and hundreds of lesser ranked all-sports magazines, as well as sports departments for general news magazines.

- *Electronic publications.* New sports publications enter cyberspace regularly, and many have lured sports editors or experienced professionals with similar titles. Computers and the Internet have spawned untold numbers of on-line periodicals (see Chapter 14), and more will surely continue to find their way to PC screens across the globe.

- *Newsletters.* Print and online newsletters are published by editors at a variety of companies and organizations to further their sports business, products, and services.

- *Wire services.* Those services with a considerable sports focus, such as Bloomberg, have a staff of writers and editors managed by a sports editor. Jay Beberman manages the Bloomberg Wire Services sports section, with a dozen sportswriters in Princeton, New Jersey, and six in the company's London office.

Of course, even as a college graduate, you shouldn't plan on attaining the lofty position of sports editor until you've been in the business for ten or more years, and then only if you're good. Only at newspapers with smaller circulation (under 50,000) would you expect to see a sports editor with minimal experience as a reporter and/or copy editor. Most have been in the business for many years—or their uncle is the publisher. But sports editing is an exciting, important, and prestigious occupation for an ambitious writer or editor to set as a career goal.

Educational Background

The educational backgrounds of typical sports editors are much like those of the professionals they supervise (reporters, editors, columnists, and photojournalists). Mark Anderson, sports editor of the *Gaston Gazette* (North Carolina), majored in journalism at the University of North Carolina, with heavy emphasis on copy editing courses and none on editorial management. Most of his sports editing knowledge comes from his three-year position at the *Winston-Salem Journal* under Terry Oberle. Although the *Gazette* is a small-circulation (40,000) paper, Mark manages a staff of two editors and five reporters. Drawn to journalism by the chance to combine his writing talent with the sports he loved, he first got involved as a freshman on his high school newspaper.

On a larger scale, Steve Blust is sports editor of the *Sacramento Bee* (California), which has a daily circulation of 285,000. Blust graduated from Northern Illinois University with a Bachelor of Science degree in journalism and a minor in English. "I was about fourteen when I realized I wasn't going to be great at sports, but I wanted at least to be involved with sports peripherally," he remembers. "Fortunately, when I was seventeen, I landed a job at my local paper in Joliet, Illinois, solidifying my desire to be in the business."

Sports editing is also an important position in new media publications. (As described in Chapter 14, new media involves a variety of on-line publications, as well as new technologies in television.) Mike Emmett was the first sports editor on the Web, with the earliest of the on-line news and sports servers at the *Nando Times*. His journalism degree is from Marshall University in Huntington, West Virginia, where he was the managing editor of the school newspaper in his senior year. He is now the managing editor for *Total Sports* on-line publications, which provides live sports sites for companies such as the *Wall Street Journal,* for its on-line sports section in the *Interactive Journal.*

John Rawlings, the editor of America's most popular all-sports publication, *The Sporting News,* headquartered in St. Louis, began his career with a bachelor's degree in journalism. He suggests that, in addition to the standard English and journalism curricula, budding sports editors should invest in psychology courses, "because dealing with people is the most important talent you can have. Business courses are also very helpful; that's one of the areas in my education I would have approached differently. I aggressively avoided any business class, and that was a mistake."

Jay Beberman graduated from the State University of New York at Oswego with a degree in communications and later worked at *Good Morning America* for ABC-TV. When he interviews candidates for writer openings for his wire services, he says, "I look for journalism majors with a knowledge of sports."

Mike Rathet, executive sports editor of the *Philadelphia Daily News*, majored in history and English literature, with a minor in journalism at New York University (NYU). "When I realized I couldn't be a great athlete, I decided to try sports journalism," he says. "I still think a broader education serves you best in the long run." Rathet took a position at the Associated Press (AP) right out of NYU and considers it a good training ground. He had to be fast and he had to be accurate. But he also had to wait five years to get a writing assignment. When the AP's baseball writer left to take a job in St. Louis mid-season in 1961, Rathet was thrown in as a substitute to cover Roger Maris's chase of Babe Ruth's home run record. "It was a very, very interesting assignment," he says. "It wasn't like going to cover a baseball game, but an event. It was about as exciting as it could be."

On the Lookout for Internships

Most newspaper sports editors belong to Associated Press Sports Editors (APSE), a national organization involving editors in all circulation ranges. Ed Storin, secretary/treasurer of the association, reports that 439 news organizations belong to APSE. This year's APSE president, Tim Ellerbee of the *New Orleans Times-Picayune*, notes that the association has a successful diversity internship program. In this program, ten minority university students are selected each year to work in the organization for two weeks, producing APSE newsletters and learning some of the intricacies of journalism and deadlines. Attesting to the program's success is the fact that sixty of these former interns are currently working in sports departments across the country.

Professional Development

Sports editors come from many journalistic positions, and not all of them studied English and/or journalism. Most came from the ranks of sports reporters and some were copy editors. Jack Gibbons, assistant managing editor for sports at the *Baltimore Sun*, explains how his many years as a reporter are invaluable in relating better to the daily problems of his staff: "We can help by empathizing with them and giving them the instruction and guidance necessary to handle a situation." Many sports editors with reporting experience agree that this gives them a better appreciation of writers' problems and therefore they can do a better job of managing their staff. They know what reporters face when they encounter an irate coach or athlete who is extremely upset with their commentary.

While attending the University of Baltimore, Gibbons met Royal Parker, broadcaster at WBAL radio and television, who introduced Jack to John Steadman, then sports editor of the *Baltimore News American* and now a columnist at the *Sun*. Lacking any employment prospects for the upcoming fall semester and needing income to pay tuition, Gibbons was pleasantly shocked when Steadman offered him the job of horse-racing agate clerk. "I jumped at the chance, worked hard, and fell in love with newspaper sports. Because they knew I was eager to learn, they allowed me to cover high school games and summer recreation stories that no one else wanted to do. Eventually, they made me a full-time sports writer."

After further experience as a sports reporter, he began to suspect the imminent demise of the *News American* and moved on to the *Philadelphia Daily News*. This was possible, in part, because the *Daily News's* sports editor, Mike Rathet, liked the news experience Gibbons had gained as assistant city editor and metro editor. After two years at the *Daily News*, the *Baltimore Evening Sun* became interested in Gibbons as its sports editor. He took the big jump and returned to the friendly environment of Maryland sports.

Only thirty-five years old when he became the *Sun's* sports editor, Gibbons remembers having "to learn about the budget and make my own decisions, instead of just watching how other people made them." He has been making those decisions ever since.

Donna Eyring followed another atypical route to becoming a successful sports editor. At the *Orlando Sentinel* where she worked for many years, management had a "job club" where editors could trade jobs for three months with other editors. She had been the news editor but came over to sports for three months. They ended up reorganizing the paper's management and she has enjoyed being sports editor ever since!

Today, Mike Rathet also would be considered an exception to the standard procedure for moving into the sports editor's chair. "I had never worked directly for a newspaper," he explains, "and I had never edited, other than public relations publications. That path would be unheard of now, because to become a sports editor, you almost have to come up through the ranks, not even as a writer, but as a desk editor. It has really changed. It is very unusual for a writer to expect to become a sports editor."

John Rawlings started out as a sports reporter and editor at various newspapers, after which he became assistant sports editor at the *Philadelphia Inquirer* for two years. He moved into the fast lane when he next took the position of executive sports editor at the *San Jose Mercury News*, which he held for seven years. He candidly admits that he was first drawn to the editing side of the business by two things he learned in journalism school. "I was surprised to find that there were a lot of talented people graduating from journalism school, and my writing was not quite as good as most of them," he says. "Also, at the time, I was drawn to an editing teacher who was a great mentor and who took an interest in me. She was very passionate and articulate about the importance of good editors and how they could make a great contribution to the final product by carefully shaping a reporter's story."

Many of the sports editors of electronic and new media publications learned their craft in print media before they moved to on-line pursuits. Mike Emmett began his career as a newspaper news reporter, but also did a lot of sports freelancing for United Press International (UPI) wire services and other publications. After stints as a print desk editor in news and in sports, he moved to on-line journalism full time in the early 1990s. "On my staff," he says, "my sports editor, his assistant, and two of my wire editors were all ex-newspaper sportswriters and copy editors. I got into it because I was always into computers; a compulsive Internet and computer junkie."

Leadership and the Sports Editor's Job

Most sports editors seem to get along very well with the people they supervise. Interaction with management, however, is often another story. Many sports editors report that they suffer from a separating wall between sports and news—often there is little or no interaction between the two.

Nonetheless, those in charge of sports sections at large papers have a much higher degree of job satisfaction than those at smaller papers. This seems to reflect how much hands-on work they must do. At papers like the *Gaston Gazette*, it's common for sports editors to also work at reporting and the copy desk, in addition to their responsibilities of planning and supervising. Many young journalists in this position had to learn their leadership talents on the job. Unfortunately, journalism education usually neglects the training of managers or leaders.

"You're a good reporter and somebody sticks you into a job as an assistant city editor," says Mark Anderson. "Or you're a good copy editor and somebody sticks you in a job as sports editor or assistant." He and other sports editors bemoan this lack of emphasis on training for the management role. Journalism schools should take heed of the need for a leadership element in today's curricula.

Women as Sports Editors

The position of sports editor is now open to women, but it's still a position that is difficult and challenging to achieve. Although they are few and far between, the number of female sports editors is growing. Ed Storin, secretary of the Associated Press Sports Editors (APSE), reports that there are approximately twenty women sports editors among APSE's 681 members. Many more women are assistant sports editors. Storin is an ex-sports editor and currently a sports columnist for the *Hilton Head Packet* (North Carolina). He and APSE member Donna Eyring agree that sports editor jobs for women will continue to increase because so many newspapers and periodicals, as well as APSE, are committed to diversity. "I've seen progress," she says, "but there could be a lot more."

On a newspaper such as the *Orlando Sentinel*, with a daily circulation of 290,000 and a large sports staff, Eyring doesn't get much time to actually work with reporters on stories, although she would like to and occasionally does "jump" on a story. Like most sports editors, most of Eyring's work is managerial, including preparing the annual budget, planning the expenses, and assigning staff to cover the big events.

As for the prejudices women sports editors endure, Eyring says that she was fortunate because there were women sports reporters and editors before her who pioneered against such biases. "But people still call my office and ask to speak to the sports editor," she says. "When they find out that it's me, a 'she', they refuse to talk to me . . . which is their loss." When Eyring originally interviewed for a reporter's job at the *Sentinel,* the personnel department specialist said, "What do you want to write about—fashion?" That's the way it was for women sports journalists only a few years ago. Thankfully, attitudes, expectations, and hiring practices have changed.

The Job Search

If you're watching for openings for a sports editor position, you'll find very few. When they do appear, they are mostly for small-circulation papers, like this one which appeared on an Internet website for journalists. It is typical of what managing editors are looking for.

> Sports Editor—Reporting experience required, Quark skills helpful. Will supervise sports desk for a seven-day A.M. paper. Will write analysis columns on local sporting events and teams, plan local sports coverage, and cover local and area prep and pro sports. Will lay out daily sports section. Great opportunity to cover [major metropolitan area] sports from a small town with a dedicated local readership. Supervisory experience helpful.

Asked how many years of experience he thought it would take for a copy editor to advance to a sports editor position, John Rawlings estimated seven years minimum and no maximum. There are talented people who wait until their forties or fifties before they finally have a chance to run a department, and usually they are great at it. It's not at all unusual for columnists or beat reporters to jump into sports editor positions. Many of the better sports editors have significant beat experience, "but," says Rawlings, "it's not the goal of most writers to run a department."

Mark Anderson hopes to spend a good portion of his life as a sports editor. He says, "I love sports, writing, and people; a perfect combination for me. From a career standpoint, I could keep looking to move to a larger paper, or I could move over to be a managing editor. The best advice I can give about this profession is that you have to love it because the pay isn't great. You have to love it because you must pay a lot of dues at small papers, working on stories that seem small and plain before you can move up the ladder."

Even the smallest of newspapers require experienced people as sports editors, and they almost always need a journalism degree. But, as Anderson puts it, "If you have a few years solid experience as a writer, they forget all about that degree stuff. Then experience and talent are paramount. A great way to learn about sports editing is by watching others."

For sports editor openings and job opportunities, networking and word of mouth are the most common avenues. *Editor and Publisher* magazine and its website are other places to check on job availability.

Finances

We surveyed a representative range of sports editors at many newspapers, the circulation size of which, of course, had a direct relationship to their salaries:

Size of Circulation	Average Annual Salary
Small	$29,000–$40,000
Medium	$42,000–$80,000
Large	$70,000–$90,000

To confirm these results, we went to the Newspaper Industry Compensation Survey (1997), published by the Inland Press Association, which, because of its larger coverage (from papers with circulations under 10,000 to those over 500,000), showed even greater extremes. For a sports editor who "is responsible for editing and makeup of sports pages, supervises employees, makes or recommends hiring decisions," the Inland Press surveyed more than 500 newspapers and found that base pay rates ranged from a low of $15,576 per year to a high of $129,017, with an average annual base pay rate of $40,033.

Of course, there are also many who make more than these averages and—believe it or not—a few who make less. In the smallest of markets, this supervisory position has its financial shortcomings, especially in a sports section that has a staff of only one or two. Although many sports editors at small papers have limited experience in the business, they usually cite low pay as their biggest personal problem with the position. Most make more than their writers do, but that's slight consolation when the rung you're on is so low.

As far as moonlighting goes, sports editors seem to be universally short of time. Therefore, not too many have time to freelance for extra income as members of their staff do.

The Daily Routine

The skills sports editors need, such as interpersonal and organizational talents, are similar at newspapers of all sizes. Planning and organizing the daily sports section has to be done on a long-term scale in terms of content and personnel supervision and management.

Although Mark Anderson plans sections a month or so ahead, he reschedules daily because events are constantly changing. Much of his day is taken up with planning what stories will be covered. His staff consists of two full-time copy editors/layout people, a general assignment reporter, a prep reporter, a National Association for Stock Car Auto Racing (NASCAR) writer, a Charlotte Hornets beat writer, and a Carolina Panthers beat writer. In contrast, the size of Jack Gibbons's sports staff at the *Baltimore Sun* is sixty, including the copy desk, with assistants, sports reporters, and editors.

Steve Blust has a full-time staff of twenty-nine, which is split almost evenly between editors and writers. Because he feels understaffed to cover all of the professional teams in the Sacramento market and San Francisco Bay area plus local high school sports, some of his editors must do some writing and some of his writers occasionally edit. Most sports editors are responsible for the entire day-to-day operation of their department and thus must be involved in all facets of the operation. The best are able to put out interesting, entertaining sections while keeping track of day-to-day beat coverage. Blust says that he is "responsible for everything good and bad that happens in the *Bee*'s sports department, whether I am working in the office or vacationing on a beach at Lake Tahoe at the time. In previous roles, I was able to hand off much of the responsibility to others." The most satisfying part of Blust's job is the challenge of putting out a different sports section every day.

Many of the activities of putting out a daily sports section can be planned in advance, as Donna Eyring explains. "Because you know what games are coming up, you can prepare a space budget a week or two in advance," she says. "As part of our annual budget, I allot space for coverage for each year. So, part of my job is anticipating coverage of big events like the Daytona 500, a potential NBA playoff, or a college football national championship and how much money and space we'll need to cover them."

Unlike most large-circulation sports periodicals, the editor of *The Sporting News* has a surprisingly small staff. Most of the written input is from freelancers, with an average of 150 freelance contributions a week. John Rawlings has five staff writers, twenty editors, and two full-time photographers to manage. Sunday is the big production night for this weekly publication, which is published every Wednesday and distributed nationwide. He also enjoys writing the weekly editor's column.

Rawlings feels strongly that the standards of sports departments have changed for the better and so has the quality of sportswriting. "It keeps getting better and better, and I think the sports section standards are much closer to the rest of the newsroom. That's definitely a benefit, because a sports department should be run just like any other department of the newspaper." He enjoys the responsibility and impact he has on each *Sporting News* edition that hits the newsstands every week. "I make sure that we deliver exactly what readers want."

Mark Anderson's greatest satisfaction comes from seeing a good sports section in his *Gaston Gazette* every day, as opposed to waking up and seeing something that makes his heart sink. His best reward is to see a multifaceted plan that he has been working on for several weeks come together with graphics, photos, and in-depth reporting. "I like to print stories about ordinary people who aren't used to the limelight but manage to accomplish something unusual," he explains. "It's refreshing when you're working with real people instead of the athletes you normally deal with, and it's nice to bring some 'fame' to someone in the community."

Although there are some sports editors who spend some of their time copy editing, Mike Rathet doesn't. "I think I'm something of an anomaly in that I'm not a hands-on editor," says Rathet. "I don't sit and change copy. I have a sense of what a story should be and how it should be told. I think I know good writing because I've read good writing, and I like to keep emphasizing that. It's amazing to think of the number of words, headlines, pictures, captions, and hours of expertise that go into a sports section or newspaper every day to try to make it come out right. From the day I arrived here, it still amazes me that the paper comes out every day. You wonder sometimes how all the required elements come together like they do. It's still fascinating and tremendously satisfying to pick it up and know we did a good job."

The Ten Special Talents of the Best Sports Editors

Sports editors cite several vital skills required for their job over and above those needed for the job of reporting. Aspiring sports editors should evaluate their potential for the job in terms of the skills and knowledge that experts rate as critical to success. As you advance in your career, develop the skills needed to answer each of the following questions with an unequivocal "yes!"

1. *Can you manage people, projects, and budgets—even under pressure?* Some of the greatest sportswriters could never tackle the complex role of managing budgets and people. "As an editor and manager in the world of on-line sports," says Mike Emmett, "you have to get things done as quickly as possible, no matter how hard they are."

   John Rawlings says, "I like being in charge, and I have developed a reasonable way of getting people heading in the right direction."

2. *Are you willing to take responsibility?* Mark Anderson explains, "As the editor, you're *it*; no passing the buck.

Reporters, too, should take responsibility, but too often they pass the buck in situations they prefer not to deal with. They'll say 'You'll have to talk to my editor about that' when a complaint or request is being made that they could have handled."

3. *Do you respect your readers?* Treat all of your readers courteously and, above all, respect their intelligence. Be motivated to think like sports fans, give them the kind of coverage they are looking for. Jack Gibbons explains that his readers know more about the subject in his section than they do about any other section in the paper. Many follow their favorite sports passionately and thoroughly and expect their newspaper to bring expertise, insight, and interpretation to all stories. "It shouldn't become routine to you," Gibbons says, "because if things start to look the same and get boring, you should be moving into something else. You're probably not going to do the job for the reader that you should."

4. *Do you respect your staff?* Treat each person on your staff the way you want to be treated yourself. "But, as the manager, you must realize that problems with your staff don't fix themselves," says Jack Gibbons. "You have to take full charge. If you allow unsatisfactory personnel situations to continue, you send the wrong message to the rest of the staff."

5. *Are you a good judge of talent?* Editors must be able to match people with what they do best. "You can't please everybody, nor can you assign reporters to what they prefer," notes Gibbons. John Rawlings adds, "The best in the business distinguish themselves by successfully dealing with the variety of psyches on a diverse staff of pros. They can sublimate their own egos and get the best out of the people who are working for them, whether it's someone who requires high maintenance or low maintenance."

6. *Can you take control and make hard decisions?* A sports section, like all other departments, has to have a boss,

someone to take control when it's necessary and make the tough decisions. "When I first became sports editor," says Jack Gibbons, "I placed too much importance on wanting to be liked. You always want to be fair and it's a very subjective environment, but not everybody's going to end up covering the Orioles or the NFL Ravens."

7. *Can you be a good "coach" to your staff?* As a coach, you must support and reassure your people. You need to let them know how important they are and how good their work is. When criticism is necessary, it must always be positive and constructive. "Place great importance on your ability to motivate other people, which is so important as a sports editor," offers John Rawlings.

8. *Do you have a "nose for news"?* "Know a good story when you see it," advises Rawlings. "One of my best talents is an intangible news judgment," which explains why *The Sporting News* is one of the best in the business.

9. *Are you organized and efficient?* The first boss Rawlings worked for at the *Miami Herald* was Ed Storin, a former sports editor who taught him about being organized, being prepared, and never getting caught short. He remembers that "the biggest sin you could commit, if you were running the desk for Eddie, was not having a plan for every contingency."

10. *Are you passionately dedicated to your work?* Dedicate yourself to the quality of your published product and have a passion for what you do.

Frustrations of the Profession

"Managing a large staff of sportswriters and editors for a major newspaper and dealing with all the political and financial issues is a daunting enough job," says Donna Eyring, "but one of my biggest frustrations is the lack of sufficient space for sports in the expanding Orlando sports market." The main problem, as with other newspapers, is the cost of newsprint, which went through the roof a few years back and caused a reduction in space budgets throughout the industry. After payroll, newsprint is probably the second most expensive item to Eyring's newspaper. "There are a few other frustrations, but to tell you the truth," she says, "I feel really lucky that I made it past forty and have a job I enjoy."

Mark Anderson agrees that space limitation is a major headache. "The toughest part," he says, "is trying to cover everything that could and should be covered and not having enough space, writers, or money to do it all. It's frustrating when you have to let some things slide." He is also bothered by the apprehension he experiences as sports editor when he goes home at the end of the day, leaving the sports section in the hands of others.

The business end of print media has become much more bottom-line-oriented in recent years because many newspapers now are part of publicly traded companies. Steve Blust feels that sports editors' "biggest challenge is in dealing with ongoing change in the newspaper business."

John Rawlings dreads talking to people on his staff who have had a series of poor performances. He's had to substantially revamp the staff of *The Sporting News*, including terminating some people and having very difficult discussions with them. "I don't care how many times it happens, I hate it," he says, "but it's part of the deal. If you don't want to do it, then you shouldn't be a sports editor."

Tales from the Top

Most sports editors have been around the block a few times and have, as a result, some fascinating recollections of the business. The group we surveyed is no exception.

John Rawlings shares a personal and commendable story to which young readers can relate. He grew up in a small town in the Texas panhandle and always wanted to go to the University of Missouri. On the night before he was to leave to begin as a freshman, he got cold feet, scared of being that far away from home. "My mother, bless her heart, said 'If you don't go, you'll always wonder. Try until spring break, and if you still hate it, then you can come home.' Can you imagine how hard that must have been for her?

Like any mother she knew that once I left home, I wouldn't be coming back. It would have been really easy for her to say 'Okay, that's fine, don't go.' But instead, she wanted the best for me."

Female sports editors share many of the headaches their male counterparts have in running a sports department, and public relations with readers is certainly one of them. But Donna Eyring had a unique problem when she was accused of having a macho attitude! Shortly after she became sports editor, she received a "letter to the sports editor" from a woman complaining about what she perceived as the *Sentinel's* light coverage of the Ladies Professional Golf Association (LPGA). Given that the tournament was in Orlando, Eyring felt the *Sentinel* had consistently presented good LPGA stories at the front of her sports section for the two weeks leading up to the tee-off. The letter writer complained the "poor coverage" was an example of the macho attitude of the paper's biased sports department. Eyring called her and said, "How do you do, I'm Donna Eyring, the *Sentinel's* sports editor, and I'm the one you're blaming for the macho attitude." According to Eyring, "the reader just couldn't be reasoned with. She assumed that somewhere a man was behind my decisions about the space we gave the LPGA and wouldn't accept that it was a woman's decision."

Jack Gibbons cites two examples that show how experience as a reporter helps a sports editor to understand and support his reporters. "An exciting time for Orioles baseball fans was the year Cal Ripken broke Lou Gehrig's consecutive games record. Readers wanted to know as much as possible about Ripken's exploits and how he felt, and they expected no less from our beat writer and others at the *Sun*. They assumed that we had easy access to the seemingly cooperative star Orioles shortstop. What they didn't realize was that our baseball writers were prevented from talking to Ripken himself or getting photos because everything had to be funneled and approved through his own marketing group, making our work very difficult."

Gibbons also explains how he and his publisher stood up for his reporter, Mark Hyman, when Hyman and the newspaper were being pressured "big time" by one of the baseball team's owners, Eli Jacobs. "When Camden Yards was being built," Gibbons recounts, "Jacobs [then an owner of the Baltimore Orioles] wanted a lot of credit for his vision and role in the stadium's design and success.

Although he had, in fact, played a significant role, so did many others in getting the project off the ground long before Jacobs got into the picture. When he learned that we weren't going to play up his role as he would have liked, he began to put pressure on the reporter, Mark Hyman. As a member of the *Times Mirror* Board of Directors, he appealed directly to our publisher to have Hyman removed from his beat so that he would get the kind of coverage he wanted. Jacobs was rebuffed by the publisher and the reporter was allowed to do his job as he saw fit." It's ideal for a reporter and the paper's journalistic integrity that a sports editor, management, and the publisher stand up and go to bat for him or her when it comes to "crunch time."

When Mike Rathet became interested in the war between the National Football League and the now-defunct American Football League in the 1960s, he was fortunate to cover Joe Namath's best years as quarterback of the New York Jets. "It really helped my career explode," he says. "The Namath exposure led to excellent contacts for me.

"Later, after the merger of the two leagues, [in 1972], Joe Robbie [of the Miami Dolphins] and Hank Stram [of the Kansas City Chiefs] were looking for a PR guy. Robbie offered me a nice salary and half a player's share of team postseason winnings, which was unprecedented. I took the Miami job, and Miami immediately won two Super Bowls, back to back (1972 and 1973), netting me about $25,000 from the two and a half player shares, which was a lot of money at that time.

"I remember the first Miami Super Bowl at the L.A. Coliseum. We PR guys were in the box right next to Commissioner Pete Rozelle's box, jumping up and down and hollering the whole game. People in the next box were waving to us to keep it down. We were a bit out of hand, but they didn't know I had a significant stake in the outcome."

Rathet stayed only two seasons with the Dolphins, because "I had had enough of the owner," he says. "But I like to point out that Dolphin coach Don Shula didn't win any Super Bowls after I left." On Rathet's last day with the Dolphins, Ed Storin, former sports editor of the *Miami Herald* called and asked him, "Are you interested in becoming a sports editor?" The Knight Ridder chain had an opening in Philadelphia, which he interviewed for and accepted. The rest is history. He is one year short of twenty-five years at the *Daily News*. "I never thought I'd be here this long," he says, "because I'm the type who's always looking for new things to do, but this job has never been boring."

Competition for Readership

Not too long ago, the only competition sports editors had for readership was neighboring newspapers and a few magazines. Now they compete for sports fans' attention with many other types of media, such as sports on cable television, on-line sports publications and e-zines, and a plethora of magazines about sports. On-line editors such as Mike Emmett must compete with a growing number of electronic sports publications as well as on-line newspapers. He thinks that his industry will have competition from the "Dead Tree Society" (newspapers) for a long time to come. "The print media, where I grew up, may be around for another fifty years," he predicts, "but new media is the shape of things to come. It is the future."

Jack Gibbons feels the growing pressure on his paper and on the writers who cover the beats and produce stories each night. An Orioles baseball beat writer, for example, is under the gun every day because he or she competes against other fine periodicals like the *Washington Post*. Gibbons explains, "We want to own Orioles coverage in Baltimore, we don't want to read anything first in the *Post*, so our beat reporter really has to stay on top every single day." His staff also feels competitive pressure from ESPN. They must bring an insight on the subject different than ESPN had the night before. Cable channels dedicated to sports are strong competition because they not only show highlights, but have strong statistical packages and "it seems to be the place people go now to get their sports fix," Gibbons says. "That's why in a town like Baltimore, you have to make sure that you cover the Orioles, the Ravens, and basketball more thoroughly than others have the time or capability to do. We're going to explain sports with the kind of insight that real sports fans desire."

"I like to look at the sports section as a grocery store in which there are a lot of different things on the shelves, a lot of different brands, and people who shop for what they like," says Mike Rathet, executive sports editor of the *Philadelphia Daily News*. "If I only had games for them to read about and they had already seen it on television, they would be in and out of our store in a minute. Because I'd like them to stay in our store for an hour, we give them in-depth pieces and a surprise every day. I want them to feel they're getting their money's worth."

Sage Advice from Sports Editors

Donna Eyring advises that you must have a real passion for the role of sports editor. "It's not a nine-to-five job," she warns. "There are weeks when I'm here fifty-five hours and, of course, during an event like the Olympics, I worked until 10 P.M. or 12:30 A.M. every day." She is called at home frequently, and if a story breaks on the weekend, she's on it. "I'm more of a workaholic than some in the business, but it's a job I enjoy, so I don't want to miss anything."

As far as advice on joining her profession, she recommends that young women journalists or aspiring reporters definitely set their sights on sports editing, if they're capable. "When I got into the business twenty-one years ago, there weren't any women in sports, and although I was always a football and basketball fan, sports editing never occurred to me. But now the profession is ready for good, young, female journalists."

Jack Gibbons advises newcomers to the profession that to become a good sportswriter or editor, you must first become a good journalist. He feels that sportswriting attracts people who are passionate about sports and it's unique because there's so much fun connected with it. "But," he warns, "don't think that covering sports is any different than covering general news like the metro section. Use the same journalistic standards for all."

"You must be patient with your career," advises Mark Anderson, "because you are not going to climb to sports editor at a 200,000 circulation paper in five years. You must do the little things at each stop along the way, and they will pay off. Then, too, you must be patient with everyone around you—your staff, the public, everyone. Hot heads will not get anywhere as good managers or sports editors."

Mike Rathet repeats a theme we heard often from the experts throughout the development of this book. "I still think the key to anything in journalism—not just sports journalism—is reading good writing. That's what writing is about and editing is about—the finished product: good writing." Also, he advises, "I don't think any qualified, interested person who wants to attain the position of sports editor should be deterred by all the changes and pressures in the nineties, but they should be aware of them. This is a tough business."

Mike Emmett believes the most important thing is to "first learn your craft as a writer or as an editor; a bad writer or editor will not be successful in any medium. Then beat the competition by learning the special things about your industry. If it's in on-line publications, learn things like HTML language and website building. There are many good writers, so the competition is keen. The trick is to know how to do things others cannot."

John Rawlings strongly advocates that a journalist interested in sports editing spend some time in other departments. "You learn many things, including good discipline."

Finally, experienced sportswriters, editors, or novices contemplating sports editing as a career should note the respect, pride, and praise that Rawlings expresses for his profession in this testimonial: "It's so highly satisfying when, at the end of the day and in spite of all the problems that come up, you know you have shaped a fine product. There's an incredible energy level in our business that you feed on when you've got everybody focused on the same goal. It's exhilarating. I love it. I love it every day."

5 Investigative Reporting

In typical sports reporting, a writer covers a game or sets up an interview through a publicist to write a feature on an athlete. But with investigative reporting, it is totally different. You're searching for people and records that can substantiate a tip. Usually, you must talk to people who have nothing to gain by talking to you. You're challenging people, threatening, and intimidating them by what you're doing.

Elliott Almond
Investigative reporter, *Seattle Times*

It's not *who* stole second base, but *why* . . . and *who* gave the orders. Fans can find out the details of who stole second base from television, radio, and the newspaper. But if they want to know why it was pilfered, who gave the orders, and who will profit from the theft, they will read it in the stories written by investigative reporters. As sports sections devoted more space to business with the growing impact of player agents, multimillion-dollar contracts, and heightened media and fan interest, newspapers began examining the reasons and controversy behind the news. This has led to investigative or enterprise reporting, which lets fans know why something happened in sports, what events led to the current condition, and what the impact has been.

This chapter defines this fascinating profession and the reasons talented and resourceful sportswriters gravitate toward it. Many find it full of excitement and challenge and enjoy both the danger and the thrill of accomplishment. We examine the unique demands and risks of investigative sports reporting through the eyes of some of the nation's best investigative reporters and newcomers as well. We conduct our own probe of why investigative reporting has become a major beat at some major periodicals and broadcast media, as well as the prerequisites that sports editors demand in candidates for such a position.

Why Investigative Reporting?

This question haunts many athletes, coaches, and owners who find investigative reporters sniffing around for a story. Good investigative reporting wreaks havoc with the daily existence of public figures in the sports world. Were it not for the vigilance of such reporters, those figures' personal and financial lives would remain safe from the prying eyes of the media and the public. Their questionable or allegedly illegal behavior might go unnoticed and often unpunished. For fans, however, the sports pages could become numbingly boring and much less informative without such scrutiny. Hard-hitting investigative reporters are the scourge of those in sports who circumvent the system or commit illegalities.

For journalists, investigative reporting is a new and growing career field; one that is interesting and rewarding for those willing to go far beyond the obvious facts and get to the real dirt—the story behind the story. What motivates this relatively new breed of journalist, spawned by the trend-setting success of Bob Woodward and Carl Bernstein who broke the story of the Watergate scandal in the 1970s?

Breaking a huge story is much more fun than covering a football game. Too many sports reporters just want to go along with the crowd, satisfied with getting their stories for a feature on an athlete from press conferences or one or two personal sources. Although in the past only a fraction of all sportswriters and broadcasters were in investigative reporting, there is now an increasing number throughout the print and broadcast media. Unfortunately for readers and viewers, many newspapers and stations consider investigative reporting a luxury. They do not have such positions or are not willing to take that extra journalistic step of thorough news reporting. The fans are the ones who suffer in these cases.

Investigative vs. Enterprise Reporting

At this point, we should define some key terms, because what the layperson considers "investigative reporting" may really be what the sports industry views as "enterprise reporting." There is a distinct difference.

Most of the in-depth stories written about off-the-field inquiries or the underside of sports actually fall under the category of *enterprise*, that is, taking readers deep into the news of the day to tackle its underlying issues. Enterprise pieces react to the news rather than find it. An example is the national Associated Press Sports Editors (APSE) award for enterprise reporting given to author Kevin Mulligan and colleague Ted Silary for their series on the impact of the NCAA's Proposition 48 in 1986.

Investigative reporting makes the news; it unearths or breaks the basic story and follows it until it has run its course. Most sports journalists agree that enterprise reporting is fully within the role of the everyday reporter. It is his or her responsibility to not only report the important sports news of the day but, during or after writing the initial article, to examine the buried elements that will make tomorrow's or next week's sports pages. This is often achieved in a series of articles to properly cover the subject.

Investigative reporters are constantly on the prowl for the potential scandal, the illegal deed, the immoral or shady sports activities. Such stories may take months of research; of watching and waiting patiently; of chasing erroneous, frustrating leads. They may play themselves out with only periodic bylines during which the writer becomes occupied with normal sports section assignments until an important break occurs. Many fine sportswriters alternate between the two types of reporting, depending on what is called for by current events in their world of sports. But, for our purposes, because the underlying skills are similar, this text focuses on the skills, stories, and experiences of investigative reporting.

Armen Keteyian of CBS and HBO Sports, one of America's finest reporters, says that, in his mind, investigative reporting is really just "solid" reporting. Sometimes it's enterprise reporting, but much of it is digging beyond the obvious and beneath the surface. "Unfortunately today," he says, "given the state of our business, if you have the courage or the gumption to ask a tough question, that's defined as investigative reporting; the kind of reporting symbolized by Howard Cosell and David Halberstam." Cosell, of ABC's *Monday Night Football* fame, was one of the best-known and most controversial sports journalists in history. Halberstam is a prolific, award-winning author who has written about American sports and mores in books such as *The Breaks of the Game* (1981) and *Summer of '49* (1989).

What Investigative Reporters Cover

Most investigative reporters look into stories that happen *off* the field. Here are some examples of activities leading to potential investigative stories:

- Scrutinizing the local university when alumni boosters are found to be paying star players illegally, and the coaches and athletic directors try to cover it up

- Finding documents and interviews showing that the NFL's drug expert mishandled test samples and did not follow protocol in testing the players, rendering an entire drug-testing program invalid

- Hearing that USA Track and Field, the domestic governing body for the sport, allegedly withheld results of positive drug tests for stars so they would not be banned from important competitions

- Examining the academic success statistics for local high school athletes

- Checking the arrangements for exclusive seating at the local arena or stadium

- Reviewing credit card privileges and residence facilities for athletes on scholarships

- Uncovering the criminal activities or records of professional or college athletes

- Delving into the unfair, discriminatory allocation of school funds between women's and men's athletic programs

This is only a sample list, of course. Others fill not only the sports pages, but also intrude into the daily news sections.

Investigative Television and New Media

Most investigative reporters are in the print media, but, as you will see in other chapters, that is changing as in-depth reporting becomes a staple in the broadcast and electronic new media. Armen Keteyian found this out during the 1988 Summer Olympics. "It was also the summer of the Pete Rose baseball betting scandal, and ABC had been getting steadily beaten on the story by the other networks, particularly NBC. ABC was looking for a hard news, sports correspondent who could reverse that trend and I applied. You won't find many investigative reporters who have been fortunate enough to climb that high in sports at the networks."

For eight years, from 1989 to 1997, his stories were seen and heard on ABC's *World News Tonight* with Peter Jennings, *Good Morning America*, *Nightline*, and *World News Weekend*. They all had some kind of sports theme, whether the business of sports or some medical, social, legal, or philosophical subject relating to the sports world. He averaged about fifty-five to seventy-five stories a year, many of which were used on various network news shows with different lengths and focuses. For example, while viewers watched the entire saga of Mike Tyson's ear-biting episode during his heavyweight boxing title fight with Evander Holyfield in the summer of 1997, Keteyian's various stories on it appeared on television at thirteen different times over the weeks of the story's life. That's a lot of television mileage for a little chunk of ear.

Television has become a comfortable haven for a few accomplished, experienced communicators such as Keteyian. Positions for broadcast reporters, especially in sports, are by no means numerous, and hopefuls should plan to experience the print journalism business for many years before attempting to breathe this rarefied air.

"There are no other people who do what I do on a regular basis for a network," Keteyian said. "I think the closest are probably Jim Gray of NBC and Jimmy Roberts at ESPN. Dick Schaap certainly did it when he was full time at ABC News. Dick, Ray Gandolfi, and I were the only three who were really devoted to covering sports as news for a news division, which I think is an enormous asset in covering the world of sports, but unfortunately, since I left for CBS and HBO, no longer exists."

Although print media is the most fertile field for the would-be investigative reporter and will be for many years to come despite the often self-serving "prophets of doom," inexperienced sports journalists should also consider the new or electronic media. As Chapter 14 explains, there are currently many popular Internet sports websites that carry opinionated, investigative types of articles similar to those in today's newspaper sports columns. This growing phenomenon may provide a place to emulate the best in the business.

Gender Aspects

Our research indicates that there are not many female investigative reporters. Women writers considering this career, however, should take note of the advantage that Suzanne Halliburton of the *Austin American Statesman* thinks women have over men.

"I think we have an advantage, and having an engaging personality also helps," she said. "Male athletes seem to talk more freely to women than to a male reporter. Conversely, female athletes don't know how to take me, and it's more difficult to get them to talk freely. One of my first stories was in the uncharted territory of female Olympic athletes and serious, hospitalizing eating disorders among a large percentage of them. But these women athletes were hard to pin down. The methods of their veteran coach, who had coached numerous Olympic swim teams, were forcing some University of Texas female swimmers into eating disorder clinics and a few into hospitals for care. That story, as well as many others, took six months to complete."

Halliburton belongs to the Association of Women in Sports Media, which has panels on investigative reporting and enterprise reporting and, like the Investigative Reporting and Editors organization (IRE), provides an opportunity for networking and professional exchanges among women journalists.

Dealing with Intimidation

Investigative reporters feel that a common problem is the level of intimidation they sometimes encounter. Although almost always meaningless, it can be disconcerting to a young, inexperienced journalist. When Doug Looney first arrived in Nashville as a reporter for the *Banner*, he faced the problem for the first time but learned early on not to let anonymous threats against his reporting affect him.

"I learned from a very unlikely teacher," he recalls. "At that time, the last phase of the jury tampering trials of Jimmy Hoffa was occurring in Nashville, and I was often in attendance. One day, there was a break in the federal court proceedings and, out of the blue, Hoffa turned to me from his place at the defendant's table and said, 'Wanna go out to lunch?' 'Sure,' I said, but on the way out of the courtroom, I asked, 'Why do you want to go out with me?' Without blinking, Jimmy said, 'Because no one else wants to be seen with me.' I explained that that wasn't a problem with me, and we had a wonderful conversation. As we ate, I told him that I had been covering the local Teamsters and their strikes, and that my wife and I were getting a lot of phone threats about the stories I was writing. I said to Hoffa, 'Why don't you call off your thugs? It just scares my wife and has no effect on me.'

"He looked at me and said, 'Young man, I'm going to give you some advice that should serve you very well: you never worry about the people who tell you in advance that they're gonna kill you. The ones you worry about are the ones who *don't* notify you in advance.' He was dead serious. So, over the years, any time I get such a call, I always smile when I hang up because I know there's a guy who's not going to kill me. He's already notified me!"

Finances

You'll probably be surprised to know that the average investigative reporter is paid at about the same level as his or her sportswriting colleagues at most newspapers. Salaries, of course, are heavily dependent on circulation, experience, skill level, and the type of medium (magazines, papers, television, etc.). Certainly, the bigger names in the business or the best-known writers at periodicals like *Sports Illustrated* command some of the highest salaries in sportswriting.

For most, though, salary standards are very similar to those you saw in Chapter 2, unless after years of experience and career-defining stories you hit the jackpot. It is important to note that there are magazines, like *Sports Illustrated*, where salaries for many reporters exceed $100,000. The very best of those reporters probably earn close to and over $200,000.

If your sights are set on television investigative writing, you may have selected the highest-paying career. It's possible to make a rather dramatic jump from print media earnings to higher salaries at major networks.

Becoming an Investigative Reporter

The educational backgrounds of veteran investigative reporters we spoke to had little to distinguish them from those of sports reporters for magazines and newspapers. It's the attitude, the depth of research, and the doggedness of the investigators that sets them apart.

Armen Keteyian started as a reporter on campus newspapers and basically established himself through the print business. After graduating from San Diego State University in 1976 with a journalism degree and a brief reporting job, he worked for the *Escondido Times-Advocate* (California). For two years, he usually wrote two stories a day on everything from high school teams to the San Diego Chargers. "I learned rather quickly," he says, "and got my feet wet on a very good paper."

Next, he enjoyed a year of learning the sports marketing and public relations business, but still wrote for the *San Diego Union* and San Diego magazines on a freelance basis. "I was trying religiously, at that time, to get a reporting job at *Sports Illustrated*, something I had dreamed about. After a piece I wrote for the *San Diego Union* won the *Sporting News* award for the best feature story of 1982 and was published in their annual 'The Best Sports Stories of the Year,'

Sports Illustrated hired me as a reporter." He stayed for seven years, learning the art of writing and reporting.

Although he worked at *Sports Illustrated* for seven years, Keteyian thought that his career took a decided turn for the better during a temporary assignment for NBC at the 1988 Summer Olympics in Seoul, Korea. He had taken a leave of absence from *Sports Illustrated* to work for NBC as part of a group of sportswriters dubbed the "Seoul Searchers." Seven well-regarded print reporters were hired by Michael Weisman, then the executive producer at NBC Sports, as a sort of protective league, to represent NBC at the major Olympic venues.

Keteyian explains, "Weisman teased us about it, implying that we would be able to do stories and interviews on camera and act somewhat as sideline television reporters for our venues. I took it seriously and, before traveling overseas, I went to a famous television coach in New York. That was very effective, and I did well in Seoul, breaking a story on swimmer Angel Myers, who at that time had been banned from the U.S. Olympic team for alleged steroid use. She disputed it, but I talked to some people who had seen her test results, and I produced the big story on it, which Bryant Gumbel presented on the air. That story resulted in my developing a good resume tape from the Olympics, which was very important in moving toward my role as the lone sports reporter for ABC News for eight years before I was hired in late 1997 by CBS and HBO."

He advises that, instead of having unlikely hopes of achieving success in too short a time, "it's best to have solid goals and a mindset that this is what you want to do. Set a realistic time frame in which to try to achieve your goals."

Most forms of sports journalism require a broad education to enable a writer to excite readers, no matter what the medium. This applies even more in investigative reporting. Plan to enjoy a well-rounded scholastic program that includes history, geography, the arts, and great literature, as well as the journalistic necessities.

Practitioners of this field recommend a few schools of journalism for specialization in the investigative skills and knowledge you will need. They include (in no particular order):

- University of Missouri (Columbia)

- Columbia University (New York)

- Northwestern University (Evanston, Illinois)

- Indiana University (Bloomington)

- University of Oregon (Eugene)

- University of Texas (Austin)

- University of Southern California (Los Angeles)

- University of Colorado (Boulder)

The special demands of this business require most young writers to become accomplished reporters long before they jump into full-fledged investigative reporting. We found that few universities teach the necessary skills, and it is unusual for a newspaper to hire a young student or graduate to focus on investigative writing. As with many new professions, this field may soon become important enough to the success of the news business to force more schools to establish specific educational programs for writers.

Many print, broadcast, and electronic forums are now giving great emphasis to investigative reporting because of its impact on readership and circulation. Some of these forums provide a learning environment for young reporters to become full-fledged investigative writers. One paper that prides itself on the quality of its investigative reporting is the *Seattle Times*, which won the 1997 Pulitzer Prize for investigative reporting (awarded to Eric Nalder, Deborah Nelson, and Alex Tizon). Not surprisingly, the newspaper also has a special focus on sports investigative reporting and news.

Elliott Almond is a seasoned investigative sportswriter for the *Times* and has been working in the field off and on since he was twenty years old. He earned a bachelor's degree in communications with an emphasis in journalism and a minor in political science from California State University at Fullerton. His success as a sports reporter is an excellent example of how a sports journalist benefits from a broad education. While still in school, he worked part time at the *Los Angeles Times*, for a local daily newspaper as a general assignment reporter, and for the school paper. After many years as a sports copy editor, he made a full switch to investigative reporting. "By the 1984 Olympics," he says, "I was looked at as an investigative guy. It was a tough struggle to find a place that permitted me to do this kind of work."

Almond's early experience at the *Times* included writing stories on such issues as Olympic athletes who were involved in steroid use. "I've always enjoyed learning more than simply who won or lost a game," he explains. "I think I've always liked the underbelly of life. My interview subjects say I'm good at getting people to open up and talk. I think it is simply a sincere interest in others and a talent for listening."

Doug Looney, now a senior sports columnist for the *Christian Science Monitor*, graduated from the University of Colorado School of Journalism and began his newspaper career as a general assignment reporter at the *Nashville Banner*. It was at the *Banner* that he started investigative reporting on his police beat. He got his start in sportswriting in Washington for the now-defunct *National Observer*, a national weekly newspaper and a sister publication to the *Wall Street Journal*. Originally, he applied for a job reporting on politics but was turned down. Surprisingly, a few months later, the *Observer* told him that although he had seldom written about sports, they would give him a try for a year, and if it worked out, they would transfer him into politics.

Looney was their entire sports department, going anywhere he wished to chase a story. As long as he had a sports story written every Friday by 9 P.M., he had complete freedom. After a year, the managing editor, prepared to keep his promise, asked him to start covering Richard Nixon. But Looney asked to stay in sports because he was enjoying his work so much. They agreed and that was how his five-year role as the paper's main sports journalist began, after which he joined *Sports Illustrated* where he was a senior writer for more than twenty-one years.

The Ten Characteristics of a Good Investigative Reporter

To be good at this business, you must begin with or accumulate a number of characteristics and skills, some of which are distinct from other journalism careers. The first three are obvious and, of course, important for all good sports journalists, but many of the rest are what separate the ultrainquisitive investigative reporter from his or her colleagues.

- Knowledge about sports and the world

- Writing talent, the ability to tell a story

- Outgoing personality and excellent people skills

- Sources, sources, and more sources

- Doggedness and persistence

- Patience

- Attention to details

- Ability to get people to open up and talk

- Ability to handle adversarial interviews

- Ability to actively listen to people

Doug Looney has his own personal criteria for being a successful investigative reporter: "You must (1) have nerves of steel; (2) be very calm and levelheaded, because you're often coping with extremely difficult and volatile situations; (3) be very persistent; and (4) be absolutely tireless." Looney attributes this lasting advice on doggedness to Armen Keteyian, who told him, "You'd be surprised how many people are home (to interview) at 4 A.M. Although sometimes the answers you get at that time aren't quite what you're hoping to hear.

"I have sometimes put in a horrendous, exhausting day," he adds, "with the only result being that I acquired an unlisted phone number! My secret of success is that I get up earlier than everybody else involved in the story, and I stay up later than all of them. You have to just wear people down until finally they tell you what you need to know just so you'll go away. You can't be shy about asking, because you're seeking the truth. I'm continually amazed at what people will tell me if I just ask."

Although he admits he is a rookie in the business, Tom Fuller, *Seattle Times* reporter/intern speaks knowledgeably about journalistic requirements: "You have to like to write about issues or do in-depth people features. If that's not appealing, you won't succeed. You have to be detail oriented and check everything. Be willing to put weeks of work into background and interviews for the story, then an equal amount of time writing it. Such stories are longer and have the biggest impact, so they have to be well written to keep a reader's interest. You get a chance to actually make readers think about an issue, and maybe even change their perspective. That's the most exciting part.

"First of all," he says, "you have to be perceptive. You're not just reporting what happened. You have to consider all sides of an issue and think more closely about the angle you are going to take. Information gathering is at an even greater premium. Investigative stories always go on the cover if you do them right. Your facts had better be right. On average, you may talk to as many as ten times the number of sources or more to do an investigative piece as opposed to a feature or news story. Investigative reporters are supposed to make an impact. They won't unless the reader knows right off the bat that they've done a thorough job. He or she won't get through a forty-inch story otherwise.

"Another element that sets investigative reporting apart from other forms of reporting is sources," Fuller adds. "You must make certain that your sources trust you thoroughly. You can't go and write something you've told them you wouldn't write."

Author Kevin Mulligan agrees that "trust development" is a vital investigative capability that a reporter must have to obtain information during research. The trust that a source needs to feel before he or she is willing to confide details of potential wrongdoing to a reporter comes from establishing a comfort zone, a confidence in the writer. Sometimes it may take months for a source to become comfortable with you. It usually occurs after a number of face-to-face meetings with the person and after he or she has read your reports on the topic in question or a similar story line. Sources come forward more willingly when they know things are being done wrong which they want to help correct.

Mulligan cites an example of trust development he encountered while working on an investigative story for the *Philadelphia Daily News* with reporter Paul Domowitch. The story followed a two-month investigation into allegations that Villanova University's wrestling program, funded heavily by millionaire John duPont, had been committing NCAA violations. These violations allegedly included duPont's use of his money and private Lear jet for recruiting purposes. "In researching the story," Mulligan says, "we interviewed many wrestlers in the program who were allegedly recruited through illegal means. It was usually after a few meetings, at odd hours and places, such as on campus benches or in the library, that interviewees felt the comfort zone necessary for them to come forward with information that made the story possible. As a result of our investigation and the published story, Villanova dropped the wrestling program."

Armen Keteyian advises that to become a good reporter or investigative reporter a writer must learn to tell a story. Investigative pieces, features, and human interest accounts all consist of storytelling, "whether it's for a minute and five seconds or for seventeen seconds of broadcast time. There has to be a beginning, a middle, and an end; there has to be a purpose to the piece. There has to be something that a viewer takes out of that story at the end of however long you have to tell it. The good storytellers, the ones who can write for television (which is different from writing for print), are the ones who make it on the air most often. A lot of people look terrific in front of the camera but can't execute the craft. Young writers in and out of college must learn storytelling as a fundamental in the fine art of writing for broadcast."

Life on the Beat

"In typical sports reporting," explains Elliot Almond, "a writer covers a game or sets up an interview through a publicist to write a feature on an athlete. But with investigative reporting, it is totally different. You're searching for people and records that can substantiate a tip. Usually, you must talk to people who have nothing to gain by talking to you. You're challenging people, threatening and intimidating them by what you're doing. These activities have no resemblance to regular sports reporting. We often go to the same people as the other reporters—coaches, or players, or administrators—but we also go to the courts, public records, and law enforcement officers."

The investigative reporter's relationship with newsmakers is also altogether different. "We are identified as 'hit' people and universally hated," Almond says. "Word gets out. But if you keep publishing the truth, eventually the coaches come to respect you for not just trashing people with unfounded information. But it is tough. We all feel the sting. Once you're onto one thing, it leads to another. You gain a reputation. Readers aren't stupid. They notice. So do lawyers, police, coaches, etc. They start asking for you as *the* person when they have something. They need to find a mentor who will help them."

One important characteristic of Doug Looney's successful investigative work on newspaper articles, magazine stories, and books, is his persistence, a vital tool in the day-to-day life of an investigative reporter. An excellent example of his indefatigability took place when he was developing a story with Armen Keteyian for *Sports Illustrated* about illegal payments being made to basketball players at Memphis State University. "One of the key figures in this investigation was a wealthy man, who was unwilling to meet with me to talk about his role in the payments," Looney says. "One of our magazine's editors called me to ask if I'd been able to pin this guy down to talk. He said, 'We need to make sure we talk to him face to face, so he can never say that we never confronted him with the information we had.'

"I had his address, so I flew from New York to Phoenix to track him down. When I arrived at his house in an exclusive neighborhood, I found that his home was protected by a tall brick wall. I tried the gate and it was locked, so I was in a quandary; I had come all this way, and I had to at least see him. We needed some face-to-face contact with this guy before we could go with the story. So, I'm standing outside trying to figure out what to do when this truck comes down the street. It's a painter and he has a ladder in the back. I waved him down and asked if I could borrow his ladder to climb over the fence. He was reluctant to have anything to do with this enterprise, so I said to him, 'How about if I buy your ladder; I'll give you $50 for it.' He thought for a moment and said, 'Okay, $100 and the ladder's yours.' So, I said, 'All right, here's $100.' I propped the ladder against the fence, climbed up, and hauled it up after me so I could get down the other side.

"By this time, my adrenaline was really pumping. I knocked on the front door, and the guy opened it with 'What the hell are you doing here? How did you get in here? Leave, before I call the cops and get you for trespassing!' He saw the ladder and opened the gate so I could get it out. Although he didn't talk to me about the story,"

Looney adds, "I had accomplished my mission of confronting him and offering to run the facts of the story by him to ensure that our information was correct. Now, at least, he couldn't deny that we had offered. We honorably gave him every chance."

Many reporters would have given up when presented with the locked gate and tall fence and told their editor, "I tried, but I couldn't get in; the gate was locked."

Tools of the Trade

Whereas the tools used by conventional sportswriters in their work are mostly what you would expect—telephones, computers, tape recorders, television cameras, and press passes—investigative reporters have much more technical "stuff" in their professional tool kits. To research their stories about the underside of sports, these journalists need all or most of the following:

- Access to a world of information via the Federal Freedom of Information Act, which can provide

  —Data on equality of facilities for men and women athletes to determine compliance with Title IX mandates for equal access to sports programs for females

  —College athletic budgets

  —Hiring policies for women in school administrative jobs

  —Incomes of college athletic personnel

- Access to state open records to determine the possible illegal use of

  —Phone records for coaches and recruiters

  —Use of college-issued credit cards

  —Unauthorized use of state funds in school athletic recruiting

  —Ticket allocations for coaches and players

—What businesses or wealthy alumni control choice university stadium/arena seating

—Who benefits financially from sales of stadium/arena seats

—The academic records of a school with regard to scholarship athletes (grade point averages, test scores, etc.) compared to the rest of the student body

—Travel expenses for recruits and players or coaches

—Coaches' work histories and resumes

- Telephone directories, utility company records, and deed records to determine

—Who occupies and owns apartments and other living quarters for school athletes

—Who is paying utility bills for them

—Whether athletes are being housed in off-campus facilities paid for by boosters

—Whether recruiters or coaches are illegally contacting prospective players

- The NCAA manual for regulations on proper conduct of athletic programs, to determine whether a school is engaging in

—Illegal recruiting

—Improper scholastic and academic grading

—Ignorance of the rules governing college athletics

- IRS tax forms 990 or 990S for universities operated as nonprofit, tax-exempt institutions to determine potential inequalities in incomes of coaches and athletic directors compared with those of faculty and administrative personnel across the state

- State motor vehicle offices, many of which will provide driver license and registration information, to determine whether student athletes, their friends, or their relatives are receiving automobiles as financial considerations from boosters or others

- Athletes (current, graduated, transferred, or disgruntled) who will cooperate with a reporter's investigation into wrongdoing by providing

  —Grade transcripts

  —Financial documents

  —Various other internal school documents

- Computer databases (newspaper archives, local university or community library) for researching a major topic or person

- U.S. Government Publication 78, which provides a listing of nonprofit organizations, for use in requesting tax returns

Investigative Reporting and Editors Organization

Only one organization represents and provides a forum for investigative reporters and editors, but it is a good one. It is appropriately called the Investigative Reporting and Editors (IRE) and is based at the University of Missouri School of Journalism in Columbia, Missouri. It provides its 3,500 members with a resource center, computer database access, and an Internet website (www.ire.org). The IRE publishes special publications for its members, including the *Reporter's Handbook*, considered a bible of investigative reporting. Armen Keteyian strongly recommends that college students join the IRE and also attend its regional or national conferences because it provides a "master's course in journalism."

In Search of Internships

Although there are newspapers at which the inexperienced intern can learn sports investigative reporting, they seem to be few in number. Even at newspapers where investigative reporting is stressed, an intern or new writer has to first prove herself or himself as a sports or general assignment reporter before being considered for weighty investigatory reports. You need years of training, improving your writing skills and building up sources and your reputation. You usually do not start out wanting to do this kind of reporting, but then you do a story and both you and your editor discover that you have the ability and you are on your way.

The *Seattle Times* employs one of the few intern reporters we found in a program that permits him to do enterprise and investigative reporting on his own. Exemplifying the common theme espoused by sports editors that a broad education is important for sportswriters, Tom Fuller graduated from the University of Washington with a degree in economics. After testing that profession for a year, he decided to try newspaper work.

"I sent out nearly 100 resumes to Northwest newspapers, promising to work temporarily for free in order to prove myself," Fuller says. "The *Corvallis Gazette-Times*, a daily with a circulation of 15,000, offered me a part-time job at $6.86 an hour." In eight months there, he accumulated helpful clips on subjects such as drug testing, high school coaches who don't teach, and booster club operations/functions for his portfolio. After a brief stint at another small daily, the *Times* hired him as a three-year intern to cover prep schools. "It's been a pretty miraculous ride up the chain," he admits. "I was at the right place just at the right time. To be at this level doing enterprise and investigative reporting work with as little experience as I have is remarkable."

At the end of his internship, the paper can choose to hire him full time or let him go. The uncertainty is frustrating at times, but it makes the intern work harder, benefiting both parties. At the majority of newspapers, interns work as they are assigned, often at menial tasks. But Fuller covers his beat, mostly high school sports, like a regular reporter and makes frequent investigative topic suggestions to his editor, most of which he is allowed to run with until they become printed pieces.

Reporters like Fuller often write more than five stories a week. But because of the emphasis the *Times* places on enterprise and investigative reporting, stringers are usually hired to cover their beats for a few days while they are off researching. Although they are given as much time as possible, they are sometimes rushed to complete a story.

There are also opportunities in television reporting for interns to test their talents and learn about this profession. As with other types of writing internships, most are advertised at schools of journalism throughout the country. Intern candidates for ABC can write to:

World News Tonight Internship Program
ABC
47 West 66th St.
New York, NY 10023

If they qualify, they can work throughout the company. The news division usually employs four or five interns in the summer. After serving as an intern for Armen Keteyian, one young writing student was offered and accepted an entry-level position at ABC Sports. He started at the bottom, but it is a great place to have his foot in the door.

Reporters' Favorite Stories . . .

Because investigative reporting involves issues and subjects much different than celebrity profiles and details of games, many of the stories are unique and intriguing. Elliot Almond remembers when the Green Bay Packers came to town to play the Seattle Seahawks. "Brett Favre (the Packers' quarterback) had been playing hurt for much of the season. Instead of recycling the obvious material on his situation, we thought it would be more interesting to take on the bigger issue, and I wrote a broad-based piece about playing with pain in the NFL. I covered Favre's physical condition in a sidebar to accompany the major story line."

Doug Looney recalls a story that he was involved in for *Sports Illustrated* that exposed some financial dealings between agents at Florida State University and members of its football team. The situation illustrates how investigative reporters can become intimidated or frightened into inactivity. "They took players on a free shopping trip to a local sporting goods store. I was called into the investigation because our reporters were making little headway;

they felt it wasn't safe for them to go into the dorms to interview players. After I got involved, I approached approximately fifty football players before I ultimately got five, a high percentage, to talk to me. One of them, an insider who was at 'the scene of the crime,' told me what was going on at the sporting goods store where the agents were buying clothes for the players and the story started there."

On another story about Barry Switzer when he was coaching at the University of Oklahoma, Looney recalls receiving numerous phone calls suggesting he "stop pursuing this story," "get out of town," and "don't leave your hotel room." In many investigations, reporters are threatened by verbal intimidation because people do not like what the reporters are doing, but it is almost always anonymous. "Once," Looney remembers, "Dave Parker, then of the Cincinnati Reds and currently hitting coach of the St. Louis Cardinals, became agitated and actually grabbed me in the locker room. Other players quickly came to my rescue, and then Parker fell all over himself apologizing. But I don't want that aspect to sound like a huge deal. Those episodes don't unnerve me or have much effect on me."

In researching the book *Under the Tarnished Dome,* which he coauthored with Don Yaeger, Looney tells of intended intimidation by anonymous persons. The book was subtitled *How Notre Dame Betrayed Its Ideals for Football Glory.* "There were a lot of threats," Looney says. "Our sources for the book were almost all named players and coaches. I was always strongly against the idea of quoting unnamed sources. There was one main source, a player who first tipped us off about the goings-on at Notre Dame, but whose name we never used. There was also a high-level school administration person with whom I talked constantly. He would often call me from a phone booth because of his fear of calls being traced from his home or office. I would tell him what we had found out about this player or about that game, and he would confirm or deny what we had learned, or tell me that we were 'completely off-base' or 'that's not true and here's why.'

"The book pointed out what was wrong with the way head football coach Lou Holtz ran his program," Looney continues, "recruiting hoodlums and thugs to play football, and stories of drug and steroid use. The school denied it all, as we expected. Eventually, the administration began to worry about their image—not what they were doing wrong, but what people thought. Notre Dame was trying to correct its reputation instead of its behavior. Finally, the pressure became too great and the school finally forced Holtz out. But now Notre Dame has much classier people; they're back on the rails.

"During such investigations," says Looney, "sources tend to be people near the story, ones who don't like what's going on at their institution or who have personal axes to grind, like an ex-wife or a coach fired from the team. Since Lou Holtz left as coach of Notre Dame, people who worked there but wouldn't speak to us while we were writing the book now come to me with other stories that I would have loved to have had then."

Tom Fuller remembers two favorite stories: "I really enjoyed writing a major piece on drug testing of athletes, a relatively new concern, in Washington State high schools. I focused the article on a young athlete who was a great story himself. As a result, I had the personal satisfaction of explaining an important sports issue to readers while enjoying my involvement in the personal angles."

His second favorite was a profile he wrote on the boys' basketball coach with the most wins in state history. "He's not very well liked, but I got into some aspects of his life that had never been written about. It seemed that after my story was printed, many people understood and appreciated him better. As a perfect bonus for him and our readers, the story ran the Sunday before the state basketball tournament, which his team ended up winning."

. . . And the Tough Ones

Frequently the job calls for the investigative reporter to develop a positive story about an unpopular player or coach or to write about the death of an athlete or about athletes with disabilities. You are never sure how to approach it. You cannot be condescending and you don't want to overwrite.

You also have to realize that the toughest stories will make people mad at you and that your stories may ruin someone's career. Some pieces can result in serious repercussions. Suzanne Halliburton of the *Austin* (Texas) *American Statesman* reports some problems she has faced but terms "minor, such as broken porch lights, obscene phone calls, and verbal threats. If you are to enjoy this work, you must quickly dispose of guilt feelings and realize that you are writing what's true."

During their investigation of the Villanova University wrestling program, Kevin Mulligan and Paul Domowitch say they received several anonymous phone calls threatening harm if they continued to pursue the story. According to Mulligan, the callers were believed to be from influential Villanova athletic boosters who were fearful that the *Daily News* investigation might lead to NCAA sanctions affecting other university sports.

One of Doug Looney's toughest stories involved the football program at the University of Colorado in Boulder during the early 1980s. He was born and raised in Boulder, and the university was his alma mater. Some of the main characters in his story had even been dinner guests in his parents' home. Obviously, that made his investigation of financial improprieties concerning the program and the team, coached by Chuck Fairbanks, all the harder. His story for *Sports Illustrated*, "Gold in Them Thar Hills," was an extremely difficult one that he really did not want to write because he loved the university. "It turned out to be an excellent story," he says, "which helped to turn the university around and scared them straight."

Frustrations

Investigative reporters tell us that one of the toughest parts of the job is dealing with editors to get more time for the story. Tom Fuller cites pressure as a distinct negative in his young career. "The pressure here at the *Seattle Times* comes from its being the biggest newspaper in the state," he says. "If you get beaten on a story, people tend to notice more. Also, because investigative or enterprise stories are often front page, there's more editorial scrutiny. Unlike other papers, getting beaten at this paper is the worst that can happen. It can get you fired."

Another common frustration is the lack of understanding by newspaper colleagues, particularly in sports, who get defensive about their teams and coaches. There is also the occasional lack of understanding by management about how much is needed to do the job right. Many sports editors consider this work a luxury instead of an essential element of the newspaper industry.

What Makes It All Worthwhile

A legitimate question for the uninitiated sports reporting candidate at this point is "What's really in it for me?" On the surface the question is appropriate for several reasons:

- The salary is on the same level as those for the rest of the print media.

- Most investigative reporters, even the best, bide their time between investigative stories and general assignment work.

- It seems riskier than straight reporting. The anonymous phone calls at night with verbal threats are tough to take.

- Some stories take months or years to develop, with boring waiting time and disappointments.

- At many places, investigative reporters are not too well liked by their more orthodox colleagues, possibly because of professional jealousy.

If you're looking for a reason not to enter the field, these will suffice for the faint at heart. But, if you read carefully between the lines of people discussed in this chapter, you will find they don't just seem satisfied with this business, they *love* it. Have they duped you with the minor work concerns, like the Floridians who tell us not to come to Florida because it is too crowded? Take a look at what they say when they're asked to evaluate their careers:

- Suzanne Halliburton: "It's much more exciting than regular reporting."

- Doug Looney: "Investigative reporting can be the most rewarding because it's by far the hardest form of journalism. It's very challenging, you're always living by your wits. It's a wonderful, beyond wonderful sort of feeling. When you start getting documents you're usually not supposed to have, the exhilaration is just terrific."

- Elliot Almond: "It is satisfying to delve into a story in depth and discover something that has not been publicized. The biggest reward is when a story is the catalyst for change."

Words of Wisdom

Suzanne Halliburton advises interested newcomers, "You have to have guts, a nose for news, and an ability to look deep beyond the obvious facts, almost being cynical about what you're told. You need a sharply tuned antenna to pick up buried information, such as that which is found during tedious examination of police records. Don't get into this business because you want to make money or become a media star, but because you truly believe in and enjoy the work you'll be doing."

Elliot Almond gives this counsel: "Games only appeal to so many people. A good investigative reporting story can hold the interest of virtually anyone, regardless of occupation, education, or outside interests. This is one of the places in sports where you can make people really think. But it helps to be humble, listen to advice from editors, and work as hard as you can. It also helps to meet as many other professionals as you can and show initiative. For college and high school students, I always suggest they should be well read and well rounded to have an enjoyable career."

Doug Looney summarizes the plight of would-be investigative sports reporters by noting that in this profession, unlike conventional sportswriting, you must progress as a baby does, "crawling before you walk. You must first become experienced at the basic elements of reporting before you can tackle the tougher work of investigative reporting. For example, you have to become proficient at interviewing sources in cordial interview environments before being faced with tracking down adversarial sources and trapping them in their offices to get a brief interview."

"Get into the business with your heart and with your soul, and be passionate about it," is what Armen Keteyian advises a young writer interested in investigative reporting. "I was lucky, certainly at ABC News and at *Sports Illustrated* where I was one of the few to be hired. I think I earned the right to be hired by *Sports Illustrated* by putting in an enormous amount of time when I was working on a daily newspaper in California."

In a revealing article in *Writer's Digest* (August 1996) about Pulitzer Prize winner Bob Woodward, of the *Washington Post*, Mitchell Bard writes:

"The difference between investigative reporters and other journalists," Woodward suggests, "is that most journalists have a deadline to gather as much information as possible, whereas the investigative types work on a story as long as it takes to finish it. The length of the story is not the issue. I've read very short articles that have really gotten to the bottom of things. I've read whole books that haven't. The full explanation is more authentic. That's what's fun. I admire good people who do that every day."

6 Magazine Sportswriting

An average of forty-one new sports magazines are launched every year, so a new media outlet for sports news opens almost every week.

Melvin Helitzer
Author, *The Dream Job: $port$ Publicity, Promotion and Marketing*

Writing for a national or regional audience in one of the dozens of sports magazines sounds great, doesn't it? Yes, but in this chapter you will find that the magazine market is one of the toughest to crack, especially if you want to be a staff writer for respected publications. Freelancer Mark Kram, an award-winning sportswriter for the *Philadelphia Daily News*, tells us there are very few such jobs out there. "It seems to be a freelancer's world," he says.

Not long ago, only a few magazines focused almost exclusively on the major sports (baseball, football, basketball, and hockey). Today, magazine racks bulge with a proliferation of special-interest periodicals with surprisingly large circulations. There are top-quality monthlies for skiers, snowboarders, golfers, cyclists, bikers, tennis enthusiasts, and bowlers, to name just a few. Recently, such fields have become extra specialized. For example, *Golf Digest* is no longer sufficient to satisfy the varied interests of golfers; now there is a wide variety of magazines on highly specific topics available,

such as *Golf Travel, Golf Resort Living,* and many others. The same is true for enthusiasts of most other sports.

Obviously, someone writes the fascinating material favored by these readers and, although it is quite competitive, there are opportunities in this branch of sports journalism for those who can not only write well, but can also market themselves and their work. Many specialized sports periodicals require that writers have technical expertise in and/or knowledge of their particular sport, including familiarity with specialized equipment, hot topics in the sport, geographic circuits, associations, and personalities.

The Scope of Magazine Sports

The actual number of magazines with sports news and features published around the country numbers into the hundreds, and as author and teacher Melvin Helitzer stated in our chapter opening, new ones start up or crash each week. The list in Table 6.1 is only a sampling of the hundreds of national, regional, and local sports magazines. It focuses on those available to the golf and recreational markets.

William Wagner, senior associate editor of *Football Digest* and *Auto Racing Digest,* has a staff of five full-time editors and writers who work on these magazines and others published by his parent company,

Table 6.1 Sample List of Sports Magazines

Golf magazines	Sports and recreation magazines
California Fairways (California)	*A Breed Apart* (retired greyhound racers)
Colorado Golf (Colorado)	*Alpine World* (outdoor sports)
Costa Golf (Spain)	*American Windsurfer*
Golf Business (NGCOA)	*Baseball Weekly* (USA *Today*)
Golf Digest	*Beckett* (price guide for sports cards)
Golf Digest Travel	*Black Belt Magazine*
Golf Houston (Texas)	*College Football Weekly*
Golf Illustrated	*Cycling Plus* (from FutureNet)
Golfline (India)	*Dive Destinations* (diving)
Golf Magazine	*Fly Fishing Online*
Golf Network	*Full Court Press* (women's basketball)
Golf Shop Operations	*GoSKI* (snow sports)
Golf Travel	*Go West* (outdoor sports in the western United States)
Golf Travel (Thailand)	*The Hockey News*
Golf World	*Horses Monthly*
LINKS	*iGolf*
Michigan Golfer (Michigan)	*Indy Car Racing*
PAR Excellence (Wisconsin)	*Mountain Biking* Pro (from FutureNet)
Philadelphia Golfer (Pennsylvania)	*Mountain Biking* UK (from FutureNet)
Shore Golf (Maryland)	*Mushing* (dogsledding)
Southern Golf Journal (Florida)	*Ocean Navigator* (boating)
Tournament Golfer	*Outside*
Washington Golf Monthly (District of Columbia)	

Ride! (equestrian sports)	Sports Illustrated for Kids
Scuba Diving	Tennis Magazine
Soccer America	Tennis Online
Sea (western U.S. boating)	Triathlete
Ski	VeloNews (cycling)
Skiing	Virtual Pathways (backpacking)
Sports Illustrated	Way Ahead (horse racing)

Century Publishing, including *Baseball Digest, Basketball Digest, Soccer Digest, Bowling Digest,* and *Home Health and Fitness.* Most of the writing for these publications is done by freelance writers.

Freelance vs. Staff Status

Because Chapter 15 focuses completely on the business of freelancing, we will say here only that throughout this industry, magazines are written as much by freelance writers as by in-house staff. Some are under contract and average about one story a month. Most, however, average only one or two pieces a year.

Although Wagner is primarily an editor, he does a fair amount of writing. He contributes to every issue of the magazines. The moral here is that although there are large numbers of publications on the country's magazine racks, this is not a business in which large numbers of sportswriters are permanent staff employees. Unless you are very well known, with great connections in and around sports and the sports business, it is best to have a day job if you're planning on freelancing.

"We go to freelancers who have the inside track in sports," Wagner says. Over the years, players and coaches who have become broadcasters, such as Randy Cross, Bob Trumpy, Doc Rivers, Chuck Daly, and Bill Walton, were special contributors to the magazine he previously edited, *Inside Sports.* "We 'ghostwrite' many of the articles of sports personalities," says Wagner. "We prefer to hire professional writers who do freelancing on a full-time basis because if you go to newspaper beat writers, they obviously save their best for their newspaper, and there's a conflict for quality material. If you send Joe Blow from the *Atlanta Journal-Constitution* to interview Greg Maddux, and he says something earth-shattering, of course the reporter's first inclination is to save it for his newspaper." Freelancers for major magazines are usually writers who have worked for newspapers and are very well connected.

"Freelance magazine writing is something of a nomadic existence," Mark Kram explains. "I prefer the stability of a newspaper to the kind of haphazard lifestyle that a lot of magazine writers live. And you can't make a lot of money as a freelance magazine writer. Some do, but it's a tough dollar."

Making the Bucks

Magazine writer incomes vary tremendously, especially between freelancers and staff writers. Most freelancers never know when their next check is coming. Staff writers get one every week or two. Writers and editors in the profession say that, at some publications, an average for less experienced reporters is $30,000 per year plus overtime, which is frequently required. Writers/reporters and associate editors earn $35,000 to $38,000. Editors or senior writers average about $50,000.

"As a young journalism graduate at *Sports Illustrated for Kids*, I started out at close to $25,000," says David Scott, who until recently was one of the magazine's staff writers. "Only a few are making great money in this business, but many are living quite comfortably on their salaries. It's a matter of realizing that if you pay your dues, you'll be able to make a good living, if not a great one."

Our experts tell us that it is practically impossible to stay financially stable attempting to write for sports magazines as a full-time freelancer. Too much time is needed to query editors in an effort to sell articles before the writing begins (in most cases). Steady income is needed to be successful. Kram, a successful sportswriter, can afford to moonlight because his full-time newspaper income supports him. "You can't make a living on freelancing, unless there are exceptional circumstances, which are rare," he says. "Getting top dollar in this business is unusual, but there are writers who get up to $30,000 a story. Most, however, earn fees from the largest sports magazines in the range of $1,000 to $5,000 per story."

The financial view from the top of the industry seems quite good, however. We learned that most of the top writers at *Sports Illustrated* earn more than $100,000 a year, and the very best make up to $450,000.

On the Prowl for Internships

It stands to reason that because there are fewer jobs in the magazine business, there also are fewer internship opportunities. We are told that *College Sports* magazine hires a few interns during the summer, but pay is small, when available. The problem with an internship at a small magazine is that, although the experience may be excellent, there is not much staff movement and expansion; consequently, there is little chance of being hired for full-time work after graduation. There are exceptions, such as one intern at *College Sports* who was offered a full-time job after six months.

E. M. Swift, a staff writer at *Sports Illustrated,* speaks of a student intern he worked with at the magazine for a summer. "Whether he returns or not," Swift says, "he has his *SI* internship on his resume, and that will indicate to his next employer that he's had impressive experience."

Networking for Career Opportunities

As in many other professions, networking is the most productive method of learning about new job and career opportunities. For David Scott, networking was the linchpin in starting his magazine career at *College Sports*. "You hear it all the time, and it's definitely true," he says. "Bill Strickland (University of Massachusetts associate athletic director) definitely helped me. He put me in touch with Norm Garrett, the *College Sports* editor, and I sent him a few letters, constantly nagged him, and kept in touch with him. Finally, when management knew they were going to have an opening, they already had me in mind. What helped me was that I had worked with Bill in sports information, and he must have been satisfied with my work and my character; that's what networking is all about. If you're doing a good job and helping others, they may help you down the road."

Mark Kram has done freelance work, including sports-related pieces, for major metropolitan city magazines, such as *Philadelphia* magazine, *Baltimore* magazine, and *Washingtonian* magazine. "The key in magazine writing," he notes, "is building relationships. Editors move around a lot. Freelancers write for a magazine, but if their editor moves to another magazine, they'll tag along." The message should be clear: never burn a bridge, because you never know when you'll want to cross it to another job or career.

The Opening Pitch

There is no set scenario for entry into magazine sportswriting, but let us examine how a few have managed it. Ed (E. M.) Swift got his first job after college in television news in Billings, Montana. After a short stint at a very small station with some on-air time, he became frustrated with the required brevity of stories for the newscasts. He wrote and aired a series of news broadcasts on the strip mining of coal, and from this initial exposure, he expanded the series into a novel, which he wrote after returning to his native Boston area, eventually submitting it for publication.

At that time (1976), Swift, a former goalie at Princeton University, tried out for the U.S. Olympic hockey team. While he was trying out, a writer from *Hockey* magazine working on a story about the tryouts noticed Swift's experience as a freelance writer on his resume. "He asked me if I'd be interested in doing some freelance work, and before I knew it I was writing a few stories for *Hockey* magazine over the next year," Swift recalls. He managed to write a story a month for *Hockey* while rewriting his novel on the coal-mining industry.

When the *New York Times* sold *Hockey*, the new buyer offered Swift the position of editor, which he accepted. While in this position, he wrote a story on the worst college team in history, entitled "Practice Makes Imperfect," in which he chronicled the 1970–1971 Princeton University hockey season. "I was the goalie for that team, which went 1–22 for the season," he explains, "The story found its way to Bob Creamer of *Sports Illustrated*, who bought it and published it. Soon after I went to Canada on a freelance assignment and did a story on a sixteen-year-old named Wayne Gretzky." That was his first assignment at *Sports Illustrated*; because of it, he was offered a staff position there. He's been on staff since.

David Scott started his education at the S. I. Newhouse School of Public Communications at Syracuse University, but after two years he transferred to the journalism program at the University of Massachusetts. As did most of our writer experts, he worked on the school newspaper there and agrees that "there is no substitute for the early hands-on experience you get reporting on games. Despite what the professor teaches you about it in the classroom, it's not at all the same as doing it yourself." That is why he feels that college sports information work is helpful—for the seasoning.

Currently a staff writer at *Sport* magazine, David Scott started in the business at *College Sports* magazine, which at the time was a start-up publication. It was a good beginning because the magazine was smaller than most and only two years old. "When you're at a smaller magazine, you can get a taste of everything," states Scott. "I started by doing what they considered fact checking and back-of-the-book details, such as notebook sections and information on Division II and III and NAIA and junior college sports." Eventually he was assigned to larger features and all types of stories. "On a small staff of writers (six or seven), you also learn the business side of the magazine quickly, because you're into everything. If I had begun my career with a big magazine, I wouldn't have seen things as clearly."

William Wagner's first job out of college was magazine writing for the Chicago Cubs baseball team. Next, he became sports editor of a small daily newspaper, the *Leader*, in Corning, New York. "It was a great place to get experience," he attests, "because at a small daily, you learn everything." He was sports editor there for two years while also working at a weekly newspaper. He had always had an interest in going into magazine work and finally landed at *Inside Sports* in 1994, where he worked for four years, until Century Publishing sold it.

Responsible sportswriters who are regarded as experts in a certain sport are approached by magazines to write freelance stories. Scott was not very familiar with the magazine writing business, so he set newspaper work as a goal, as most young writers do. "Now that I'm writing for magazines," he says, "I don't think I would like newspapers, because in my work I have the freedom to involve myself in a story, learning everything there is to know about it and fully immerse myself in it. As a beat writer at a daily paper, you don't have that luxury because you have a daily quota of stories to produce. I like the magazine pace much better, and that's where I'd like to stay."

Writing for Magazines vs. Writing for Newspapers

Some newspaper sports feature writers see many similarities between their types of stories and magazine writing. But most aspects are actually different. Our experts cited the following major distinctions between newspaper and magazine writing:

- *Less restrictive deadlines.* Writers are often forced to "crank out" stories for newspapers and weekly magazines, such as *Sports Illustrated.* Monthly sports magazines offer easier deadlines. William Wagner, who spent his early career in newspapers, enjoys having the extra leeway. "You can spend more time crafting the stories, with more in-depth coverage, a big-picture look with more polish," he says. "We look more at trends, issues, and personality profiles. We want the writing to have a little more of a lasting effect on the reader."

  More workable deadlines afford writers the opportunity to become more involved in a story. Wagner recalls a magazine feature he wrote about rising star Warren Sapp, a Pro Bowl defensive tackle for the NFL's Tampa Bay Buccaneers. It took him two weeks of research—traveling to Tampa, watching a game, and spending time with Sapp—and then a couple days to write the story. Wagner may not have had as much time to work on the Sapp story at many newspapers, although many of the nation's top sports sections do afford feature writers as much time as necessary for such in-depth profiles.

- *Writing in advance.* "At *Inside Sports*, we had an 'early close' and a 'late close,'" Wagner says. "The late-close stories were the most time-sensitive. We closed them out about two weeks before the magazine hit the newsstands. Early-close pieces are sent to print three and a half weeks before the magazines were distributed. We were working far in advance of the print version, but you had to make certain the piece didn't contain elements that would enable it to go stale or be overcome by events before publication." When some ex-newspaper writers start working for a magazine, they have trouble with the problem of working in advance. They're not used to wondering how the facts will hold up by the time the magazine comes out weeks later. In many cases, newspaper journalists are used to writing about daily happenings. "For a magazine," Wagner says, "what's true today might not be true tomorrow, and there's a real art to straddling the fence."

- *Space.* Decreasing space per story in magazines, which used to have the luxury of more room to play with, is becoming a growing frustration for writers. "Our stories get shorter, and our pictures get bigger," Ed Swift says. "When you shorten stories, you lose depth. We used to provide more depth than you could find in a newspaper, but I'm not sure that's true anymore, except in isolated instances. We're just infatuated with these 'notes' columns which you can read in a good Sunday newspaper."

- *"Editor's magazines."* A current difference that displeases writers like Swift is that some magazines are becoming "editor's magazines" rather than "writer's magazines" as they once were. At an editor's magazine, "editors change more than they ever did, and your stories are shorter," Swift explains. "Readers still admire good writing, but it's almost an accident when they get it." He realizes that this is caused by the competition with television for readers' attention. "But," he adds, "it's true, we are worried that our audience of young males is not reading much any more."

- *Unfamiliar face syndrome.* Mark Kram focuses on the difference between the team personnel's acceptance of the freelancer compared to the beat writer. "Although I didn't particularly want to be a beat writer because I didn't want to be limited to one sport, that has its drawbacks and advantages. The drawbacks of freelancing are that you're always a new face to somebody. If you're from the beat, they know who you are, so you can easily strike up a conversation. When I go into a situation, I'm always explaining who I am and what I'm doing. I'm a stranger, and that entails a leap of faith on the part of the athlete."

- *Greater flexibility.* David Scott uses one of his experiences at *College Sports* to illustrate the differences in resources allocated for stories by magazines and newspapers. He was to write a story about Marcus Harris, a wide receiver at the University of Wyoming. The school had been touting Harris for the Heisman Trophy early in his senior year. "If I'd been a national college newspaper writer," Scott says, "I might have flown to Wyoming for a quick interview with Harris and covered a game the following day. I would have read some other material and then written my story in two or three days."

  The magazine approach is rather different. Scott flew to Wyoming, walked the campus with Harris, hung out with him for a while, did a photo shoot with him, and took him to dinner. In short, Scott was able to get up close and personal with the player. "In Wyoming," he notes, "I learned what he had to deal with weather-wise, and what it's like in a small town being the big man on campus. I had time to talk to his coaches, his parents, and even his sister. It gave me a better chance to tell Harris's story and be absolutely accurate."

  Ray Didinger, a Pro Football Hall of Fame sportswriter now writing for NFL Films, has extensive magazine writing experience. He disagrees with our other experts about the many differences between the two media. "I've always found magazine writing to be very similar to writing a 'take out' [long story] in a newspaper. I approach both pretty much the same way. It's a much more leisurely style of writing [magazines]. You generally spend more time with your subject to get a fully flushed-out kind of picture about who they are and what they're about. They're really fun to do."

Although magazines allow staff more time for research and craftsmanship, freelancers like Didinger and Kram have had time limitations because they write on their off-hours, after their regular reporting. "Freelancing is hard because of that," Kram admits. "The last thing you feel like doing after writing all day at the newspaper is to write all night for the magazines, but if it's an interesting subject, I enjoy it."

Preparation and Access

Because of the length of most major magazine stories, writers usually are given more preparation time than that granted to other sports journalists. The real key to a good magazine story is extensive preparation, which entails reading everything you can on the subject before an interview. "You have to build a frame of reference," Mark Kram advises.

The single hardest part of getting a story is gaining access to the people you need, because there is so much competition from news agencies and television. According to Kram, "Athletes seem to understand that television doesn't make too many demands on them, because they mostly stand there in front of the microphone, do their interview, and they're done. But a writer, if he's going to do his job well, needs as much access to the subject as possible. The old expression 'access is king' *is* true."

William Wagner agrees that gaining access is a difficult part of magazine writing, especially because there is so much money in sports now. "Sometimes when I'm working on a story," he says, "I have to go through so many hoops to arrange an interview with the athlete, it's like trying to arrange an audience with the Pope. It can be frustrating."

The Art of the Interview

The best magazine sportswriters exude excellence in their writing. Most of them agree, however, that their best stories resulted more from outstanding interviews than from writing talent. Although he knows he is a good writer, E. M. Swift considers his interviewing skills a major part of his writing talent. "I think Gary Smith (of *Sports Illustrated*) is a great writer," he remarks, "but I think it starts with his being a great interviewer. He gets people to trust him. You have to care about the subject and listen to the answers. If the person believes you're really listening and not just going through the motions, as some writers do, they'll tell you much more."

A thorough interview also requires time, and an uncooperative subject is what frustrates writers such as Swift. "We can't get the time with the athletes that we once could," he said. "We're not as important to them as we used to be, so they don't want to give us their time. Early in my career, if I said I was from *Sports Illustrated* and wanted to do a story on them, I could take almost as much time as necessary, maybe three or four days. Now, I'm lucky to get three hours."

According to David Scott, another thing not taught in all journalism courses is the interviewing process and its importance. "If you ask a question, listen to the answer," he advises. "If you're not getting an honest answer or a direct answer, you have to ask a different question to get that answer. Getting the person to open up to you, to trust you, and to tell you things that he hadn't intended to is what characterizes a good interview."

Most of our veteran journalists have a favorite magazine interview story. Ray Didinger's favorite was a piece written for *Pro* magazine several years ago on "Mean" Joe Greene, the Hall of Fame defensive lineman for the Pittsburgh Steelers. Didinger found him to be a nice, interesting guy, contrary to common perception. "He was very bright, and I liked him a lot," he remembers.

The interview took place in the mid-1970s when the Steelers' vaunted "Steel Curtain" defense was the scourge of pro football. Didinger traveled to Greene's hometown of Duncanville, Texas, and found Greene to be very quotable and insightful. Afterward, the football player showed off his game room and challenged Didinger to a game of billiards.

"I hadn't played pool in a million years," Didinger says now, "and I wasn't very good at it, but I beat him. 'OK,' Joe said, 'you're better than you thought you were. Let's play another.' He racked them up, we played another game, and I won again. In the middle of the second game, Joe started to get mad, because he doesn't like losing and he thought I was 'sandbagging' him, which I wasn't. Those first couple of games we played for laughs, then I could see his mood was starting to get a little darker. Joe wanted one more game, which needless to say he won. It was an insult to such a great competitor who hated losing. That scene made my story even better. Here was a guy who couldn't take any contest lightly; he was so competitive. It's sort of ingrained in the personality of pros such as Greene, like bedrock. They never do anything just for fun."

You never know when you will find a personality who will really open up beyond the normal interview situation. Be alert to that possibility, because it provides excellent story material, over and above standard material such as player achievements. Spend time with your subject and see how he or she reacts, interacts with others, and deals with certain situations. Observe behavior, such as how he or she spends free time, because it can tell you a lot.

Similar to his experience with Greene, Didinger learned a great deal about another former NFL star, ex–Baltimore Colts quarterback Bert Jones, by sharing in one of his hobbies. "I flew to Shreveport, Louisiana, and he met me," Didinger recalls. "What I didn't know was that he was a licensed pilot, and he was going to fly us from Shreveport to Ruston in his private plane. When I arrived, we walked across the tarmac to his little plane and flew off to Ruston. I wrote most of the story about his being a pilot, because I found such interesting parallels; the way he flew was much like the way he played.

"I got very few quotes from Jones, but a lot of the story was about the thrill of flying, the sense of freedom and of being in control. Then, when I met his father, Doug, who had played for the Cleveland Browns, he talked about how he viewed his son, his career, and how 'Bert had never changed.' It was one of the more fun stories that I've written. When I was done, I thought I'd captured him really well, and yet, I bet there weren't more than two or three of his quotes in the whole story."

Some of the nation's top feature writers feel that one of the best ways to spend quality time with an athlete or coach is to invite him or her to share a meal. "If time allows, I like to break bread with an athlete I'm interviewing at a place where he feels most comfortable," says Didinger. "While I watch how people interact with him, I take notes, because every little thing you can learn, whether he's aware of it or not, shows you a little more about him. You learn a lot from the way he goes about things. You gather all that together in order to paint a full portrait. Some writers, such as Peter Richmond or Rick Reilly [of *Sports Illustrated*], are very good at taking those things that define the person and painting a clear picture for readers."

Didinger cites a piece he read about Karch Kiraly, the U.S. Olympic and pro volleyball player, in *Gentleman's Quarterly* (*GQ*) magazine. "I had interviewed Kiraly earlier, and I thought Richmond really captured everything about him, the way he walked, the way he talked, the way he looked, the whole thing. Whether or not you'd met Kiraly, after reading the story, you felt like you'd known him for years." That is what the art of painting a picture with words is to a fine writer.

In some cases, writers add color to a story through their own words. At other times, they simply let everything happening around them become their paint. Both methods have proven to be effective devices for excellent writing.

Sitting Down to Write

Our experts unanimously agree that regardless of what publication you work for, a well-written story will always find a home. "I tell youngsters who are very interested in writing that when I write about sports personalities or events, it's exactly like what they do in school when they write a paper on a subject they know little about," says E. M. Swift. "It could be about *Moby Dick* or hunger in Africa—any subject. Do your research, find out as much about the subject as possible, by whatever means you can. Use first-person interviews, background research, library work, and newspaper checks. Then you assemble that information in your best organizing style (e.g., note cards or outline form). Write it to the specified length, just as we must when we do a story.

"Write to cover the subject as concisely and entertainingly as possible, because you don't want to lose the interest of your teacher when you're writing a paper," he adds. "You don't want it to be dry, uninteresting writing. It's got to have the information which the writing brings to life. You can't have a dry section in the middle of your story, because you're going to lose your reader. One paragraph has to lead into the next, almost like telling a mystery story. It must flow freely. What drives us crazy at the magazine is when our story is edited, editors tend to throw out transitions, which we've included to keep the reader moving to the next paragraph, so they don't stop reading until the end."

David Scott compares writing magazine sports for certain age groups (such as children) to technical writing. "When you're writing down to your audience," he says, "you're becoming a better writer. I can't take anything for granted. If I write a sentence that says, 'They got an illegal procedure penalty,' I have to take the next two lines to explain what an illegal procedure penalty is, rather than assuming that my reader knows. It's helpful for adult sports magazines, too, because some of those readers aren't as knowledgeable as others. To write that extra line may make the reader feel they're a part of the story and more comfortable reading your stories. Although it's harder to write for children, in the long run it helps me, because if you can write for children you can write for anyone."

Fact Checking Is Job One

The one characteristic of magazine writing that editors demand is accuracy. As a famous reporter, Arnold A. Dornfield of the City News Bureau of Chicago, once said for the ages: "I don't care if your mother says she loves you. Check it out."

Dornfield would like the way *Sports Illustrated for Kids* magazine ensures accuracy in its stories. David Scott says, "The job description for a reporter is basically fact checking and research, even though you're given the opportunity to write some. Fact checking seems to be paramount at all Time-Life magazines, including *Sports Illustrated for Kids*; a really strict way of going through each story and literally making a red check through each word. If the story says, 'Michael Jordan scored 23 points and had 12 rebounds against the

New Jersey Nets on December 19,' you have to get the media guide and make sure that Jordan's name is spelled correctly and other things writers don't ordinarily worry about. You become so worried you'll get something wrong that you pretty much check everything."

It sounds like copy editing rather than reporting, doesn't it? It is at magazines. A reporter in the magazine business does little or no writing. According to Scott, "If it's a feature story and one of us is checking something about Eric Lindros [of the Philadelphia Flyers hockey team], such as when he began to skate, we have to contact his mother and ask her if young Eric did in fact begin skating when he was two years old. We expect that his mother would confirm or deny it, enabling us to incorporate that into the story. That's our basic task as reporters: fact checking. We must make certain that everything that's printed in our magazine is 100 percent accurate. It gets tedious, obviously, but it teaches you to be a good reporter. You can't be a good writer at many magazines without being a good reporter first."

The Stories Behind the Stories

Magazine writers are noted for their storytelling, never hesitating to spin a yarn if you are willing to listen. E. M. Swift's favorite "story behind the story" emerged from his work on the "Sportsman of the Year" retrospective on the 1980 U.S. Olympic hockey team several months after they pulled off the historic gold medal-winning "Miracle on Ice" at Lake Placid, New York. "I traveled the country interviewing seven team members individually, and corresponding with others," he remembers. "Getting the various personal stories was very effective. Unfortunately, such in-depth research and storytelling are things we now don't usually have time for. It was a luxury, and an important one. I wish we would do it more often instead of constantly writing about the Rose Bowl on Sunday night—when the game is played on Saturday. A little distance helps everybody, and at *SI* we don't do that as much as I would like.

"The fact is that a well-told story is timeless," Swift continues. "You see this in books such as *Into Thin Air* and *The Perfect Story*, which are basically magazine stories that have been expanded into books. It doesn't matter if it happened last week, last month, or eight months ago. You can make it just as vibrant if it's well done, and the Olympic story was like that: everybody knew the ending, everybody knew the story, but it actually helped the interviewing process to go back eight months and have the players recall it. After eight months, they hadn't been recently barraged with questions, so they had had time to put it all into perspective within their own lives. They could now ask, 'How did this change my life?' Also, they just remembered the highlights and the important points; they didn't remember all the little details. They were better able to put their story into perspective with that distance in time. So, that helped me retell the story and readers seemed to enjoy it ten months after it occurred."

Sage Advice from the Writers

Ed Swift has this advice for young people who say they love sports and want to write for *Sports Illustrated*: "That's fine, but the important question is Can you write? Do you love to write? If you're not writing about sports, would you be writing anyway?" If the answer is unequivocally yes, then we agree—go for it.

William Wagner highly recommends starting a career in newspapers even if magazine writing is your ultimate goal. "It's a good springboard," he notes. "I think a lot of the best magazine people got their start in newspapers. It's a high-pressure atmosphere that teaches you the meaning of a deadline and all the fundamental skills you need to make the jump into magazines. Not every newspaper writer is suited for magazines, but if it's something you have your eye on, newspapers are a good way to get all the fundamentals down. The people I've seen fail, especially at a monthly magazine like ours, are people who never came from newspapers and never knew the meaning of a deadline."

"My advice would be to take a long view of your career," Mark Kram says. "By that, I mean don't get terribly discouraged if by age thirty you're not where you think you should be. If you're really serious about writing, you'll get better as you age. Keep improving the quality of your work. You might be working at a small paper, but if you're doing work you're proud of and know you're improving, that's what's important. It's very tough to get to the upper ranks."

David Scott also urges patience: "Don't expect to be an overnight success as a great writer. All the top writers and authors whose stories and books you now read started as copyboys or in entry positions at various publications. You can't think you're going to become a top writer overnight. Make connections in college, search for internships, and do as much freelance writing as possible, no matter what the pay. If you come into an interview and you don't have anything that you've written, you're hurting yourself right out of the blocks."

Finally, Swift points out one cardinal rule for all young writers to remember: where a story appears does not define its quality. "Great writing is great writing, wherever it is published. There's no different style at *Sports Illustrated* that isn't being done elsewhere in newspapers or other writing outlets throughout the country."

7 Sports Media Relations in Colleges and Universities

by Kathleen M. Mulligan

A good media relations department will take some arrows for you and stand up for what is right.

John Calipari
Head coach, New Jersey Nets

John Calipari probably received as much media attention as any college basketball coach in the country from 1994 to 1996, while he was head coach at the University of Massachusetts (UMass). Now head coach of the NBA's New Jersey Nets, Calipari is articulate, outspoken, well dressed, good-looking, and an expert at the game of basketball. He has a presence, and whether they like him or not, the media can't get enough of him. Massachusetts's rise to the elite of the college basketball world, capped by an appearance in the 1996 NCAA Final Four, made the UMass campus, nestled in tiny Amherst, the focus of the college basketball world.

"In any school or program I've been in," says Calipari, "media relations is probably the most vital part of the job, aside from the actual coaching on the court. Image and perception end up becoming reality, and it's your media relations people who help a coach or a team form that image. They put you in good positions, and many times shield you."

Media attention at any school is a prized commodity. A successful athletic program can mean tremendous visibility and free media exposure to a university. But have you ever wondered how all of those television interviews are arranged, and where newspaper writers get so much background on the team and players they cover? It's because of sports media relations or sports information personnel. In the field of collegiate athletics, it is not only one of the most exciting careers to pursue; it is also one of the most important positions in an athletic department.

What Is Sports Media Relations?

Sports media relations, also referred to as sports information or athletic communications, has become, over the past twenty years, an increasingly important arm of a university's athletic department. A sports information director's (SID) countless responsibilities are not easy to pinpoint in a brief job description. A sports information office has its hand in almost every area of the athletic department. Why? Because it is the SID's job to publicize the school's athletic programs to the best of his or her ability. That means getting the school's name in print, on television, or on radio. Publicity is the best-known tool in sales, and the SID's main job is "selling" the university, its players, and its coaches.

A career in this field is an exciting one, but keep in mind that it certainly is not a nine-to-five job. Long hours, nights, and weekends are the norm, and the job requires a wide variety of skills. Some of them include:

- A considerable amount of writing, some of it dry and concise, some more creative

- Public relations and marketing skills to help promote programs and individuals

- Constant interaction with the local, regional, and national media, to not only provide them with information they seek, but to pitch story ideas that will increase exposure of the athletic program and the university

"There were many times at UMass," Calipari says, "when the importance of our media relations office was evident. In particular, three stories come to mind. The first is a story that ran in the newspapers about brothers on our team, Edgar and Gidell Padilla, whose parents were deaf. They moved their family from Puerto Rico to get a better education for their sons. It wasn't a story about the players themselves, it was a human-interest story about how two sons and their parents would converse in sign language and the parents would come to games to watch, but could never hear the radio broadcasts. It was the type of story that a good media relations department gets across. They help create a story that grabs people's hearts.

"The second example concerns our battle with the *Boston Globe* when they printed our UMass players' transcripts. At that time, we needed a strong media relations department that could put out the true facts and wasn't afraid to stand up for the truth. And that's what our people did. They informed the media that not only did the school have a great graduation rate, but that the graduates went out and got real jobs and contributed to society."

As his other example, Calipari remembers when the Minutemen were ranked first in the country. "When your team is No. 1 in the country for twenty-five weeks over two years, someone has to become the gatekeeper. Not just for the players, but also for the coaches. Our media relations people put us in a position where the public could see the true side of our team. Instead of 'catching the ball *after* it was thrown,' they were there moving *before* the ball was ever thrown."

Although the job a media relations staff does is very important, a career in this field will not make you rich. The following might be a typical job description for a sports information director:

Provide service and information to the media and general public. Publicize the university's athletic program. Disseminate information to local and national media on school, team, and individual accomplishments through daily interaction, timely press releases, and the university's athletics home page. Produce athletic department publications, including media guides and game programs. In addition, handle press operations for home sporting events by arranging for statisticians and public address announcers; coordinating postgame press conferences; and providing the media with necessary information, such as game notes, updated statistics, and coach and player quotes.

It's a very demanding job, but it's also rewarding.

But why is the role of the SID so important? According to Bill Little, the associate athletic director for external operations at the University of Texas, "I've always thought that the university should view its athletic department as its window to the world. It is the SID's job to open that window."

He explains the common philosophy of the sports information profession. A young person learns about a school by seeing its name and information about it, mainly via television. A school can be one of the best in any number of academic fields, but it is those schools who can get their names on the television screen that have the best chances of attracting, not just the best athletes, but the best students in all academic areas. Through sports, a school can gain the exposure and capture the interest of a broad base of people throughout the country and beyond. As Little says, "It is not just about the high school football player who saw Texas on television and wants to go there now. It goes way beyond the football program. It goes back to the man or woman who, as a youngster, saw someone or something on television that attracted him or her to the University of Texas. Later, as a businessperson or an architect, he or she gives back to the school. Although the introduction had nothing to do with athletics, it was his or her opening to our school."

Bill Strickland, associate athletic director of external affairs at the University of Massachusetts, agrees that athletics can serve as the university's window. "Some people in academia may think this is crazy, but prospective students getting ready to make their choice of colleges are influenced by their favorite athletic teams. I'm an example of that. From the time I was seven or eight, I grew up watching Mike Garrett, O. J. Simpson, Anthony Davis, Sam Cunningham, and Charles White run the football at the University of Southern California [USC]. Through television, I became a USC fan. When it came time to apply to schools, I applied to UMass, Syracuse, and USC. I knew nothing about USC other than the fact it was in Los Angeles and it had a good football team that would occasionally bring joy into my life by beating Notre Dame. And don't think that rooting interest isn't a factor with today's kids when they look at schools. Is it the determining factor? I would hope not, but I'm sure in some cases it is."

The field of sports information hasn't always been what it is today. Its numbers have grown, the field is more recognized, and job descriptions have changed. Some of the experts, such as Larry Kimball from Syracuse University, a Collegiate Sports Information Directors of America (COSIDA) Hall of Famer, remember the COSIDA national conventions in the 1960s and 1970s with 100 people crammed into a room in a Chicago hotel. Today, there are over 1,000 people at the annual national convention. Most universities, colleges, and junior colleges in the country with athletic programs have one or more persons acting in the position of SID, with a staff of one to five full-time assistants and any number of interns, graduate assistants, and students. COSIDA, the primary organization for sports information professionals, has approximately 2,000 members. Many other professionals in the field and assistants or interns aren't members. The opportunities are out there. It's a matter of finding them, as we discuss later.

The Evolution of Sports Media Relations

The media explosion that has occurred with the advent of cable television, twenty-four hour sports talk radio, and the Internet has led directly to the growth of the sports media relations field. More and more people crave information about sports, and there is an infinite number of newspapers, magazines, Web pages, and radio and television shows that thrive on anything from game stories to in-depth looks at the lives of pro and college athletes. It is the sports information director's job to feed this ever-growing media as much as possible. The SID's ultimate goals have probably not altered substantially. How those goals are achieved have changed drastically.

Take media guides, for example. Media guides, the informational books a school's athletic department produces for each sport, used to be just that—a guide for the media. They simply supplied background information on teams, coaches, and athletes. There was no real need for them to look fancy as long as the information was useful. That all changed around 1986, when the NCAA set limitations on the number of publications that institutions could send to a prospective student-athlete. Now, they are allowed to send only one publication. That publication is the media guide. The media guide has become the major recruiting tool for schools throughout the country. Ever since 1986, it has been a race to see whose can be the best, the biggest and the flashiest—anything that might help bring a star athlete to a given school is considered well worth the effort. It became the SID's job to not only find out all of the information about the players and put it into a useful written format but to make it look good in the process. At first, media guides were done mainly for basketball and football, because they were the only ones that got any significant attention. But, as recruiting became more and more important in other sports, that changed things. So did something called Title IX.

Title IX, more formally called "Title IX of the Education Amendments of 1972 to the 1964 Civil Rights Act" stated:

> No person in the United States shall, on the basis of sex, be excluded from participation in, be denied the benefits of, or be subjected to discrimination under any education program or activity receiving Federal financial assistance.

The adoption of this law meant that all schools must provide women with programs and activities (including athletics) in the same manner as they do men.

Obviously, Title IX has had a huge impact on the sports information world. It has helped create more jobs and a lot more work for every SID. For example, media guides must be produced for the women's teams in a similar manner as those for the men's. The same goes for game programs, schedule cards, posters, press releases, and everything else produced by the sports media relations office.

What Does It Take to Be a Sports Information Director?

The standard answer we received from SIDs was "Be willing to work a lot of hours." Outsiders' perceptions, however, tend to focus on the more glamorous aspects. Some look at the SID as someone who works with big-time coaches and athletes, sits front and center at every game and travels throughout the country and overseas with their teams. Although these are benefits of the job, it's the 100 million other tasks the SID performs that balance the scales in this career.

According to Mike Tranghese, now the commissioner of the Big East Conference, who was an SID at Providence before joining the conference, "It used to be that a school might have eight to ten sports to deal with, but the two main ones, football and basketball, were the only ones given much attention. Now, in order to offer equal opportunities to all of its students, schools are offering twenty to thirty sports."

Larry Kimball uses the words of inventor Thomas Edison as an example: "Genius is 97 percent hard work, and 3 percent inspiration. You could say this about sports information as well. It's great when you are playing Georgetown University on national television, and Billy Packer and Jim Nantz are raving about Syracuse, and you are basking in the limelight. It's funny, the game itself is really the only time you are relatively free. You work on everything leading up to the game, and then once the game is over you start doing it all over again. That hour and a half for a basketball game, and three hours for a football game is our 3 percent. The other 97 percent is in the office."

Bill Little remarks, "Last year, I staffed eighty events, and from September to December, I was on the road for forty-six days. I think it's really important to realize that other people think our work is recreational. Other folks die to go to the games on the weekend because it's a release for them. It's not a release for us; it's our full-time job."

As an SID you have to love what you're doing. "I didn't do it just because I wanted to be in athletics," explains Mike Tranghese, who began his career as an SID at St. Michael's College in Vermont. "I loved the idea of being creative and finding ways to get our story across. I would recommend this field to people if I knew they were willing to work hard and had a real thirst for it. But if they just want to get into athletics, they are barking up the wrong tree."

It's also important to be a people person. To publicize your school or team, you initiate, develop, and nurture relationships with media members, coaches, athletes, parents, and alumni. An SID may deal with fifty different people every day, each with a different perspective. If you are unfriendly or uncooperative, the media will lose interest in writing stories about your players. If you are unapproachable, coaches won't suggest story ideas or make themselves accessible. If you are too demanding or hard to deal with, athletes won't want to do many interviews. "As an SID," says Little, "you serve and try to satisfy eight different levels: the student, his or her parents, your coaches, your administration, the media, the fans, the alumni, and the student body."

Tranghese takes the role of people skills a bit further. "To be a good SID, you need basic writing skills, but more important are people skills," he affirms. "I see people who are very talented but have difficulty relating to other people. You must be able to relate to people you work with, the coaches and the media, because you are the middle person. You're often placed in difficult situations and have to know how to sort your way through them. The quality of your people skills usually resolves them."

Joe Paterno, Penn State head football coach, told us, "A good SID or public relations [PR] director is essential to any athletic organization. That's because there are PR implications to almost any issue and good advice in advance often will head off potential problems. Through most of my career at Penn State, I worked with one of the business's foremost professionals, Jim Tarman, and his contribution to spreading the message of Penn State football cannot be overstated. I think any athletic team benefits from a strong SID who can tutor players on media responsibilities; help organize players' time to minimize interview distractions; and provide the national and local media with timely, concise, and useful information on the university's athletic teams. I encourage sports journalists to learn as much as they can about the sports they cover, to take into account the impact of what they do on the lives of the people they write about, and, most of all, to be accurate and fair in all of their dealings."

The Skills Required

In addition to people skills and a willingness to work hard, SIDs must have the following talents:

- *Writing.* Most sports information and publicity consists of the written word in a variety of forms, including press releases with the five W's (who, what, where, why, and when) satisfied, biographical material to help the media prepare stories, and season outlooks for teams and feature stories for university newsletters and publications.

    Our SID experts agree that writing is the most necessary skill for someone in their profession. Bob

Kenworthy, veteran SID at Gettysburg College, a Division III school in Pennsylvania, states, "Writing is at least 75 percent. There are two things you have to know in this business—that's how to write and how to use a computer." Larry Kimball adds, "Some people want to write the great American novel, but that's not what is needed. A clever, practiced writer isn't overcome by tough deadlines."

- *Desktop publishing.* This is another qualification required of many SIDs for producing professional media guides as recruiting tools. In most schools, the sports information office writes and edits media guide materials, as well as doing the layout and design of the book. Experience with Pagemaker and QuarkXpress software, which are the two main desktop publishing programs on the market today is also very important. "Anyone who applies for a job at Syracuse must have desktop publishing skills," says Kimball.

- *Knowledge of sports.* Another obvious but necessary tool of the SID is being able to see the big picture, including understanding the rules and rankings of a variety of college sports. You needn't have been a star in the sport, or even have played it, but it is important to know the basics of how to keep a scoresheet or at least have the ability to learn.

- *Record keeping and managing game operations.* You must be able to keep game scoresheets and statistics and set up personnel to run the scoreboard and serve as announcers.

The Daily Routine

We keep mentioning that one thing necessary to be successful in this field is a willingness to work long hours. Sixteen-hour days are not uncommon during the peak of sports seasons at many schools, depending on the size of the staff and the level of competition. A major time commitment comes with the job. If you aren't willing to put time into your work and be happy doing it, this career field might not be for you.

Typically, during the basketball season you go into the office at 8:30 A.M. and work throughout the day making the usual preparations—working on media guides, talking to press people, interacting with coaches. This is followed by a basketball game at night which starts at 7:30 P.M. and lasts two hours. Then you work with the media until about midnight. On the positive side, most schools are pretty flexible with SIDs taking time during the day to attend to personal business.

Most sports information jobs also require significant weekend work. At a football school, for example, the home games are played on Saturday afternoons, which means that you get to the office early to prepare for the game, attend and work at the contest, and then deal with media needs. Sunday, you are back at the office to file reports with the conference office and the NCAA, and update statistics and game notes for the media.

On the road, your schedule changes. Friday is usually the travel day, which puts you somewhat behind in office work. Even if you don't work at a football school, there are still countless weekend events such as soccer games, lacrosse games, cross-country meets, and so on. Larry Kimball, a person who loved his job, admits that on many weekends he'd rather be doing other things. "There are a lot of Sundays and beautiful spring days when you would rather be anywhere but in the office, such as home watching the NFL games or taking a nap." Simply put, it is important to love sports, love your work, and understand how long it takes to do it right.

Out of the Blocks

To get a good start in this career, a college education is a must. Actually, selection of a major isn't all that important because SIDs come from all types of educational backgrounds, with a wide-ranging number of degrees. Those with journalism backgrounds have less of a learning curve, but it's really experience and willingness to work that are preferred over a degree in English or journalism. "Some student workers in our office weren't journalism majors," says Rick Brewer, assistant athletic director for sports information at the University of North Carolina. "They came to school primarily to work in our office because they liked sports and wanted to get involved in the business."

Charlie Bare, assistant SID at the University of Virginia, was a math major at his alma mater, Notre Dame. "I was looking for something to do," he recalls. "I liked sports and there was an ad in the school paper for volunteers to work in the sports information office. Even though I was a math major, this career seemed like something I would really enjoy."

Some schools, however, offer majors in sports administration/ media relations, as well as public relations and communications. Others, such as the University of Southern California, Syracuse University, and the University of Massachusetts, even offer courses in sports information/media relations.

Experience is a must to enter this field. Leigh Torbin, a senior intern in the University of Massachusetts media relations office, remembers a well-educated applicant who lost out because he wasn't experienced. "In one of our sport management classes, I met a guy who had graduated a few years ago with a 3.97 grade point average, which he thought would open many doors for him in this profession," Torbin remembers. "But he finally realized that his GPA wasn't nearly as important to employers as experience. While he was at home studying for top grades, others were getting real on-the-job experience in undergraduate internships."

If you are interested in becoming an SID, it is important to think ahead. Build your resume. The more experience you have as a student, the more likely you will be able to get a good internship at a school and that will help you to attain your first full-time job.

"Get started early," emphasizes Bill Little. "Students who want to be in SID work should go to their sports information office and pitch in. Too often, "seniors come in after they've been at the school for four years. They learn too late that this would be an interesting career for them. My question to them is, 'Where have you been for four years?'"

Mike Tranghese agrees. "We have 25-year-old applicants for these jobs who ask about getting into sports information," he says. "I tell them, 'I don't care how well you write, how well you think, or how creative you are. If you don't have some type of practical experience, there are very few people who can afford the time to start training you from scratch.'"

Unfortunately, most universities can't get enough help. But keep in mind that everyone starts at the bottom and most of the work is not glamorous. Tasks like clipping newspapers and stuffing envelopes must be done on a daily basis in a media relations office. At the beginning of the school year, the University of Massachusetts, for example, gives prospective student workers a pamphlet advising those who are interested in SID work not to expect to work directly with the football and basketball teams, but rather with less popular athletic teams and perform the mundane but necessary busywork in order to learn.

Volunteering

Volunteering is an unavoidable concept in the SID world. Most schools can't afford to pay all of the workers they need. Many student workers we spoke to started out as volunteers and worked their way into a paying position. Leigh Torbin began as a sports information volunteer when he was a freshman at the University of Massachusetts. "I used to go to Boston Bruins games, and I always thought how great it would be, instead of spending forty bucks on a ticket to come home with a paycheck after the game," he says. "That's how it got started for me." He volunteered his first two years, working mostly on sports information grunt work, clipping articles, stuffing envelopes, and even delivering lunch for staff members. His training included some unusual talents. "I learned things like the quickest way to seal a paper cut," he recalls, "how to jiggle the toner in the copier so the toner light would go off; and exactly how long it took to stuff, seal, and stamp 300 releases."

But Torbin always volunteered to write articles and hometown stories about local athletes. Even though he wasn't paid for his work for two years, it did pay off. As a senior intern, he received an hourly rate ($5.25—minimum wage), and covered his own sports. And after graduation he landed a full-time job as assistant SID at Vanderbilt University.

Some students become frustrated with clerical work and give up. Larry Kimball told two student volunteers who said they wanted to help in the office, "Well, we can always use help clipping newspapers, stuffing envelopes, and the like." He recalls, "We went through a long list of things, none of which sounded interesting to them. All they wanted to do was go to games, and that was all. I told them when they wanted to do something productive to let me know. They didn't come back again."

Capturing the Internship

As in many journalism career fields, the next step after graduation is a full-time internship, where you learn different approaches and ways of dealing with the media. Full-time internships don't pay too well, but they are usually the only way into the SID and sports administration world. Intern wages vary depending on the school. Some offer stipends up to $1,000 a month; others offer less money but provide room and board. UMass, for example, pays $750 a month and offers housing, which is a major benefit. Other schools, such as Syracuse, offer graduate assistantships (GAs), which are usually two-year appointments, in exchange for the tuition and a small stipend. Syracuse pays a stipend of $8,000 for about ten months of work, plus full tuition in the graduate program. Wagner College on Staten Island, New York, also offers a graduate assistantship in which the intern receives a very small stipend, but is provided free graduate school and housing in campus dorms.

The Big East Conference, one of the better paying places to intern, pays $12,000 for nine months of work. It also provides medical coverage, which most do not. "We just think that if an intern has a medical problem, it should be our responsibility," says Mike Tranghese. "They're not going to get rich making that kind of money, but we assist them in finding housing and we can point out other opportunities to them. It's what I call survival money."

Charlie Bare followed a typical path from student volunteer to intern to full-time job. "When I started as a student volunteer at Notre Dame, it was really exciting," he explains. "When you are around a high-profile team, as I was with the football team then, it's fun, even though I was just stuffing envelopes or answering the phones. It was great just to be a part of it. The longer I stayed, the more responsibilities I took on. Early on in my senior year I decided I might like it as a career."

Like many others, Bare found that the field was very competitive, despite his experience. "I interviewed for three internships and was only offered one of them," he says. "The field is still hard to get into, despite low earnings, because there are so many interested in it." Bare went on to a two-year internship at UMass. He gained excellent experience handling media relations on lower profile Olympic sports, such as soccer, field hockey, swimming, and volleyball. He was also required to do a lot of writing, including feature articles for the monthly publication the *Maroon and White*, game stories, team outlooks—you name it, he wrote it. In his second year, Bare worked primarily as the main assistant with the men's basketball team which was bound for the NCAA's Final Four. "In my second year, I learned more about dealing with the national media, because they came to us for help rather than us going to them," he recalls. Bare also points out that it really wasn't too bad living on a low salary. "At first you think, there's no way I'll be able to live on this. But then you realize that with all the work, you probably will not have much time for a social life in which to spend money anyway."

While internships are one of the best ways to enter the field, there are critics of the practice. Rick Brewer believes that many internships prepare people for jobs that don't exist. "All these schools have internships, more like cheap labor, and are turning out candidates for jobs that just aren't there," he argues. "There isn't as much turnover as there used to be and not that many jobs anymore. Many veterans have left the profession and been replaced by younger people who aren't about to leave. Marketing has become so important to athletic directors these days that when they add an assistant, it is for marketing, not for sports information."

Brewer has a point. Some young people trying to get into the business work two or three internships and still can't get that first full-time opportunity. Schools are now more apt to add internship positions, which don't cost them as much as a full-time employee with benefits. Although many schools would gain by hiring another staff member, the addition of a full-time assistant at two or three times the internship salary plus benefits is not always viable, especially when many athletic directors are looking at ways of cutting their budgets rather than expanding them. Unfortunately, intern-

4	Guest editorial	7	Football	20	Three in a month
	Counselor says media play a big role in proliferation of sports gambling		**Final Division III individual and team statistical reports**		**NCAA, USA Wrestling review recent deaths of college wrestlers**

The NCAA News

ships may go the way of bachelor's degrees—necessary, but no guarantee of getting a full-time job.

The Job Search

So, where do you find these jobs? They are not advertised in the newspaper. The weekly NCAA News is the one publication to which virtually every NCAA member institution subscribes. We recommend it as the place to start your job search. The sports information jobs are typically listed in "The Market" section under sports information, but some are occasionally listed under public relations or media relations. If your school doesn't subscribe, order a subscription or tap into the NCAA website at http//:www.ncaa.org. Keep in mind that most hiring is done in the late spring and summer. Therefore, you should start sending out resumes in April or May. But, don't be overambitious. Some places don't hire until near the end of the summer, so be patient.

A more specific publication for the sports information field is in the COSIDA Digest. The organization sends out a monthly newsletter with a "Jobseekers" section. Another tool is COSIDA's yearly directory, which identifies sports information office contacts at every school in the country, plus conferences and other organizations. COSIDA also runs a summer convention that includes a "Jobseekers" session. Through membership in the organization, job seekers have the opportunity to send resumes to a central location where prospective employers interview interns, graduate assistants, and full-time assistants. It's a great place to meet people, see

Cosida Digest

Monthly Newsletter of the College Sports Information Directors of America

VOL. 47 NO. 11	KINGSVILLE, TEXAS 78363	DECEMBER 1997

what schools are looking for in a candidate, and compare your resume with those of others around the country.

The Importance of Making Contacts

As with other careers described in this book, media relations requires that you become adept at networking and making contacts. Because media relations is a public relations business based on dealing with other institutions and media outlets, it is very easy to research job openings. Someone always knows someone who knows someone else. So, the goal is to make your name and work known.

Keep in mind, though, that knowing people who might come in handy in the future isn't enough. It is the impression you make on them that will be remembered. This is a big business but a small, tight-knit network. Others in the field will know something about your work ethic, your writing skills, your personality, and so on. It is always important to be at your best.

For those who may be timid about networking to find jobs, we have this advice: don't be afraid of it or you will lose out. When you get into this business, it is your job to push ideas to the media, to make calls to people you hardly know, and to be outgoing and likable. That's essentially what you are doing when you use your networking skills. Make a call. Let people get to know the real you. Be proud of your work.

Women SIDs and Family Life

Job opportunities are certainly out there for everyone, including minorities and women. There aren't as many SIDs from minority groups as there should be, but women are now beginning to play a major role in sports information departments throughout the country. Despite the growing number of women in the profession, there are too few in the top positions. Of the approximate 1,000 schools in Divisions I, II, and III, only 10 percent have women as head SIDs.

"There definitely aren't enough women in the field," agrees Sue Edson, director of athletic communications at Syracuse. "There are plenty of opportunities in the field for men and women willing to work hard, but there are different issues and stereotypes a woman must deal with that men don't." Since Edson was just recently promoted to the position of sports information director, she has encountered all of these issues in the recent months. For example, "For postgame football, I don't go into the locker room, my male assistant goes in to get players for interviews," she says. "That's one barrier that I'm not going to be able to overcome because I don't want to make the athletes uncomfortable."

Women have some choices, such as avoiding the men's locker room as Edson does. But there are other areas over which women have no control. "There still exists the stereotype that only males are SIDs and females are assistants," notes Edson. She remembers a trip to the 1997 Fiesta Bowl. "I was sitting near the phone in the press box, when I overheard a male reporter on the phone. He said, 'I don't know where the Syracuse SID is, but I'll go find him.' So I stepped up and said, 'Hi, I'm the Syracuse SID. My name is Sue Edson.' He was really taken aback."

Putting stereotypes aside for a minute, there is a reality issue for prospective female SIDs. Many of those in the profession, including women, believe that it is virtually impossible to handle both family and a career as demanding as sports information. And for some, it is. "We had a panel at the COSIDA convention one year about having a life outside of work," recalls Bill Little. "One woman, who worked at Notre Dame at the time, was on the panel with me, and she got up and said to all of the rookies, 'I have no life. I go to the office, I go home, I go back to the office.'"

For some people, that kind of daily existence is enough to make them rethink their decisions to pursue or stay in sports information. For others, though, it is simply a matter of balance. "For the female, of course, it's harder because she is looked at as the primary person holding a household together," remarks Edson. "If you have a husband and are planning a family, you have to have someone who understands your job. I'm fortunate because my husband works in athletics." That's a blessing, but what if it's not the case?

Rick Brewer finds it amazing how people manage to enjoy happy marriages while working in the business. "I've never been married, and I don't see how anybody who is married does this job," he says. "That's why I have such great respect for people in this business who are happily married and have managed to balance their family and business lives."

"It takes a really disciplined person to be able to have a life outside work because the hours are so demanding," confirms Edson. "I'm able to get out and golf in the summer, play in two softball leagues, and in the spring semester teach a class at the Newhouse School. I'm also a Girl Scout leader, so it's true that you can do other things if you want to. It's just a matter of balancing."

Despite the conflicts, women are becoming fixtures in sports information and are gaining widespread respect in the process. "I have great respect for women who have to deal with men's sports," says Brewer. "It's tough to do that. Sometimes those coaches just don't understand that women are fully capable of handling them."

Where to Work

There are several options for working in sports media relations. There are NCAA Division I, II, and III schools, NAIA schools, conference offices, and even professional sports (see Chapter 9). Where will you fit in? What's the best place for you? To answer those questions, it is important to know that the job varies at each level.

Colleges and Universities

Most colleges and universities with athletic programs have one person or many who serve in the role as the sports information director. There are definitely pros and cons to both large and small sports information departments.

Working in a small office of a small school provides many positive experiences. It may be less glamorous, but you can have a more well-rounded experience than if you work in a bigger office, where your responsibilities focus only on one or two sports. A common question is "If I have a choice to work either as a Division I intern or at a full-time Division II or III job, what should I do?" Rick Brewer advises: "I always tell them, if you have a chance at the full-time job, take it. You'll learn more at one of the smaller schools, because you have to do everything—and I mean everything."

That's a major consideration when investigating the differences between job opportunities at different schools. For example, the difference between a "big-time" Division I school (e.g., University of Texas or University of North Carolina) and a smaller Division I institution is enormous. Schools such as Texas, Michigan, Ohio State, and North Carolina have large staffs. The University of Texas, whose offices are divided into men's and women's sports, has sixteen employees, one of the largest in the nation. The University of North Carolina has six full-time staff members, a secretary, and about ten student workers. Other schools cover as many sports with half as many staffers. How can that be? It boils down to exposure. That is the big difference in the big-time schools. They receive so much media attention that the extra help is a must. They employ several assistant SIDs to help handle the load. At schools whose teams aren't as successful, the administration doesn't see the need to employ more than one or two people. And that makes for a lot of work—and experience—for the director. "I've worked in Divisions I, II, and III, and in pro football," says Bill Strickland. "You certainly get a more well-rounded experience at the Division II and III levels, but sometimes it is hard to break out of those schools. If your goal is to work in major college athletics, it can be an uphill struggle to go from the lower divisions. Most departments prefer someone who has experience dealing with major media, who is used to being under the microscope, and who has crisis management experience."

Problems can occur, however, when a small school has a good year and experiences instant fame, as St. Joseph's University in Philadelphia did in 1996 and 1997. Its men's basketball team, the Hawks, went to the finals of the National Invitational Tournament (NIT) in 1996 and advanced to the "Sweet 16" of the NCAA tournament in 1997. Such success had not occurred at the school in decades, so the sports information office had to handle hundreds of media requests with a two-person staff. To complicate matters, in 1997, the St. Joseph's women's basketball team won the Atlantic 10 Tournament and were also busy with media requests and travel needs of their own. Larry Dougherty, assistant athletic director for sports media relations and one other full-time staffer were saddled with the massive challenge of handling all the publicity. "We were lucky our athletic director, Don DiJulia, was so supportive during that time," recalls Dougherty. "We were so short-staffed, we had to hire 'freelance' SIDs. We hired a person from the university's external relations department and added student workers. It was doubly hard, because our St. Joe's women's team was also in the NCAA tournament at the same time."

Dougherty wanted to make certain, however, that the school took advantage of the national exposure, which was rare for a school the size of St. Joseph's. "It's not often a small Catholic university gets the kind of national exposure we received," Dougherty said. "We didn't want to shortchange ourselves by not having enough staff members to handle it."

At the Division III level of sports information, the business is much different. Bob Kenworthy, who has been SID at Gettysburg College since 1958, believes that working at a Division III school is actually worse from a media standpoint, but better from a pressure standpoint. "Division I schools mostly generate their own following in the media," he explains. "Even some good Division II schools do, but in Division III where I work, there's none. There definitely isn't the same pressure in Division III as in Division I. You don't have big-time players and pressure to promote them at a school like ours. Nonetheless, you still try to maintain the same professionalism as SIDs do in Division I or II."

Athletic Conferences

Another recommended target for your job search is athletic conferences. There are thirty-two Division I athletic conferences and approximately 125 other collegiate and junior college athletic conferences throughout the country, as listed in the COSIDA Directory. Each employ at least one sports information professional. A conference media relations director acts as a service bureau for the league member and the media. He or she typically generates releases, notes, statistics, and other exposure for each sport in season on a daily or weekly basis, depending on the sport. The focus, of course, is on the entire league rather than on one school.

The other major difference in working in a conference office are the hours. Granted, you won't be working nine to five, but there is more structure in typical conference media relations jobs because they can be handled in a normal business day. The hours begin to build up during basketball or football season, for example, when attendance at games as a representative of the conference is expected as part of the job. Conference media relations people also are usually involved in other conference happenings, such as championships. They travel to several of the league tournaments throughout the year to promote the schools and help run the tournament. Denise Gormley, the assistant commissioner for public relations at the Northeast Conference thinks the lifestyle in a conference office is somewhat easier. "My work in the conference office is more structured and businesslike than at a school," she says. "Although I am not working an eight-hour day by any means, I don't have to be at a sporting event every night of the week either, as some school sports information directors do." Gormley does see the lack of interaction with the student athlete as a downside of working in a conference setting. "One thing you miss in a conference office is the relationships you make with the student athletes. You might get to meet and interact with some of the elite athletes in your league, from the media end, but rarely do you get to build any kind of relationship with them as you could at a school."

Moving up the Ladder

Many people remain as assistant SIDs for several years before a sports information director job opens. The typical line of progression for sports information professionals is shown in Figure 7.1. Not all schools use this progression or the same titles. Nor do all SIDs want to move up the ladder into athletic administration. Many, such as Larry Kimball, love sports information so much, they stay in it. Others move out of the field to other jobs within their school's athletic department or to other related fields.

For example, Rosa Gatti, senior vice president for communications at ESPN, was an SID at Villanova and Brown Universities early in her career. Val Pinchbeck, director of broadcasting for the NFL, was the SID at Syracuse before Kimball. Chuck Steedman, former

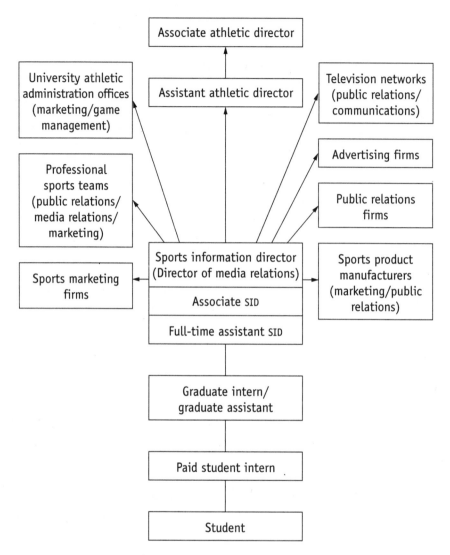

Figure 7.1 Career paths in the sports information field

vice president of Raycom Sports, was the assistant SID at University of Connecticut.

Mike Tranghese started in the sports information office at American International College in Springfield, Massachusetts, and worked as SID at Providence University. Later, he became public relations director at the Big East Conference, and nine years after that became its commissioner. "In the seven years I worked for Dave

Gavitt, then athletic director at Providence, I had the opportunity to be involved in various jobs within the department, such as marketing and promotions," Tranghese recalls. "I was exposed to so much as a result of Gavitt providing those opportunities."

If you start out in sports information, you hope that in time an administrator will allow you to interact and become involved in other areas, helping you to take the next step. Whether it's another year as the SID at a school you love or a job in a related field, the experience and education you gain in the sports information field will aid you throughout your career. Head basketball coach of Duke University, Mike Krzyzewski credits his school's SID with a measure of its success in collegiate sports. "In my opinion," he says, "SIDs provide an invaluable service to players, coaches, writers, and other media people covering college sports. I have found the SIDs at Duke to be extremely insightful and have an amazing work ethic. They also all seem to have a great sense of humor. Thank God for great SIDs."

A Rewarding Field

Some call it a dream job. Familiar comments to an SID include, "Wow, you get to sit at courtside and watch all of those sporting events and get paid for it," or "You must have the funnest job ever," or "You call that work?" Well, to repeat, the job is a lot of work, but there are great benefits if you are a sports lover. Leigh Torbin says, "I always thought the people in the press box had the best seats in the house, and they are the ones walking home with a paycheck." True, people in the profession usually get the best seats in the house, but they work very hard for them. "I used to joke with people that the best part of my job was my seat," says Larry Kimball. He was only half-kidding, but there are a number of other reasons why this field is such a rewarding one.

There aren't a plethora of jobs where you actually see the outcome of your work. Doctors can observe the improvement of a patient; lawyers know whether they've won or lost a case. But many other workers don't see the fruits of their labor. In sports information, you can pick up the paper the day after a big game and see the results of your phone calls, notes, arranged interviews, and press releases. Your team's story is in the headlines. That feeling of satisfaction can last throughout the year, as a marketable star player wins awards for which you promoted him or her, or you see the clip files on your athletes, or your teams grow and grow. "If you do your job," says Little, "you are able to tell a story that matters and possibly make a difference in someone's life. You have a chance to make a hero."

Another reward in sports information is feeling like part of a winning team. You might not think that sports information directors and their staffs have much to do with wins and losses, but they do. There are some in the profession who mutter things like, "I can't shoot the jump shot for them" if their team is doing poorly. Or they say, "I didn't score the winning touchdown, don't congratulate me." But that's negative thinking. Although the SID may not be on the field, he or she is the person working behind the scenes to make things happen. "If people in the media relations business are doing their jobs properly and are giving their maximum efforts to promote and publicize their teams, then their work can be a positive factor in helping the coach to recruit better players, which does affect wins and losses," notes Bill Strickland. "I think people need to realize that everyone in the athletic department has an effect on wins and losses, not just the coaches and players."

Remember our earlier example of the media guides. Although their intended purpose is as an information tool for the media, they have become coaches' recruiting tools. "Media guides are vital to recruiting," says Calipari. "They are the first thing players see. Your school's image and perception come from that book. If it looks cheap and another school's is big and glossy, then in the eyes of a high school student, who has the better program?" That philosophy trickles down through every aspect of the SID's job. By making your guide better than those of your competition, you may have contributed in a positive way to your school's eventual win–loss record.

One of the areas of greatest fulfillment from a career in sports information is intangible: the relationships formed with players, coaches, and others in the business. Without a doubt, such ties are the reasons many stay in the business for a long time. "The greatest reward," says Bob Kenworthy, "is my association with the athletes, because it is often a lifelong relationship. I still keep in touch with many of them." Sue Edson from Syracuse agrees: "When you work in a college atmosphere with athletes who want to be there and like the media attention you get for them, you have an opportunity to help them grow as people."

Veteran SIDs were unanimous in saying that their greatest enjoyment came from the friendships formed during an athlete's four-year career. "I think interacting with the kids is still the best part of the job," stresses Mike Tranghese. "It is seeing naïve seventeen- or eighteen-year-old kids come to your school and then seeing them at graduation grown, developed, and matured. And then ten years down the road you see them out in the world, hopefully being successful. You look back and say, 'I was a part of their experience. I helped develop them so they could enjoy this kind of success.' "

Enduring friendships also are formed with other professionals in the field. "There is no way that Dean Smith and Mike Krzyzewski can be best friends as they compete for athletes and against each other on the basketball court," Rick Brewer said. "SIDS get along better than anyone. They probably talk to each other more than any school professional. That's what I enjoy most about the profession, the camaraderie."

"You develop such great friendships," Kenworthy agrees. "That doesn't exist in other parts of athletics. I can't think of a better field to be in because of my association with others in the business."

What's the Downside?

Sports information is like many businesses—it has its drawbacks. One frustration that SIDs eventually come to terms with is the income. Their salaries vary with experience and the size of their school, but seldom approach the salaries of coaches and other athletic administrators. "I think this is a fantastic career field," says Rick Brewer. "But don't go into it for the money. Do it because you love college athletics and living in and around a college campus."

Another disadvantage is that many SIDs cannot avoid the feeling they are fighting a losing battle. It is hard to please everyone, but that's what is expected of a sports information director. Many times, the SID is the liaison between coaches, media members, athletes, and parents, each wanting something different. The following are just a sample of the problems that come up on a day-to-day basis:

- Coaches complain about not getting enough attention.

- Athletes complain about having to do too many interviews.

- The media need statistics, schedules, profiles, interview appointments, and the inside scoop on team gossip.

- Parents want to see their kid's name in the paper, even if he or she only sits on the bench.

All of these make an SID feel like he or she is doing a juggling act.

Some think of travel as a frustration; others see it as a reward. As an SID, you have opportunities to travel the country and even the world with your teams. "We have played all over the globe in football," says Larry Kimball. "We played in Japan, California, and all over. In basketball, we've gone to Hawaii, Alaska, Puerto Rico. It's a great way to see the United States and the world."

Kimball is right, but for some, after years of trips, opportunities become obligations. Bill Strickland says, "I've been fortunate to go to places like Hawaii, France, and Japan because of my association with athletics. But, honestly, after being in it for a number of years, the travel does start to wear you down, especially if you have a family. It can be exciting, but there definitely is a trade-off."

Money Doesn't Always Talk

We'd love to tell you how you can make millions in sports information, but we can't. It is, however, a profession where you can make a comfortable living. Some sports information directors at large universities earn as high as $60,000 to $70,000 per year, while those at smaller schools make as little as $20,000.

An independent survey of Division I schools lists the average salary for a head SID as $42,000, while assistants in those schools average approximately $22,000 to $26,000. Information on salary ranges from an independent membership services survey in 1996 lists the range of salaries for 165 random Division I media relations employees as between $20,000 to more than $46,000. Positions included full-time head SIDs, assistants, and interns. The bottom line is that salaries are quite varied, depending on the size of the school and the funding its athletic department receives.

To Sum Up

"There are many things a person learns as an SID that can be taken into almost any area of the athletics profession," says author Kate Mulligan. In her experience as an assistant SID at both St. Joseph's University (Pa.) and the University of Massachusetts, there wasn't much going on in the athletic department of which she wasn't a part. The interpersonal skills needed as an SID to navigate situations with coaches, athletes, the general public, administrators, educators, and the media prepare you for almost any job, whether in media relations, professional sports PR, as an athletic director, or in television PR. All of these professions require good communications skills, knowledge of the game and how to run it, and creativity to make your team, your school, or your television network stand out. You do all of those things as a sports information director.

Sports information is special because of its variety. If you are a writer who is a sports enthusiast, but the newspaper business is not for you, this may be an attractive career alternative. You'll use your writing skills in many and varied ways, but you will also use your interpersonal skills to build relationships with athletes, coaches, administrators, and the media. It is a job that is very demanding, but very rewarding. As Sue Edson puts it, "I just like the pace of it. I enjoy dealing with all of the challenges thrown at you. I could never sit behind a desk in a nine-to-five job. Sports information allows you to have variety in your profession, and that's one of the best things about it. I can honestly say that, in eight years, I have never had the same day twice."

8 Sports Advertising and Marketing

In the game of business, you don't have to outspend them to outsmart them. Just find a hole in their game plan and break away.

Sparky Harris
Sports marketing specialist

Most of us over thirty years old remember a time when the clothes we wore functioned to cover us or keep us warm. Now, the T-shirts we wear and the uniforms of college and professional athletes all carry an advertising message in one form or another, such as logos and names. The only information printed on ballpark walls a few years ago was the distance to the fences; now they're covered with sponsor names. The front of the basketball scorers' tables used to be covered; now they are fronted by mechanical billboards that try to draw our attention. Watch events such as a Wimbledon tennis match and compare commercial monograms on shorts, sweaters, and socks. The National Football League has "logo police" to make certain that players aren't wearing anything other than the official NFL-licensed sportswear. Wherever you look, you can see little else than advertising. It is everywhere!

Twin Sisters

Sports advertising and *sports marketing* can be thought of as twin sisters; they produce the same outcome—selling a product, creating an image, or attempting to bolster the reputation of an athlete or executive. Although they are both after the same outcome, advertising focuses on publicity, hype, and buildup of the product. Marketing, too, involves promotion but also entails sales and distribution.

Sports advertising and marketing professionals develop the ads we see regularly with high-profile sports personalities plugging various products from sneakers, to aftershave, to underwear. Remember NBA stars Charles Barkley (Houston Rockets) and Scottie Pippen (Chicago Bulls) cast in their elegant riding ensembles exclaiming that "Anything less would be absolutely uncivilized"? Those famous words sold tons of men's deodorant, but more to the point, it was financially rewarding to an advertising agency and a number of its well-paid staff, including writers. In that award-winning commercial campaign, advertisers and their copywriters helped us appreciate a product by employing sports figures we instantly recognized for their basketball talents. In other instances, copywriters help us to develop affection for a product line or with a sport itself by associating it with popular sports figures.

The writer's special wordsmithing talent is a cornerstone of this high-profile profession. Advertising and marketing of sports products, personalities, and organizations is, as most of you know, big business. It's an important ingredient of the American economy and you can become part of it if you have the written and oral communications skills that match this industry's needs.

Sports Products

In order to consider advertising and marketing of sports products, it's important to define the term. In her book *Sports Marketing*, Christine M. Brooks discusses competitive business strategies for sports and generally defines a sports product as consisting of three major elements—the sport, the team, and the participants—all revolving around the competition itself, the contest.

For each sport product to be sold, Brooks sees four basic markets:

- The *primary markets*, consisting of participants, spectators, and volunteers

- The *participant markets*, comprising the actual producers of sports

- The *spectator markets*, which includes television viewers, stadium attendees, radio listeners, and press readers

- The *volunteer market*, encompassing those who love the sport so much that they devote almost all their leisure time to helping it grow, such as coaches of youth teams

Sports advertising and marketing focuses its efforts on these groups as sports consumers. Brooks elaborates in her book on the way consumers are attracted to the sports product via advertising and marketing, but the writer plays a fundamental role in convincing potential buyers of the importance and value of the sports product.

Let's define the two major subsets of the marketing arena. *Sports marketing* refers to events and activities promoting individuals and teams, usually in competitive activities. It includes games, races, tournaments, and so on, which, because of their great spectator appeal, often cross over into the entertainment industry. *Marketing of sporting goods* involves the planning, introduction, and promotion of products used in sports and fitness activities.

Kellee "Sparky" Harris, owner of a sports marketing consulting company called MarketSpark, explains that sports marketing might involve the promotion of a major marathon, whereas sporting goods marketing would include the planning and introduction of racing shoes to be used by competitive athletes in the marathon. It is fair to say that sometimes the lines become blurred, as many sporting goods manufacturers often sponsor athletic events or teams, thus crossing over into sports marketing as well. We examine both fields further in this chapter.

Another example of sports product marketing is called "on-ice branding" by Michael Humes, vice president of sales and marketing for the American Hockey League (AHL). "We work with various equipment companies," explains Humes, "who pay a fee to us for helping to market their products for them. We permit them to expose their logos and brand or company names on skates, sticks, helmets, gloves, and goaltender gear."

The Team of Advertising, Marketing, and Public Relations

Just as in sports competition, the promotion team that plays best together usually produces a winner. Although sports advertising and sports marketing are usually thought of as interlocking, in many well-organized sports organizations, public relations (PR) (see Chapter 9) functions in concert with them. In modern sports franchises, these departments work together to achieve an organizational goal. Their messages must be consistent, whether it's in a newspaper advertisement, a sportswriter's story or column, an item in the business or local news section, or a television commercial. The theme, thrust, and content have to be the same.

The key from a marketing perspective is to have a consistent, well-planned message. Dave Coskey, vice president of marketing and operations of the Philadelphia 76ers' NBA franchise believes in bombarding a target audience with "multiple impressions." According to Coskey, it takes many "hits" before a message makes an impression on fans or potential fans. "The hits come from the combined efforts of all of us," he notes. Reporting to Coskey, therefore, is a director of marketing and a director of PR with the same goal, promoting the team. "The only difference is that the PR director doesn't call *Hoop* magazine and argue about where the story about the 76ers is going to be placed in their publication, but the marketing director does, because she's writing a check for a team advertisement.

"If our PR writer helps one of the newspaper beat writers write a great story on one of my players, that can be as valuable or more so to the team than if my marketing people place a special ad in the sports section." It's critical for writers and others in these positions to understand that marketing, advertising, and PR are all teammates.

Variety Is Bliss

Advertising

It takes a lot of different skills and talents to produce a successful sports advertising program. There are many job functions for you to consider in this field, such as news media advertising, in-house advertising for corporations, copywriting, or some of the positions mentioned later. A small advertising company or a team at a large Madison Avenue firm usually consists of the following personnel, all of whom need strong writing and communication skills:

- *Advertising manager.* The manager is responsible for running the entire operation or business. She or he oversees the staff development and planning of an ad campaign to advertise a product, service, team, publication, or organization. Depending on the size of the advertising firm, the manager may often personally create and develop the campaign.

- *Media salesperson.* A salesperson represents the advertising firm to client advertisers. He or she sells services, space, or time and may actually write advertising messages.

- *Copywriter.* This person assists in or develops an advertising plan. This includes planning and writing the ad copy; helping to plan art, photography, or layouts; and in a smaller firm overseeing final production. He or she helps to determine and write appropriate advertising messages.

- *Agency account supervisor/executive.* In addition to analyzing client needs and acting as liaison between the advertiser and the agency, this person usually writes the marketing plan for products or services.

- *Researcher.* This person conducts research to analyze specific marketing and advertising requirements.

Marketing

Writers will find that the marketing departments of major sports franchises are good places to apply their skills. Michael Humes has a full-time sales and marketing staff of four, plus four interns. He says that writing skills are one of the qualifications he looks for in an applicant for his staff: "They must have the talent to write a variety of publications, such as successful proposals, partnership reports, and press releases."

His marketing efforts for the AHL involve various components, including programs with the hockey teams in the league and product sampling reports. A typical retail promotion involves a sweepstakes agreement with a major chewing gum firm that places the league name cross-connected with the candy in all stores selling the product via sweepstakes premiums such as all-star team jerseys and memorabilia. This is another method of enhancing fan interest in the image of the league, its teams, and its players.

The Value of Quality Writing Skills

The major clients for Sparky Harris's sports marketing company consist of small to medium-sized sporting goods manufacturers, retailers, and suppliers to the sporting goods industry. They may be start-up companies, more established ones, or those that wish to remain small but look big. Usually, they aren't large enough to need or afford a full-time marketing manager. But they do need a professional level of expertise, because the industry is so competitive.

Writing skills and talent are vital in the business of marketing and advertising. Harris says that "if applicants can't communicate well in both written and oral form, they will be at a major disadvantage. This is a very high communications-based type of industry. It is what we call fashion driven, very fast. Things are changing very quickly and, as a result, you have to think on your feet and you have to be able to communicate successfully."

At Harris's company, MarketSpark, new employees must be college graduates. Most work to support clients and in the process write marketing newsletters, proposals, and press releases. "Media writers play a major role in developing sports in the United States," according to Christine Brooks. "Writers enrich our appreciation of a sport via books, publications, broadcasting, and other media."

Writers interested in learning more about working in the different sports domains should examine or become members of writers' associations. Many sports have their own such associations, which help to improve press coverage of the respective sport, ensure professional working conditions for the press, and lobby for improved media relations with tournament sponsors and players. They also keep members informed about new developments in the sport.

Marketing Plans

Writing skills come into play in a variety of advertising and marketing processes, but none more important than the development of marketing plans. These documents direct the efforts of the entire sports marketing organization and materially affect the degree of its success. An example of the scope and effectiveness of this type of work is the marketing plan that Dave Coskey's staff at the Philadelphia 76ers recently produced. The purpose of the forty-page plan was fourfold:

- Define and identify the marketplace of the franchise.

- Define and identify its strengths and weaknesses.

- Outline the methods for exploiting strengths.

- Explore the means of rectifying weaknesses.

The central point of such an organization's marketing strategy is often to spark new fan interest. In this case, the organization hoped to enlarge the youth and female fan base via a cross-promotion with the Nickelodeon cable television network, the 76ers' parent company Comcast, and a local department store chain. The program drew a surprising 18,000 fans for an unimportant (to the standings) end-of-season NBA game. It was called "Nickelodeon Night" with all the viewers' favorite characters in attendance.

"The plan was to bring a fresh new audience into the building, expose them to our product, and provide not just a game but an entertainment experience for an evening," Coskey says. "Because the original plan was well thought out from the beginning, well written, and well executed by the 76ers' marketing staff, a near sellout crowd made the program a huge success."

Educational Flexibility

In the advertising and marketing business, educational backgrounds seem to be somewhat more diverse than in other journalism careers.

Typically, those who enter these businesses have one of the following majors:

- Journalism, with concentrations in advertising and public relations or in marketing

- Marketing, with communications or journalism course work

- Business administration

- Economics

Sparky Harris graduated from the University of Oregon with a bachelor's degree in journalism and received her master's in business administration from the University of Portland.

Dave Coskey received his bachelor's degree in communications at Villanova University, in the Philadelphia suburbs. He got a good taste of the marketing world there, because after graduation, he was the university's director of athletic marketing until he left for a marketing position at an Atlantic City casino several years later.

Michael Humes came at the job from a more administrative angle. He graduated with a bachelor's degree in business administration and economics from St. Thomas University in Fredricton, New Brunswick, Canada, followed by a graduate degree in sports administration from Concordia University of Montreal.

Sports Experience

To be successful, it isn't required that prospective sports marketers own an Olympic gold medal. You don't have to be a fanatic or an ex-varsity team player. But if you haven't participated, you should love sports as a fan or spectator. In addition, you need a working understanding of what's involved in the sports you advertise. Sparky Harris thinks that enthusiasm for the game is a pretty important tool. "Without some love for sports," she says, "you'll be kind of a duck out of water."

In marketing sports products, you'll need some experience with equipment and apparel. "If you've never owned a pair of running shoes, I'd be a little suspicious of your interest in the sports marketing business," says Harris.

Internships

Internships are plentiful in advertising and marketing. The programs vary in what they offer. The University of Oregon, for example, has a grant program in which it requires the employer to pay for half of the intern's salary and the university pays the other half. At many colleges, interns aren't paid by either the school or the employer except with credits and invaluable experience. Fortunately for employers, there is such a demand for experienced men and women in this occupation, students are more than willing to work for the experience, a future letter of recommendation, and the opportunity to develop a portfolio of their work.

The traits required to be considered for a program are pretty basic:

- Good oral communications skills

- Persuasive writing skills

- Willingness to be flexible (hours, assignments, etc.)

- Good sense of humor

- Willingness and ability to work with the sports celebrities that companies use to endorse products

If you are interested in combining your education and ambition in an internship in the sporting goods business, examine those universities that sponsor a sports marketing program. Many have connections with major manufacturers. Also check Internet sites, such as Online Sports and the Sporting Goods Manufacturers Association's home page.

To learn your way around the sports world and make important contacts for the future, offer your services as a stringer or seek out summer jobs in the sports department of your local newspaper or the PR departments of area sports companies, both of which are good foundations for the work required in this profession. Or, you can apply for an internship with one of the numerous trade or consumer publications such as *Sporting Goods Business* magazine.

Places to Start in the Business

Good preparation and research are necessary to embark in sports advertising and marketing. Target specific companies that you feel your skills will benefit and for whom you would like to work. Find out the name of the product line marketing manager or promotion manager and call him or her directly to introduce yourself. Offer to send them a resume of your achievements, awards, involvement in athletics, and (if you can get them) letters regarding your abilities from coaches and other sponsors. If you are a good public speaker, volunteer to run sports clinics for local schools. Convince the potential employer that you'd be an asset to the agency's public relations programs.

One avenue to aim for in the sporting goods industry is retail sales, because that is a business driven by sales and marketing. Athletic footwear chains, including Foot Locker, Lady Foot Locker, and The Athlete's Foot, have management training programs. With this experience, it's easier to find an interesting job with a sporting goods manufacturer or sales rep agency.

Advertise your skills through networking and meeting people in the business by volunteering at sports events such as local track meets, running and walking events, aerobic dance competitions, golf and tennis tournaments, consumer sports shows, and anywhere else manufacturers and retailers are likely to be. Keep up on the market and stay on top of trends in the industry so you will be able to discuss them knowledgeably with new contacts.

Working with Athletes

Much of sports marketing work involves interacting with or supporting athletes or personalities who endorse products. It seems that sports marketing pros put up with the same spoiled and pampered athletes that other forms of journalism do. "Some of these personalities are great to work with, but some of them are real jerks," says Sparky Harris. "Quite frankly, some are on ego trips and think they're the greatest thing since sliced bread. You have to be very flexible in working with those kinds of people. They can have very sensitive egos, so you have to realize you're walking on thin ice. I've not had too many problems working with them, but sometimes if there is a major problem, we have to sit down and work something out."

Personalities involved in promoting products are often the highest paid stars of the sports world; those who can create instant identity with a product line and make a successful marriage of advertising and marketing. "If you are lucky, you'll work with some first-class celebrities," says Harris, "such as my opportunity to work with Clyde Drexler, high-scoring shooting guard, then with the Portland Trailblazers and later with the Houston Rockets." Drexler is an endorser for two companies Harris represented and she remembers him as "a perfect gentleman and wonderful with kids. I watched him at a trade show sign autographs for four solid hours, without complaint. Youngsters came up to him in droves. As they came up, he signed one of whatever item they had to sign. Some adults brought multiple items and were turned down, but would work their way up the line again and act like newcomers. Drexler was actually able to identify them and, when he did, would politely decline. He was never rude, never arrogant, just a total gentleman."

Thousands of journalists would be much happier if Drexler were the typical sports personality they deal with. But he seems to be among a shrinking fraternity of class acts. You need a lot of patience in this end of the business.

Financial Rewards

Compared with many of the sports journalism professions, the advertising game offers some high salaries. A recent *Advertising Age* survey showed that average advertising agency salaries for the top pros in the business are as follows:

CEOS	$140,000
Creative directors	$100,000
Chief copywriters	$60,000
Media directors	$80,000

Senior account executives $85,000

Account executives $60,000

Defining Success

For some marketing and advertising pros, success is in the personal gratification of being part of an industry that's always spawning new fads or new trends. Sparky Harris maintains, "It's like being in the fashion industry more than anything else. It's entertainment and Hollywood and New York glamour and fashion. Sports has gone much more Hollywood than people think."

9 Sports Public Relations

*PR, first and foremost, is a service entity. You're try-
ing to take care of people, whether it's the media,
players, or your owner. You're always doing something for someone else. If you don't want to be in a
position of helping other people out, then you're in
the wrong field.*

Harvey Greene
Director of media relations, Miami Dolphins

There are numerous opportunities for a young journalist to find
openings in the sports public relations (PR) field. A recent survey done by Ohio State University estimates that more than 14,000
(11 percent) graduates of university journalism and communications programs enter this expanding field. This chapter focuses on
why sports journalists should consider a career that includes the
excitement and challenge of sports-related public relations.

A major consideration for such journalists is the modern growth
of the publicity machines in professional and university sports that
make big money representing the personalities, teams, and products. Although they share many significant characteristics, PR for
professional sports organizations is covered in this chapter and
publicity for intercollegiate sports (sports information or media

relations) is covered in Chapter 7. We examine sports PR through the eyes of several experts who are veterans in the business:

- Jim Gallagher, recently retired as PR director for the NFL's Philadelphia Eagles

- Dave Coskey, vice president of marketing for the NBA's Philadelphia 76ers

- Harvey Greene, director of media relations for the NFL's Miami Dolphins.

- Sandy Genelius, director of communications for CBS News

- Kevin Monaghan, director of business development for NBC-TV

Modern Challenges of Sports Public Relations

The PR person's job is difficult because the needs of media personnel are so varied. Some reporters need to get stories by 6 P.M., which will not be published until the next day's newspaper. On the other hand, radio reporters get material at 6 P.M., and at 6:10 it is on the all-sports station; in television, it is all over the country on ESPN by 7 P.M. A local event can become national news within an hour, and you must be able to deal with that. Obviously, the television reporter's need for a three-minute sound bite is much different than the print reporter's need for a one-hour interview with an athlete for a magazine piece. They all must be juggled and accommodated.

Public relations professionals agree that technology has prompted enormous changes in the PR business. "Twenty-five years ago when I was getting started at Madison Square Garden," says Harvey Greene, "you didn't have ESPN, sports talk radio, or television stations producing live shots. A few journalists wrote all the sports information." When technology changed, there were three major corresponding changes in sports journalism that still affect the entire industry:

- *Investigative reporting.* Reporters no longer explain only what happens *on* the field. Their stories now tell *why* it happens. Behind-the-scenes stories about teams, coaches, athletes, and management must be analyzed and probed.

- *Formal, impersonal relationships.* The huge increase in the number of news organizations reporting on each sport has changed the interrelationship between athlete and reporter. Some players will only speak to the press through an intermediary marketing representative and some major universities prohibit reporters having face-to-face interviews with players. Instead of having eight or nine reporters in a clubhouse after a game, now, with radio stations and networks that were never before involved, there are thirty or forty. Writers have become adversarial because they are competing against so many other media outlets for fan interest and readership. Everyone is trying to create an individual niche.

- *New media and electronic communications.* Most sports organizations and many athletes now have glitzy, professional websites with more data than the average fan could ever digest. From a PR standpoint, these may threaten the future focus of print and broadcast media reporting. Until recent years, newspapers had that all-important advantage of distribution to hundreds of thousands of relatively captive readers. Teams did not have that kind of capability, but now, Greene asks, "Why does a writer need to tell readers what the Dolphins' head coach is thinking when the coach can do it himself? If I ask a coach to write a story each day on why we won or lost and put it on the team website, his opinions will be on the Internet and on everybody's PC screen almost instantaneously."

Education of Public Relations Professionals

Specific education in public relations was not available to many of the professionals working in sports PR today. Instead, they majored in a variety of other programs to get the foundation they would later parlay into successful career fields. They learned PR skills on the job.

Two of Philadelphia's professional sports teams have had PR directors who came from nontraditional PR educational backgrounds. Jim Gallagher graduated from Temple University with a liberal arts degree, and Dave Coskey received a degree in communications from Villanova University.

Coskey oversees almost everything except sales and the basketball team on the floor—marketing, advertising, public relations, community relations, fan relations, radio and television broadcasting, game presentations, and even the music played during the games. He first began working as a student intern in the sports information department at Villanova. He thinks that the best candidates for sports marketing and PR come from university sports information offices. Many of his current staffers are former sports information directors (SIDs) and ex-interns. He says now, "I had no idea when I was at Villanova, trudging through practical journalism, learning proofreading symbols and how to use an AP [Associated Press] stylebook, that I was ever going to use them." Following the wisdom of his university teachers, he has supplied his entire staff with AP stylebooks, which they use as a guide for all their publications and press releases.

Proving that you do not have to have your whole life planned out at age ten to be a sports professional, Harvey Greene turned his career goals completely around late in his college career. Always a sports fan, he presumed there were very few opportunities in sports. So, he majored in and earned a bachelor's degree in chemistry. He was even thinking of pursuing a doctorate when he learned of other prospects. Aside from his studies, he worked at his college radio station and became sports director fully expecting to put sports aside upon graduation. But midway through his senior year, after accepting admission to the Ph.D. chemistry program at Rice University, he read about graduate programs in sports administration at Ohio University and the University of Massachusetts. He applied to the latter to "test it for a year," while asking Rice to defer his acceptance for a year. "For all I know," Greene says, "they may still be waiting for me twenty-five years later."

Greene notes that because sports is now so specialized, employers want trained individuals, just like most businesses. "When I graduated, those two schools turned out approximately forty qualified graduates from their major sports administration programs, and that was all there was nationwide. Now there are fifty such programs turning out hundreds of grads available for hire each year; and most have completed journalism internships at school." He advises journalism graduates to proceed to a master's program at what he considers the best schools, such as Ohio University and the University of Massachusetts. "If you go into the best program possible, doors will open for you," he says. "Follow that with an internship that the school can help you get, gaining experience and contacts, which you just can't do from the outside."

Two public relations professionals at competing television networks have succeeded without formal PR education. Sandy Genelius majored in communications at Cleveland State University and New York University. Because she loved literature and writing, she hoped to someday become an English teacher. Instead, she became director of communications at CBS News after being number two in the sports publicity department at CBS and in charge of CBS's Olympic publicity for the 1992 and 1994 Games. Years after embarking on her PR career, she graduated from New York University with a degree in communications. Kevin Monaghan, began his long career in PR from the educational base of a history major at Manhattan College in New York. He began enjoying the world of publicity as he worked in the university sports information office, like many of the PR professionals discussed here, eventually finding his way to NBC.

Writing Skills in Public Relations

Our experts agree that there is no substitute for high-quality writing in the PR business. It is critical. "The ability to put ideas on paper is still a fundamental way by which we communicate with the media," Sandy Genelius says. "To develop an interview or a story on a sports figure, most reporters want a written bio or press release in front of them. In PR, a writer must have the ability to quickly assess such needs and come up with interesting angles for a reader. Some reporters want 'off-the-wall' stories; others just want ordinary, basic stuff; and still others like to be very creative. Knowing what they like is crucial to successful PR work."

Although he was reluctant to write at his college paper, Dave Coskey won Pennsylvania Collegiate Associated Press Awards for photography and writing. "I considered it a weakness I had to improve, because it didn't come easily to me," he recalls. Instead of press releases, which he thinks are antiquated, "I think it makes more sense to send out bulleted fact sheets for sportswriters to use. So, our writing consists more of compiling and organizing important facts than in writing releases."

Kevin Monaghan bemoans the fact that some major colleges are graduating students who expect to work in this prestigious business without the fundamental writing talent to make it. "It baffles me how many university graduates don't know where to put a period in a sentence or how to communicate by writing anymore," he says. "There are major TV personalities who, when required to write their own material for broadcast, are hopelessly overmatched. We actually stopped taking interns from one major New York university because we had a succession of ten who were unable to spell or punctuate, let alone produce good written material." Like most PR pros, Monaghan knows the great importance of learning to communicate well, both verbally and in writing. You can't get by without these skills.

Public Relations Internships

Young writers almost always benefit from internships in ways they may not realize for years. A positive internship experience can be more beneficial than many hours of course work. It also can make or break a career. "Attitude" is the key word.

Media and journalism organizations in most states provide scholarships and internships to journalism students. For example, in Ohio, a number of chapters of the Society of Professional Journalists and the Association for Women in Communications offer scholarships to deserving college students who plan to pursue a career in public relations or journalism. Grants range from $1,000 to $4,000, if academic excellence is maintained.

All television networks employ interns on a regular basis, but it is almost always the young student with a great attitude that makes it up the career ladder to success. "Some of our interns thought the world owed them something," Sandy Genelius observes. "I can't tell you what a turnoff that is to an employer. I would not recommend such a student for a job or anything else." Most of her interns turn out very well, however, and most receive glowing recommendations from Genelius. "When I learn of a position opening, I make certain the better ones know about it," she says.

As with many programs, interns usually earn college credit but no salary, although a few told us they're paid around $100 weekly. Most work for a semester and have to complete a paper for their grade. Some have to keep a weekly diary or submit a weekly status report of their activities.

Dave Coskey's interns are not paid except while putting in initial training hours. When he considers people for entry-level positions, he is not very sympathetic with job applicants who consider their journalism or public relations education of paramount importance. He tells them that, although very helpful, theory and education are not as important as how they are applied. Usually, he will hire someone who has previous intern experience. Each semester, Coskey employs ten interns for public relations, community relations, fan relations, and marketing. He warns internship candidates against the following no-no's in his departments:

- Letting your body language or your face show your dissatisfaction with grunt work

- Forgetting your work ethic, which requires a full day's work following a night game ("We work some pretty late hours in PR, up till 2 A.M.")

- Thinking you need a secretary to handle your mail

A few years ago, NBC wasn't satisfied with the talent level of its interns, so it raised standards and required students to commit to a full six months of work. Interns were challenged in this new system, making official presentations and gaining access to major meetings with clients and executives. As a result, the program became a more meaningful professional learning experience.

Kevin Monaghan recalls a typical assignment for the hardworking intern assigned to assist him. Bill Parcells, then coach of the NFL's New York Giants, was coming to NBC at 30 Rockefeller Plaza for a news conference about his upcoming appearance on WNBC-TV, the New York network affiliate. Monaghan assigned his intern to wait for Parcells at 49th Street. When the coach arrived, the intern was to take him from his car to the studios and be his host during his stay. Obviously a fun assignment, and an important one, for a young sports fan.

Getting Your Start

Sports public relations offers a wide variety of job opportunities for writers far beyond the four major sports. Some recommended places to break into the business are with figure skating, track and field, rowing, professional tennis, and golf associations. They all employ public relations personnel but are not bombarded with resumes as are the NFL, NHL, NBA, and Major League Baseball (MLB).

As with other journalism fields, there is no standard approach that guarantees entry into the business. For example, after serving an internship with the organization operating the New York Nets (NBA) and the New York Islanders (NHL), Harvey Greene had a strange career start one summer many years ago at a short-lived job selling season tickets for the Providence (Rhode Island) Reds American Hockey League (AHL) team. "Here it was," he remembers, "a hundred degrees in July, and I'm trying to sell season tickets for a minor league hockey team in a strange town." Just before the start of the season, the team, which had been around about fifty years, folded before a game was played, and Greene was unemployed. He still has the Providence team stationery framed on his wall as a constant reminder of those distressing times. "Every time I get upset about something or ticked off at the job, I look at it and realize how lucky I am to be where I am," he says. "I could be selling season tickets in a minor league hockey town. Or worse, a chemist."

Greene explains that his first real career break came after two years working for a sports PR firm in New York City, and typing play-by-play action for the New York Knicks and the New Jersey Nets. There was a newly created job, public relations director of the Madison Square Garden Network, that nobody else knew was open. "The reason I got the job," Greene said, "was because the person who was doing the hiring saw me all of the time at the Garden, knew me, and knew what kind of person I was. Rather than go through a stack of resumes, he asked me, 'Do you want this job? OK, you're hired.'"

The Making of a Public Relations Pro

To help novices obtain a sense of what it is like to grow in this field, we asked those who have "made it" to explain what it took to get there and enjoy their current success. We found one constant in their stories; they all paid their dues. Patience always led to good things for determined, high-quality writers.

Making the Rounds

Early on, Sandy Genelius realized that sports and television made a great team. "I've been a sports nut since I was ten years old, watching baseball on television with my dad on Saturday afternoons. I was always intrigued by television. Although I didn't know what a producer was, I imagined that the coolest job in the world would be as a producer for *Wide World of Sports.*" While in college, she worked at a Cleveland FM rock-and-roll radio station until its sister AM station's sports talk show hosts let her book guests and perform other low-profile tasks. She soon moved on to a Cleveland marketing firm, International Management Group, working in publicity for an over-35 tennis tour featuring greats such as Rod Laver and Ken Rosewall. She developed press kits, player biographies, and made interview arrangements at the cities on the circuit.

Pleased with her work, her employers named her to work on publicity for the women's professional tennis circuit, which was sponsored mostly by Toyota of Japan. She designed and ordered promotional materials, wrote press information kits, and made sure that the sponsor's interests were being well served. She was promoted to account executive, responsible for finding sponsorships and organizing a women's professional racquetball circuit. Her five years of work in Cleveland led to a job in New York at the Men's Tennis Council, the governing body for men's professional tennis worldwide. She acted as liaison between the players and the press and developed media guides for the tour. "Being in press rooms every week on the road, I learned what the print media and television industry need in the way of information and deadlines," she recalls. Punctuating her career advancement by completing her degree requirements and graduating from New York University was a tough combination. "If I had to do it all over again," she says, "I would have finished school before my career began. But, in life, you make the best decision that you can at the time."

She jumped onto the fast track when she was hired to join CBS Sports as an associate director of communications. During four years in this position, she dealt regularly with television and print sportswriters. Another break came when she was promoted to director of publicity for the 1992 Winter Olympics and for the 1994 Winter Olympics in Lillehammer. "CBS didn't hire a staff of people to do the Olympics," she admits, "it was just me."

Clearing the Hurdles

Although Kevin Monaghan was never much of an athlete, he loved sports. As an undergraduate, he worked in the Manhattan College sports information office and continued for two years after graduation. He then took a position with a public relations firm that specialized in promoting track-and-field athletes and international events. "Because I had graduated from Manhattan, then known as a track and cross-country college, they figured I knew something about track," he explains.

After he had established an outstanding reputation at Manhattan and the firm Joe Goldstein Communications, NBC hired him in 1981. For six years, he learned the television network ropes, eventually becoming head of sports public relations, with responsibility for promoting NBC's coverage of the 1988 Summer Olympics, the World Series, and the NBA. Monaghan's present position is director of business development for NBC Sports, which involves business development and the whole "new media" area for the network (see Chapter 14).

Women in Sports Public Relations

Dave Coskey points out how a great attitude and work ethic can pay off in the public relations field by relating the experience of Jodi Silverman, the Philadelphia 76ers' former media relations director, who graduated from Pennsylvania State University. After a year as a 76ers intern, she was promoted to administrative assistant, then to assistant PR director. After one more year, she became director of PR for the NBA franchise.

Public relations has many opportunities for young women journalists. Sandy Genelius reports that her staff of seven has only one male. "In the CBS Sports department, we used to joke that we were the all-girl PR department until we hired a male publicist," she says. "There's no reason why a woman can't know as much about sports as a guy. Gender doesn't matter, if you know your sports. I felt the need to prove to the (male) sportswriters that I knew sports, but not in an obnoxious way. Female sports PR practitioners can build credibility by demonstrating their knowledge when they talk to sportswriters."

Harvey Greene cites several successful women in pro sports public relations who are great examples of what can be accomplished: Sharon Pannozzo, Chicago Cubs director of media relations; Susie Mathieu, St. Louis Blues vice president and director of public relations and marketing; and Rosa Gatti, senior vice president of communications at ESPN. High-ranking women on NBA staffs are the Phoenix Suns' Julie Fie (director of marketing) and the Seattle Supersonics' Cheri White (director of media relations).

From Sports Information to the Pros

Journalists do not usually take their college diplomas directly into the job market and become press directors for professional sports teams. Working and learning the business of media relations as a sports information director during and after college speeds the learning process and helps open many doors into the PR world, as discussed in Chapter 7.

It is important to become fully knowledgeable about the media end of the business as well as the sports end. As is true for SIDs, a public relations person deals with all of the print media as well as radio and television stations and networks. Many move from the challenge of university SID work into network broadcasting, pro sports teams, or other sports business as a PR person. Kate Mulligan, author of Chapter 7 and an experienced sports information professional who became the assistant commissioner of the Northeast Conference at age 26, says, "There are many things you learn as an SID that you can use in almost any area of the athletics profession." When you deal with different groups, including coaches, athletes, the general public, and the media, you build interpersonal skills you can use in any number of PR positions. Both types of jobs also require excellent communication skills, a knowledge of sports, and creativity, which makes it easier to move from one field to the other. Sports information work teaches you about the media and how important college sports are to them. Kevin Monaghan advises students interested in a career in sports PR to get involved in the SID office at their colleges, which always needs interns.

Monaghan also distinguishes between two fundamental publicity techniques to satisfy the media's needs—offensive and defensive PR—which can be used by both professions.

Offensive Public Relations

This type of PR brings particularly good stories to the attention of the media, especially for those sports that do not usually get much publicity. Track and field is a good example; it is only covered periodically during big events or Olympic years. "An offensive-minded PR writer researches and develops good stories and press releases and gets them to the media," Monaghan explains. "It's important to get the athlete in front of the media at a press conference or a press luncheon." Monaghan was the first PR director of the New York City Marathon and was challenged to get reporters to cover the now popular annual race.

Some PR pros call this method "creative publicity" when experienced professionals give birth to an enjoyable story they know will promote their team, school, or organization. Readers may be surprised to learn that PR writers actually "stage" stories for publicity purposes. In fact, it is done often and is known to be an effective tool of the better PR professionals.

Defensive Public Relations

You are on the publicity defensive when your players, coach, or organization are in the media's crosshairs and are being slammed in the press. Recently, a plethora of major incidents have embarrassed college and pro organizations. Kevin Monaghan points to the examples of players arrested for assault, a coach caught with a weapon in his luggage, or an athlete caught with drugs. In each case, it's the PR department that takes the first hit and must begin defensive damage control through effective communication. "If you leave the sportswriters to their own initiative, they will usually rip the player or team," he warns. "But if you can provide each writer with a believable, convincing story that puts the incident in the best context possible, you have succeeded in defensive PR."

Monaghan describes an excellent example of defensive PR that occurred during the 1988 Summer Olympics in Seoul. "Before and during the games, the Korean people had the impression from their press that our television personalities were demeaning their country and customs," he explains. "Korea had only recently achieved freedom of the press, and their reports were often inaccurate or irresponsible. They wrote stories about NBC statements that just weren't true. They reported that we were encouraging Americans to adopt Korean babies so that we would use them as servants and slaves. This misinformation gradually grew and grew, and we had to diffuse the situation. We decided that damage control would consist of our calling a major press conference, appearing on Korean television, and apologizing. That bought us time to successfully defuse the situation."

Television Public Relations Responsibilities

The formal responsibilities of a broadcast publicity director may surprise the average journalist, but they are what makes the television publicity machine operate. Kevin Monaghan tells us that those responsibilities include the following:

- Ensure that the listing services (newspapers, *TV Guide*, etc.) know what sports shows the network is showing and when.

- Assist the television sportswriters with stories and information that help promote your lineup. For example, if you're televising a weekend NBA basketball game, prepare publicity by setting up a conference call with your news talent to talk to television writers looking for a column about why the Los Angeles Lakers may emerge as the top team in the Western Conference.

- Accommodate, to the extent practical, the radio sports show hosts who clamor for guests from your network for their shows. They call constantly for talent like Bob Costas, and, although that is usually not possible, do your best to accommodate them with other sports news talent.

- Use your defensive PR skills, such as being gracious even while you are denying media requests.

- Defend the network for any gaffe committed by on-air talent.

All the education, planning, preparation, and dues paying a writer invests may result in a professional PR position that involves a surprising mix of skills and roles. Monaghan estimates that PR responsibilities consist of the following:

- *Technical tasks (30%).* These involve researching and writing press releases, answering questions from sportswriters concerning games to be shown in their market, and preparing the listings.

- *Communicating with the media (30%).* This means selling ideas to the writers and national media.

- *Satisfying the media's needs (30%).* You need to respond to their requests, helping them do their job (with data, tickets, arrangements, etc.) and answering questions.

- *Making yourself smarter about your product and your people (10%).* Get to know your "team" better. Learn about the on-air stars and the production people. Build relationships by taking news talent out to lunch or sitting in the production truck and asking questions about their work and off-camera interests.

Sports Personalities' Responsibilities

Professional coaches and some athletes have been around the business and understand the importance of the media's job and deadline pressure. Harvey Greene has dealt with such greats as George Steinbrenner, Jimmy Johnson, Don Shula, Billy Martin, and Dan Marino. "When something happens that requires a comment, they know enough not to say, 'I don't want to say anything,' and therefore lose a chance to get their side of the story out," Greene says. "It's mainly the players you have to educate, because they're not as media conscious as owners and managers. Occasionally though, they might say things you wish they hadn't. Billy Martin was famous for that."

What Kevin Monaghan calls "patching things up with the media" after one of your players or coaches has said the wrong thing, Greene calls "damage control." He considers himself lucky to be able to work with a very PR-minded head football coach, the Dolphins' Jimmy Johnson. "He's been on national TV as studio analyst for the Fox network and HBO for two years, so there wasn't anything that I could tell him about publicity," Greene states. "On the other hand, we've had guys who didn't talk here. I thought Rickey Henderson would say some stupid things when I was with the Yankees and had to try to meet with him. The toughest thing is to convince a player why it's in his best interest to deal with it immediately, rather than to hide it or postpone it."

Stories from the Pros

Young writers should beware of focusing all of their attention about sports PR or any sports profession on just the allure of sports. Harvey Greene tells a story that illustrates "how quickly your prospect of a glamorous job can fade." It occurred on his first day working as an intern for the [then] New York Nets. "I was all bright eyed and bushy tailed, like 'Wow, I can't believe I'm actually working in sports,'" he says. His boss, the public relations director of the Nets, said, "Hey, kid, I want you to answer phones."

"Here I was, an Ivy League graduate, enrolled in postgraduate programs, somewhat taken aback. I said, 'I can do more than that, if you need help in writing things or statistical compilations, I can do anything you want.' When he said, 'No, just answer the phone,' I asked, 'Sure, is it going to be busy?'

"My boss's response was, 'Well, in an hour we're going to announce that we're trading Julius Erving to the Philadelphia 76ers.' Sure enough, we announced it and the phones lit up, and there were 10,000 Nets season-ticket holders demanding refunds of their money because, in their minds, they had bought tickets to watch, not the Nets, but one of the greatest, Julius Erving. When I told callers we couldn't refund their money, I was cursed out in five different languages over three days. So, I always tell people, the view I had about sports being glamorous lasted all of one hour! It's a fun business, but it wasn't quite as terrific as I had thought it would be."

Some of the better stories about sports public relations involve PR people communicating to the personalities on their team an understanding of what the PR job is and how they can help those personalities. Monaghan offers this example of how important it is for a PR writer to relate closely to the performers he or she supports. "At a certain point in his career, sportscaster Dick Enberg really wanted to be a studio guy, and the first chance he got was in 1983, at the Helsinki (Finland) Winter World Championships. He was viewed by some of the media as not on a level with perennial ABC Olympic host, Jim McKay, to whom he was often compared. He appreciated the fact that I came to him and said, 'Dick, my perception is that some of the media are out to annihilate you, for example, *Sports Illustrated*. They want you to pose for a photo for an article in which they're going to demolish you. My recommendation is that you don't pose for that photo.' When I got back to New York, Dick sent me a magnum of champagne and thanked me for being up-front and honest with him. The class acts of the business appreciate such candor."

Knowing Your Sports Market

Dave Coskey explains why it is important for a PR writer to become involved in the deeper aspects of his or her team's environment, such as reading the fan mail, understanding the team's market, and knowing what kind of stories local newspaper and television reporters seek. His team's director of fan relations received a letter last year from a New Jersey youngster who explained that the 76ers' Jerry Stackhouse had been his favorite pro basketball player since Stackhouse was a star at the University of North Carolina. In the letter, the fan detailed the tragic loss of his family's home and all their belongings by fire. Included among the items lost was his treasured Jerry Stackhouse jersey. To ensure that the letter was legitimate, the team's management called the *Atlantic City Press* in New Jersey and found the story to be true. The Red Cross was putting the family up in a motel. Coskey invited the family to an NBA game in Philadelphia, suggesting that the parents surprise the boy by not letting on about the game ahead of time. The family drove from Atlantic City to the Philadelphia CoreStates Center, with no idea of the team's plans.

When they arrived, the team's director of marketing took the young man to a courtside seat and presented him with an authentic Stackhouse jersey. Topping off the surprise, Stackhouse approached the boy, who was completely overwhelmed, and said, "I understand you're a fan of mine. I have something for you." He signed the boy's new jersey, a photo was taken, and the youngster was speechless. Stackhouse spoke to him briefly and returned to the pregame shoot-around.

This all occurred just after Christmas. The boy's parents said after the game that although everything had been going against them and they thought no one really cared about them, their faith had been restored and their son made happy again by the 76ers' thoughtfulness.

The story also turned out to be perfect for local sports columnist John Smallwood, who sat with the family at the game and wrote about the boy's experience. Coskey explains that "if a clerk had been opening all fan letters, we might never have realized how happy we could make that family. We would also have missed a great story."

He adds that knowing the marketplace also has its benefits from an employment standpoint. "I recently ended an interview with an applicant from Florida for our PR department with the question 'What time does the sports segment of CBS's Miami affiliate come on?' 'Eighteen after the hour,' he answered, adding 'and the NBC and ABC affiliates are on about twenty-four minutes after the hour.' I was pleased with that response because you have to know such details when you have a breaking story," Coskey says. "Working on a deadline, that's not a detail you go research."

Advice from the Experts

Sandy Genelius gives this invaluable advice to any writer who wants to be successful in the sports public relations business: never burn a bridge with a writer. "Every year that I worked the men's professional tennis event in Boston (the U.S. Pro Championship), there was a sportswriter at a small suburban daily who I helped, just as I'd help everyone," she remembers. "My philosophy was and is that it doesn't matter which paper they work for, whether it's the *New York Times* or the *Poughkeepsie Journal,* they have a job to do and it's my job to help them. You never know where they'll end up in the business.

"Eight years later, I'm at CBS Sports and we introduced a new on-air team for *The NFL Today*—Greg Gumbel and Terry Bradshaw, along with Lesley Visser. I prepared a publicity plan for this big introduction, because obviously we wanted to get a lot of attention and publicity. These three were taking over for the long-established team led by Brent Musburger and I wanted to find great feature articles about the new team, including Bradshaw in his new job in the studio.

"I learned that the Boston sportswriter from eight years earlier was now a contributor for *GQ* magazine. I called him and explained how fascinating, colorful, funny, entertaining, and smart Bradshaw is and how great a feature on this ex–Pittsburgh Steelers quarterback would be for the magazine. Well, he wrote the Bradshaw story for *GQ*, and I looked like a star. Our friendship from the early days had been beneficial for both of us, not to mention for *The NFL Today*. You just never know how professional relationships can come full circle like that."

Dave Coskey's advice focuses on the role of the PR writer: "I believe that PR people are basically there to help reporters do their job better, to create story ideas, and to perform lesser but important tasks like organizing interviews. Always do all you can to be accessible and helpful. There will come a time when a reporter will be undecided about a story line and, if you've always been available and ready to help, chances are greater that she or he will decide in favor of your philosophy or organization."

He also has practical advice for PR job applicants: "Don't mail photocopied form letters when you're applying for a communications position. If you don't have time to write a decent letter, you probably will be unable to correspond successfully with a newspaper or magazine reporter when you're on the job." Of course, there is also the opposite extreme, the overaggressive applicants. "That's another bad sign in this business," Coskey says. "You need to be aggressive, but not to the point where you irritate somebody. Find the ideal middle ground between not caring enough and writing obnoxiously."

Newcomers must realize that this field requires a tremendous time commitment with very little monetary reward, at least in the beginning. Long hours and low pay are the norm. Harvey Greene says that he goes from July to January each year without a day off. "If you tell someone you're going to work six months without a day off, they won't believe you," he says. "If you have to complain about the long hours or about the fact that you're not as well compensated as your PR counterparts are at IBM or Xerox, then you shouldn't be in this field. It comes with the territory and you have to accept it, just as you enjoy and expect the good elements of this otherwise enjoyable profession. I always feel my first job is to make friends for this organization. How do you do that? By being friendly, by being outgoing, by trying to help people out. If you don't have that kind of approach, then maybe you're better off doing something else."

Mistakes are learning tools and, according to Genelius, deadlines are times to make mistakes. "Before fax machines, we actually hand-delivered press releases to the newswriters," she recalls. "I remember being just a little bit late with a release to a writer with the result that my radio station wasn't going to be covered in the newspaper that Friday. When you're a young kid trying to do really well, mistakes like that become burned in your memory, and you make certain they never happen again."

10 Radio Sports Journalism

Even to do a two-minute sportscast, you have to be a good writer; it really makes a big difference. You have to be able to write in a conversational fashion so that when you read, it doesn't sound like you're reading.

Jim Colony
Radio sports broadcaster

With the growth of television and the convenience of cable and computers, does anyone still listen to radio? The National Association of Broadcasters estimates that there are 580 million receivers in the United States tuned to more than 11,700 radio stations. These statistics indicate that radio is still a vital part of our news and entertainment scene and, from the view of sportswriters interested in broadcast journalism, it's a good business to investigate.

An often overlooked field of sportswriting is that of the radio sports news journalist. Variously called "writers," "reporters," "commentators," or "broadcasters," these sports professionals write, rewrite, and often deliver stories, promotional spots, commentaries, and news reports. Radio newswriting presents a unique and rewarding opportunity for the prospective sports-minded writer who may be interested in the challenge of using his or her writing and speaking talents to develop tight, informative articles for broadcast reports to a diverse group of listeners.

Sportscasting as a Dream

The storybook approach to getting into sports broadcasting is to be well focused on what you would like to do as a youngster, possess the vocal and writing skills, and be able to follow through with that dream into adulthood. Jim Colony, formerly a sportscaster with Pittsburgh radio station WTAE, admits that he was not one of those guys who did play-by-play at Wiffle ball games in the backyard, but he was a "radio junkie."

"When we were kids growing up in New Hampshire, you could not get FM radio," he recalls, "so we listened to the radio at night to the big, high-powered stations that came in from far away. One of the stations that I used to listen to all the time was Philadelphia's WCAU and their broadcast of the Phillies' baseball games. I also listened, long distance, to Pittsburgh Pirates games on KDKA and to the Yankees. If the wind was right, sometimes I could get St. Louis, Chicago, or the Expos games in French from Montreal."

Harry Donahue, a versatile sportswriter and on-air personality for Philadelphia's all-news station, KYW News Radio, fulfilled his early dreams of being a broadcaster. He too remembers as a young boy delighting in listening to and paying close attention to play-by-play announcers on the radio. "When I listened to a game, I was more interested in who was doing the game and how they did it than in what was happening on the field," he says. "That was true for all the sports I loved—baseball, basketball, and football. I was fortunate enough to grow up in a major sports city that had all the professional sports teams and great announcers. It definitely helped to foster my career. I can recall as a kid not only being fascinated by our hometown radio play-by-play announcers, but also laying in bed and listening to distant radio frequencies with Harry Caray doing a Cardinals game from St. Louis, or Chuck Thompson from Baltimore, or Bob Prince out in Pittsburgh. I remember getting upset when the static would interrupt and I would miss a couple of pitches, and by the time it cleared up there was maybe another batter up there."

When he was in the sixth grade, one of his Christmas presents from his father was a Wollensack tape recorder. That was the year

(1960) the Philadelphia Eagles were in the NFL Championship Game against the Green Bay Packers. "I'll never forget it because, even though the game was a sellout in Franklin Field, it was blacked out on television," Donahue recounts. "NBC broadcast the game, but we could not watch it in Philly. My brother Joe and I placed our tape recorder microphone right up against the radio, because back then you could not patch in; you had to hold the microphone and try not to make any noise. We taped Bill Campbell, who was my favorite football guy, announcing the whole game play-by-play. Whenever the Eagles scored, you could hear Joe and I in the background cheering.

"I was fascinated by that and the fact that I could read from a newspaper or write something, record it, and then listen to my voice on tape. I would sit in front of the TV when a sporting event came on and actually do play-by-play with this reel-to-reel tape recorder. It was a huge piece of equipment, probably weighing twenty-five pounds, unlike today's compact cassette and microcassette units that you can hide in your hand. But it was high tech then and it really jump-started my early career aspirations."

Many of us, as young sports fans, liked to pretend we were "announcing" the feats of our favorite players while we were playing. How many kids, while shooting hoops in the schoolyard, have envisioned themselves courtside hollering, "Michael Jordan picks up the loose ball, dribbles the length of the court—and he jams a thunderous dunk to win the game in the last five seconds!" This is a familiar memory for many of us, but writers such as Donahue had a deeper dream they believed would come true. So, while the rest of us moved with our dreams into other pursuits, men and women like him followed up on their young aspirations with serious goals and education. They worked at campus radio stations for experience and learned all they could about the business—both writing and announcing—from any radio people with whom they came in contact.

Writing for Radio

Does the sports reporter or anchor just read what he or she is given? No way! Especially in sports, if you cannot write your own material for broadcast, who needs you? Even at larger market stations, sports anchors must write their own stories; it would be too expensive for someone else to prepare the reports. The days of reading sports over the airwaves from the local newspaper sports pages are gone, except maybe on backwoods stations.

So, a pretty face and great voice is not enough anymore. Radio is not just a vocal medium, and if you cannot write, you are not going to get very far. Radio sportscasters at almost all stations are required to research and write their own sports news pieces, and edit and re-edit them for the few moments of airtime available. Anyone with any creative juices whatever can get maximum satisfaction out of presenting the best copy possible for any medium. In radio, experts say writers are limited by time and the sound dimension, making creativity vital. An imaginative use of sound, such as weaving music or crowd noise in and out of the story line, can enhance what you have written by letting one complement the other.

At all-news station KYW, for example, Harry Donahue writes all of his own sportscasts. Radio news anchors are often responsible for writing about two-thirds of what a listener actually hears. The rest is provided either by a writer who helps three different news anchors prepare for their shows, or by the editor. But most write all of their own material.

For Richard C. Crepeau, a full-time professor of U.S. history at the University of Central Florida and writer of weekly sports essays for WVCF-FM in Orlando, the discipline of the writing is the most interesting part of radio work. "As a teacher in the classroom," he observes, "I can expand the field and take a wide look at issues, deal with subtleties, and explore complexities. But in the written form of my sports essays, which are limited to 900 words, I must deal with a few points, make them as quickly and clearly as possible without oversimplifying them, and still be provocative or humorous."

Radio veterans agree that writing is an invaluable tool. It takes talent and a lot of practice to come up with a conversational tone that won't sound stilted when it's read. According to Jim Colony, "When someone tells me, 'You sound just like you do on the radio,' I take that as a tremendous compliment, because it tells me that on radio I come off as natural, holding a conversation with my audience."

On a typical morning, such as after a Pittsburgh Steelers game, Colony had two minutes for sports on the morning drive, twice an hour over four hours. On average, he wrote a one-minute story on the game and another sixty seconds for all other sports news. So, his script had to be carefully and tightly written and also include a sound bite or two of play-by-play highlights. Our radio experts are unanimous on the idea that it is much harder to write a two-minute sportscast than a four-minute segment. It takes the skill of an accomplished writer.

A Variety of Educational Backgrounds

In today's educational environment, aspiring radio sportswriters/broadcasters can find curricula specifically focused on communications and broadcasting. Such was not always the case. A common thread in our research of professionals in this field is that sportswriters in radio have widely varied educational backgrounds that greatly enhance their written and broadcast stories.

For a writer who wants to get into sports broadcasting, there is now a profusion of courses and majors with many different titles such as radio, television, and film (RTF); radio and television (RTV); broadcast journalism; and communications. Universities such as Syracuse, the University of Missouri, and Penn State have had such programs for many years, but now almost all major institutions have gotten on the bandwagon. Many of today's broadcast sportswriters were educated within journalism majors, which taught them the writing skills and techniques necessary to communicate in this business.

Harry Donahue began his college education with three years at Philadelphia's Saint Charles Seminary (in preparation for the priesthood). He later transferred to St. Joseph's College (now University) in Philadelphia, and in his senior year took a part-time position with station WPBS-FM. From midnight to 8 A.M. on Saturday and Sunday mornings, he played records and delivered the news every half hour, gaining invaluable experience and airtime. Almost twenty years ago, after another part-time stint, KYW offered him a full-time job. He has been there since, covering sports, hard news, and special reports. The KYW exposure also led him into television play-by-play, while keeping his full-time position in radio news. "Think for yourself and be creative—that takes you to another level," he advises.

"And if you have those skills, you can hone them at a number of different places."

Richard Crepeau's educational background includes a bachelor's degree from the University of Minnesota, a master's from Marquette University, and a Ph.D. from Florida State. He is deeply involved with the North American Society for Sports History, as reflected by the title of his Ph.D. dissertation: "Baseball in the 1920s and 1930s as a Reflection of American Culture."

Jim Colony, too, was a history major, but at the University of New Hampshire. "I took some journalism courses, but I had planned to be a teacher and coach, not a radio sports announcer." He thinks that although it would be nice for a student wanting a career in radio to go to a school like Syracuse, with its fine reputation in broadcasting, it is not necessary. "Obviously, a lot of well-known broadcasters such as Dick Stockton and Bob Costas did," he allows. "But you can learn the business at any good college that has a student radio station. You just need to be able to get on the air."

Career Preparations

After they got past the broadcasting dream phase, many radio sportswriters learned in high school that they had writing skills and started to consider what type of college education would help them achieve their goals. Many started seriously preparing at campus or small local radio stations as apprentices.

Jim Colony, now a confident and self-assured professional, was one of those who started out shy and reserved. "I always wanted to be in radio, but I was afraid to walk into the campus radio station and say 'put me on the air,'" he remembers. "But eventually, as I was taking education courses at a New Hampshire state college in the town of Keene, there was an employment ad for a sports director at a little local radio station to replace someone who was leaving. Actually, I didn't get that job; they gave it to one of their sales guys to read sports in the morning and afternoon. But they hired me to do a talk show. So, I basically learned radio by going on the air with very few listeners and making a lot of mistakes, but learning how to behave." Like many marketable traits, self-confidence grows with practice and exposure.

Richard Crepeau has been writing radio sports essays since he became chairman of the University of Central Florida history department to keep his hand in sports and sports history. His inspiration comes from the work of the British Broadcasting Company's Alistair Cooke and his weekly "Letter from America," as well as the work of Haywood Hale Broune and Howard Cosell.

Harry Donahue believes that studying at Saint Charles Seminary helped his career—"Not only did it fortify in my mind what I really wanted to do, but it gave me the opportunity to meet and learn from a fellow named Joe Grady." A popular local disc jockey, Grady was just starting to teach third-year speech courses at the seminary while working as program director at radio station WPEN.

"When I was leaving the seminary, I told him that I'd always wanted to get into broadcasting," Donahue says. Grady told him to send him a letter and that he would try to help. Donahue contacted Grady while looking for a summer job. Grady said he had no on-air positions available, but did offer Donahue a job as a mailroom boy, whose duties included getting lunch for the station's disc jockeys, for $100 dollars a week. "First thing each morning at 7:30, I would get newspapers and coffee for Philadelphia's legendary morning man, Bob Menafee, and he would let me watch him work," Donahue recalls. "This was someone I'd grown up listening to, and now here I was every morning having coffee with him."

The best in the profession have succeeded with a combination of talent, creativity, and hard work. But there are also examples of laziness that we all should avoid. As Donahue tells it, "Another Philadelphia legend, baseball's Robin Roberts [Hall of Famer and former pitcher for the Phillies], was broadcasting sports for WPEN, working at the station for about three hours a day. Robbie would read almost verbatim from the sports section of the *Philadelphia Inquirer* newspaper into the microphone. You could anticipate what his next line would be." Obviously, Donahue didn't receive much enlightenment about sportswriting from the tactics of his baseball hero, Roberts, but he learned what not to do. Fortunately, he studied and emulated some of the best in the business.

Radio provides basic talents useful in other sports journalism fields. Many fine sportswriters have radio backgrounds. If you can learn the tight, crisp writing skills for sports radio, along with how to ad-lib and do play-by-play, you will probably be ready for work in the print media. Colony uses Al Michaels of ABC's *Monday Night Football* as a good example of the particular skills that sports journalists bring with them to any writing situation. "During the San Francisco earthquake of 1989, some of the on-air network people who happened to be in the city were sports guys. Michaels did a great job during that calamity. His sports background helped him to be able to think on the fly; to have a picture thrown in front of him and to be able to describe spontaneously what was occurring. Many straight news guys wouldn't have been able to handle that."

Paying Your Dues

Internship opportunities available in radio vary with the broadcasting company, but typically radio is a fertile ground for fledgling radio sportscasters. Many radio stations allow young writers to participate in not only the on-air and production functions, but also the sales department and other positions. Most often, internships are available through arrangements between universities and stations. Some companies require that college students maintain a specific scholastic level to continue in the program.

Universities award communications and broadcast students credit for internships. Of course, salaries vary from station to station, and many outlets offer experience as the only reward.

With so many radio stations, career opportunities for positions, such as play-by-play announcing, anchoring, production, and reporting are often available for the aspiring young reporter. In all cases, of course, dues must be paid, especially by the recent graduate.

College graduates are usually assigned to entry-level positions, such as desk or production assistant. They are hired not to be on the air but to assist in production and get the broadcast on the air. They update weather forecasts, bring in the late business reports, watch the wires for scores, and keep score sheets current. They perform a variety of ordinary tasks, such as putting labels on tape cartridges when reporters file audio reports. They do every type of work there is in order to learn the business. But if they are really interested in learning to be on-air broadcasters, the studio is there and they can watch the professionals do it. Remember Harry Donahue's first job in which he mostly sat in the studio, watching a veteran announcer conduct his show, and asked questions? Unlike him, today's interns will probably have to do some work now and then.

As an intern, you should try to go into an available studio on your free time and learn to perform on your own. Most stations will afford you this opportunity; take advantage of it. Put together your own audiotape, give it to one of your mentors at the station, and ask, "If you get a chance, will you listen to this?"

After receiving some entry-level radio experience, many writers have gone on to become successful national radio personalities. Andrea Mitchell, for example, is now a major network reporter covering the White House. She started her distinguished television and radio career as a desk assistant at KYW, putting labels on cartridges and researching baseball scores to be read during sportscasts, while she was an undergraduate at the University of Pennsylvania.

Many beginning writers do not perform on the air; their primary function is, of course, to write. If you show initiative and you're good, management may make you an on-air reporter. The opportunities are there for apprentices, if you know what to look for. And when you find one, it's up to you to decide how far your skill and ambition will take you.

In preparation for a career in radio, you should constantly be aware of other reporters' styles and the way they turn a phrase as they deliver the news. Listen to how the good announcers perform. Do not assume that everybody is created equal, because they're not. Ask yourself these questions:

- What characteristics make this sportscaster better than the others?

- How did he or she rise to this position?

- What attracted me to this station?

- What vocal and personal traits about his or her delivery do I particularly enjoy?

- Why do I continue to listen to his or her shows?

As you plan your career, it is important to have humility and realize that there will be a learning period in which you will be doing some relatively low-level broadcasting chores. Jim Colony moved up from the little station in Keene, New Hampshire, to Pittsburgh's

WTAE via a long and winding path. (His first sports talk show lasted only thirteen weeks.) Remember that to small stations and their audiences, the quality of your work is as important as if you were on network radio.

Stepping up to the Plate

In radio sports, one of the best ways to market yourself and possibly learn about your shortcomings in order to improve is with audition tapes. When you think you are ready to be heard and judged by experts, select a story such as a college football or basketball game or a sports news broadcast you have written up. Remember that the material has to be well written—tight and interesting. It is not only your voice and delivery in which employers are interested.

When he was sports director at a station in Vermont, Jim Colony received many letters and tapes from men and women looking for jobs, and he would always respond. When they asked for a critique, he always gave one. "One fellow wanting to get into sportscasting, sent me a tape requesting an honest assessment. 'Tell me,' he said, 'if I have a career in broadcasting, or if I should be selling popcorn outside of Fenway Park instead.' The tape was pretty bad, so I was tempted to write in my response, 'You seem like a very fine young man, but please make my popcorn buttered.' I didn't. Instead, I pointed out a few things and suggested he had a lot of work to do. I think people are more sophisticated now."

If you send out tapes, make sure to find out the name of the person in charge, such as the station program director. Make sure you spell his or her name correctly and write a finely crafted cover letter.

Opportunities for radio writers seem to be fewer now than in years past. A decade or more ago, most radio stations had news departments and there were many announcers who did nothing but sports. Even at KYW, Donahue now does both general news and sports, but many stations don't even have a news department, let alone a sports department. "Radio," he said, "except for the generic talk shows, now has little to do with creative writing. On the talk shows, it's just entertainment. The emphasis is on enticing listeners to call in—basically just a stimulus reaction type of thing, an exercise, it seems, to try to get people mad enough to react to something said on the air and flood the station with calls. Conversely, on the news shows, you can't think about that. You are doing a good job when no one is calling to complain."

Donahue's best advice for a student learning play-by-play skills at the college radio station is to work at broadcasting high school games. "Make tapes," he says "and listen to them carefully. Send the ones you're pleased with to other stations that do play-by-play or to sports teams." The normal progression is to start as you would in baseball—in the minor leagues—and work your way up. For basketball, go to a college town and try to impress the college team with your skills. Work there until you are confident enough to send your tapes to a larger market where you may be hired to broadcast for a larger conference schedule. "Eventually, you meet somebody a few years later, who says, 'We need somebody to do games. Are you available?'

"One lesson that Joe Grady taught me," he adds, "was that no matter what time of day you're on the air, and no matter how unimportant you think the game is, always treat it like it's the Super Bowl, the greatest thing that is going on that day, that night, that moment. You never know who's listening. That is still true today. No matter where you are, if it's going out over the radio, somebody is out there. If they're not listening to tonight's broadcast, they may be listening to your next one. The potential is always there for them to say, 'Hey, this guy is pretty good!' "

You can increase the odds of finding a position or internship in radio by researching the few organizations and websites that focus on this business. For starters, check the following for employment, internship, and freelance opportunities. On some sites, you can send your resume for employers' consideration.

- The Radio Employment Connection at Airwaves Media (http://www.airwaves.com)

- Radio and Television News Directors Association (http://rtnda.org)

- National Association of Broadcasters (http://www.nab.org/ech/linksjob.htm or www.nab.org/ECH)

- Radio Broadcasting Newsgroup (http://www.broadcastjobs.com)

Other tips for job seekers include:

- Visit and write to local stations to learn from them what is happening in the radio business locally and nationally, especially regarding job vacancies.

- Let all stations know you are available for part-time or stringer (freelance) work.

- Become familiar with people in the broadcasting programs at nearby schools and request that they keep you posted (via phone, E-mail, or fax) about job opportunities.

- Propose covering a crime scene, criminal trial, local high school or college game, or interviewing a visiting celebrity for a local station.

- Advise news directors at wire services and regional associations in your state of your availability to "string" for them.

The Life of a Radio Sportswriter

More so than most journalistic endeavors, the pressure of deadlines is omnipresent in radio. There is usually a newscast every hour, and you can go on immediately when a major story breaks.

Richard Crepeau spends about three hours writing his radio essays. He writes his first draft on Monday or Tuesday, polishes it on Wednesday, prints it, and then does a reading. He then tapes on Thursday, and the piece is aired on Friday mornings and evenings. "Mostly, I enjoy writing about the sports I like best—baseball, hockey, and the Winter Olympic Games," Crepeau says. "I also enjoy going into areas that I am not totally familiar with, such as the Iditarod race, which, of course, required some research. Personal observation pieces are also fun to write, and I like doing movie reviews and book reviews."

There is very little that Harry Donahue hasn't done in sports media. He has written about it, done play-by-play for it, and reported on it. In his present job, he is on the air for five half hours; a half hour on, an hour off, and then back on again. That sequence repeats five times during the day. His downtime is occupied with writing sports for two other anchors.

Working in radio can mean some very early wake-up calls. When he's working in radio broadcasting or writing, Richard Johnson, an ABC Radio anchor, sets his alarm for between 3 and 4 A.M. because he must start preparing for the morning newscasts before 5 A.M. Donahue faces a similarly early morning; his is often the first voice listeners in the Delaware Valley hear each morning, and he usually wakes up at the ungodly hour of 2:45 A.M. "You have to be friendly, you have to be up," he warns. "If you're having a bad day, you can't let your listeners know it. You always have to project a friendly tone, and always be on top of your game. That is not always easy. I can honestly say, however, that there's nothing else I ever wanted to do. It's just always a pleasure for me to get up and go. There probably aren't many people who can say that about their work."

Freelancing in Radio

Radio freelancing mostly consists of temporary employment, by the day or week, or by the assignment or story. At radio stations, freelancers (or stringers) come and go, and the best are used regularly or are eventually added to the station's staff. If the station likes your work, you can count on a good salary (as long as the station can afford to pay you). ·

A good example of making this end of sportswriting work is Richard Johnson, who turned a steady gig as a freelance writer at ABC Radio into a staff position in New York as an anchor of hourly ABC entertainment and general newscasts. He still helps make ends meet by freelancing occasionally as a writer for WNBC-TV.

Vernon Stone, professor at the University of Missouri, says that freelancing income varies widely throughout the country. He thinks that stringers often do it "more for love than money," using the example of a county seat radio station in Kentucky that pays the local jailer $30 a game for his play-by-play of local games. That is love!

The Best of the Sportscasters

The National Association of Sportscasters and Sportswriters annually chooses the National Sportscaster of the Year. In its April 1998 selections, Al Michaels of ABC Sports was named the 1997 Hall of Fame Sportscaster inductee, and Bob Costas (NBC) was the National Sportscaster award winner. The table lists the winners of State Sportscaster Awards. (A few states did not submit nominees.) Note that some winners are television sportscasters.

Alabama—Jim Fyffe, WLWI, Montgomery
Alaska—John Seibel, KIMO, Anchorage
Arkansas—Ray Tucker, KTHV-TV, Little Rock
California—Bob Miller, Los Angeles Kings
Colorado—Ron Zappolo, KUSA-TV, Denver
Connecticut—Scott Gray, WTIC, Hartford
Florida—Gene Deckerhoff, Tampa Bay Buccaneers/Florida
   State University, Tallahassee
Georgia—Jeff Hullinger, WAGA-TV, Atlanta
Illinois—Wayne Larrivee, WGN-TV/WMAQ, Chicago
Indiana—Sam Simmermaker, WCSI/WKKO, Columbus
Iowa—Ron Gonder, WMT, Cedar Rapids
Kansas—Bob Davis, Jayhawk Network, Westwood
Kentucky—Tom Leach, WVLK, Lexington
Louisiana—Ed Daniels, WGNO-TV, New Orleans
Maine—Mike Estrada, WSKW, Skowhegan
Maryland—Gerry Sandusky, WBAL-TV, Baltimore
Massachusetts—Bob Lobel, WBZ-TV, Boston
Michigan—Ernie Harwell, Detroit Tigers
Minnesota—Herb Carneal, WCCO, Minneapolis
Mississippi—David Kellum, WQLJ, Oxford
Missouri—Randy Karraker, KMOX, St. Louis
Montana—Rocky Erickson, Northern Sports Network, Billings
Nebraska—Chuck Stevens, KFOR, Lincoln
New Hampshire—Dick Osborne, WKKL, Concord
New Mexico—Mike Powers, KRQE-TV, Albuquerque
New York—Mike Breen, New York Knicks
North Carolina—Steve Martin, Charlotte Hornets
North Dakota—Lee Timmerman, KFYR-TV, Bismarck

Ohio—Tom Hamilton, Cleveland Indians
Oklahoma—Bill Teegins, KWTV, Oklahoma City
Oregon—Bill Schonely, Portland Trail Blazers
Pennsylvania—Merrill Reese, WYSP, Philadelphia
Rhode Island—Frank Carpani, WJAR-TV, Cranston
South Carolina—Warren Peper, WCSC-TV, Charleston
South Dakota—Tom Maxwell, WNAX, Yankton
South Dakota—Danny Olson, KELO, Sioux Falls
Tennessee—John Ward, VOL Network, Knoxville
Texas—Mark Holtz, WBAP, Arlington
Utah—Kent Rupe, KSL, Salt Lake City
Vermont—Ken Squier, WDEV, Waterbury
Virginia—Bib Black, Virginia News Network, Richmond
Washington—Kevin Calabro, Seattle Supersonics
West Virginia—John Simonson, WWVA, Wheeling
Wisconsin—Matt Lepay, WISC-TV/WIBA, Madison
Wyoming—George Kay, WKTO-TV, Casper

Courtesy: National Sportscasters and Sportswriters Association.

The Financial Side of Radio Sports Journalism

When Jim Colony started in his first full-time radio job in the late 1970s, he made only $200 a week as an on-air broadcaster. Although that now seems extremely low, there are still a multitude of small stations throughout the country where writers and broadcasters are learning their trade for only a little more.

Vernon Stone's recent research shows that "average radio news salaries beat inflation in markets of more than 1 million population but lost ground elsewhere. If you are interested in sports radio as a career, you should realize that the number of jobs at the higher-paying, major-market stations is limited, and because most people are working in sports in smaller markets, the salary averages for the profession as a whole are skewed by their large numbers [i.e., so many small stations]." His study resulted in projected salary averages for various radio positions, including sports anchors. These averages, which are too detailed to be included here, can be found at Stone's website: www.missouri.edu/~jourvs/.

Stone's research indicates that "all markets considered, the principal positions are paid a little more than twice as well in television as in radio news."

Tips from the Pros

For those preparing for a career in sports radio, Harry Donahue offers this advice: "Bring more than just a superficial appreciation for an event you report." As an example of such superficiality, he cites a story recently broadcast by a local television sportscaster on baseball great Jackie Robinson, and how poorly the Philadelphia Phillies treated him in his early days with the Brooklyn Dodgers.

During an interview with Bill Giles, then the Phillies' owner, the sportscaster remarked that the Phillies were "one of the last teams in the National League to hire a black player (which is true)." Donahue continues, "Then the interviewer added that even today the Phillies only have three African-American players on their roster. He didn't, however, inform the viewers that over the decades since Robinson's playing days, the Phillies frequently had many black players. Instead, he left us with the implication that even today the team is guilty of bias. He could have pointed out, for a more complete story, that some other organizations, including the Los Angeles Dodgers, currently employ only a small percentage of African Americans. He didn't. From this incomplete story, fans would focus on how prejudiced the Phillies were (with only three African Americans), when a more important facet of the story would be that the Dodgers, the team that broke the color line fifty years ago, now has only *one*. You can't reach a correct conclusion with the facts the reporter presented. If you're supposed to be doing an objective report on the state of baseball today vis-à-vis fifty years ago, I think you should get your numbers straight."

Donahue advises that "Reporters have a responsibility to present facts and reach a certain conclusion. Good reporters must delve beneath the surface to determine what they've missed." Following his own advice about truthfully presenting readers with the facts, he offers this personal recommendation (resulting from his experience in sports radio and television): "If it's sports broadcasting you want, television is the avenue to go."

Richard Crepeau agrees that the best radio sports journalists should be able to go beyond the obvious and look for meaning and values that are the underpinning of events. His advice to students is to learn to read, write, and think analytically. Know the history of the event or personality you are covering. "I find people's reactions to what I report to be the most satisfying part of my work," Crepeau says. "When I've tried to make listeners think about the subject or reevaluate their assumptions and there is an indication I have succeeded, I am delighted."

For budding radio sportswriters, the best advice Jim Colony has to give is "don't be afraid of rejection, and don't be afraid to accept criticism, because without them you may not get any better." He thinks it is worth the extra cost and effort to send your audition tapes to many stations, rather than focusing on a few. "You've got to be willing to work anywhere and therefore sending them out in great numbers may improve your chances. Even if stations don't have current openings, they may in the future and they may save your impressive tape for when they do. If someone listens to your tape, and especially if they respond to you, you may be able to build up a relationship that produces information about openings at other stations."

Finally, Donahue recommends that you constantly be aware of your responsibility for being accurate and for being there when listeners need important information. "I try never to shape opinion; listeners can do that for themselves," he says. "Make certain you're consistent and keep your product current. Provide the service that people come to expect over the long term."

11 Television Sports Journalism

Don't do it for the money. Do it because you love it. There will always be days when the last thing in the world you want to do on a nice July evening is go to the game.

Richard Johnson
Freelance television sportswriter, ABC Radio anchor

For any sportswriter considering television sports reporting, there are two important misconceptions that should be cleared up immediately. First, although many writers do excel and earn top dollar, it is not a field in which becoming rich quickly is automatic. Second, realize that it is *not* an easy transition from writing for the print media to writing sports for broadcast media.

Television sports reporting is not about sticking a microphone onto a podium with twenty other mikes at a postgame press conference and taking notes. It is about telling the story and writing to fit the video that's been shot. According to Richard Johnson, "It's about walking up to the pitcher who just gave up the winning run and asking him what happened. But that's where the fun lies, in overcoming the challenges and making good radio or television."

In this chapter we will see why television is a written medium before it becomes a visual one.

The Need for Writing Skills

Many people assume that their local sportscasters have everything written for them, but this is not true. Sportscasters, both local and national, are not just good-looking faces on the tube. They actually research, develop, and write their own material; in many cases, they become actively involved in the production process of their newscasts and pregame shows.

Our interviews indicate that sports anchors at most television stations write their own copy. Some are obviously better at it than others, but writing skills are definitely important. Ray Didinger, a Pro Football Hall of Fame sportswriter now writing for NFL Films, thinks that a sportscaster who can write well rises above the crowd. He says that if you have "a reporter's eye and a storyteller's ability, you have the two ingredients to do well in television sportswriting." Didinger's own writing skills have been highly praised in each of the media in which he has worked. For example, he wrote and partially produced *Football America*, produced by NFL Films for the TNT cable network, which recently received an Emmy for outstanding sports special and best editing.

Writing for Television vs. Other Media

There are the obvious differences between sportswriting for television and writing for newspapers, magazines, and radio. A major one is tight time limitations for stories that accompany visual presentations. "You only get one chance in broadcasting," Richard Johnson warns. "The recipient of your work can't go back two paragraphs and review. Television writing obviously depends much more on the pictures, while radio writing revolves around the sound of the news makers. But the thing they share that makes them different from print is the 'one-take' aspect, requiring much simpler writing with overt references."

The hours are somewhat the same. In both radio and television, the top jobs have the worst hours. In radio, prime time is between 6 A.M. and 9 A.M. The top television show is the late news at 10 or

11 P.M., which means you have no evening life. This is similar to newspaper sportswriting, because most games are at night, and papers must be printed for morning delivery.

The deadline pressures are very different in each medium. "In television, you build and build and build for that one thirty- or sixty-minute show, and that's your only shot," Johnson says. "When it's over, the lights go down, you go home, and start from scratch the next day. There are two very different mindsets. In television, it all has to be there for that one play: the best words, the best pictures, and the best combination of other elements for that one and only chance to grab the viewer." Print media can provide more in-depth coverage, with more than one article, a sidebar with related information, and so on.

Ray Didinger, who has also written extensively for newspapers and magazines, thinks that the biggest difference in writing for television or video is that what you are writing is mostly transitional; thoughts or information take the viewer from one point in the story to another. In print, whether it's a magazine article, a newspaper game story, or a column, you have a blank canvas and you have to paint the picture. "You have to write about the blue sky, or the paint peeling off the locker-room wall, or the pile of duffel bags in the middle of the room," he says of print media. "You have to create that world for the reader. When you're writing for film, it's there. People can see the paint, and they can see the duffel bags and the player with his head down and hear what he's saying. In the short bit of time that exists between his voice and the next piece of music, the writer may have as little as eight seconds to subtly inject a thought or information that transitions the viewer."

Didinger equates the job of writing transitions to the moving walkways in an airport. The television writer provides the moving walkway that takes a viewer from one image to another. But there are only seconds in which to do it and it has to be exactly right. It also has to be unobtrusive so the written words do not jump out and interrupt the flow of the story.

Armen Keteyian, of CBS-TV and HBO, warns print media writers against underestimating what is involved in becoming a television sportswriter. "It is a very different kind of storytelling and print writers who think it is a hop, skip, and a jump to go over and cover news for television are very much mistaken. You have to let the pictures tell the story visually," he explains. "You write in and out of sound bites, rather than explaining what viewers are seeing on screen. You must employ the art of economy; using less to say more. The most difficult transition I had to make moving from print media was telling a story with my voice; that's a very difficult transition to learn."

Perhaps the biggest difference between print media and broadcasting is that the written word is relayed to the viewer vocally. Although the vocal skills of our favorite sportscasters are mostly endowed at birth, their mellifluous tones and delivery style must be learned and cultivated. Keteyian took his training from a very good, tough New York voice teacher. He describes the process: "We did exercises, read poetry, and projected, learning how to use our voices as instruments. Those who can do that, like Peter Jennings, Charles Kuralt, Jack Whitaker, Jim McKay, Robert Krowich, Ted Koppel, and Diane Sawyer, lead you and pull you through a story. They make a vast difference in how a story is received. I remember writing some very good scripts that I look back on now and cringe at how my voice would destroy what I had written. It didn't support it—it detracted from it."

Beat the Clock

Just as a print reporter wants that extra couple of inches of space, the broadcast writer wants that extra thirty seconds to make one last point—and frequently does not get it. The clock can be a villain.

In most situations of writing hard copy, whether it is a term paper, a game report, or a letter home, a writer has a clean sheet of paper or computer screen to fill with thoughts or facts. Not so in television.

After a career in print media sportswriting, Ray Didinger's first assignment at NFL Films was *Football America*. The film's producer brought him a taped segment on football in Alaska. Didinger's job was to write one transitional bridge of seventeen seconds from one story to another. He had to write it in context, consistent with the overall mood of the piece. "When it all fits together—the pictures, the interviews, and the music—it can be very powerful, very great," he says. "Then to have your script read by a professional actor like James Coburn or Gary Busey, who may find meaning in something you wrote that you didn't even know was there, is really kind of fun."

It's Still About Telling a Story

Although the method of storytelling is different in the various media, writers must still tell the story well, even if it is only a few minutes long. Some writers just know how to do this, whether they are sitting on their front porch or making a movie. Didinger has found that there is a good side and a frustrating side to the absolute limits film and video put on what you can say and how much you can say. For this year's NFL Films *Presents* video, he had five minutes, forty seconds on film to say what needed to be said. "There were times when I wanted to cry, because I had three or four really good anecdotes to use, but I had to pare it to one or two," he remembers. "In a newspaper column or story, you can usually go to the editor and get extra inches of space, but on film, you use one and let the rest go. You learn to live with that."

Television writers, therefore, must learn to let the film tell a large share of the story and suppress the urge to write as much as they would in other media. In writing for *Football America*, which chronicles the way the game is played throughout the country, Didinger recalls a segment on a high school team in Juneau, Alaska, which had to play on a bumpy and rocky field. He did not have to write, "Imagine what it's like to play on this." It was much more eloquent to pan across the field's surface, play some music, and let viewers visualize the obstacles present. His next written line, therefore, did not deal with what the images related, but instead said, "Playing in Juneau gives the Crimson Bears an uncommon home-field advantage." Usually, pictures and music say it much better than the television sportswriter can.

There is a theory that stage presence is as important as journalistic skill in this business; that acting training and experience performing on stage are great assets. Such theories contribute to what television writers call visual media's "sizzle." The complaint regarding many sportscasters is that they provide us with "more sizzle than substance."

Television seems to have become more and more cosmetic than it was ten or twenty years ago. Harry Donahue, sports and news writer/announcer at KYW-TV in Philadelphia, has experienced this industry during its growth and maturing phases. "Inasmuch as television is a visual medium," he says, "cosmetics and sizzle are understandable, but the whole glamorization of the industry sometimes overshadows the real information and those who present it."

He sees that as a frustrating part of his business, realizing that it is not so much *what* you know but *who* you know that may get you a job in this business. His advice for someone preparing to enter television journalism is to work from more than just a superficial appreciation for the event about which you're writing. "Make certain your interviews and subsequent stories are deep and substantial, and guard against superficial research," he said. "Scratch beneath the surface, considering what your readers will want to know. Ask yourself 'What can I do to make this a better story without cheating my listeners or viewers out of the full treatment?'"

The Cosell Legacy

Most sportscasters think that one sportswriter who never cheated his listeners or viewers out of anything was Howard Cosell, an icon in his profession in the 1960s and 1970s. Sports broadcasters refer to the "marriage of journalistic judgment with stage presence." More than a few believe Cosell was a successful example of this combination, despite some problems the industry had with his style.

One of his countless admirers is Dick Crepeau, radio sportswriter at WUCF-FM in Orlando, Florida. He credits Cosell with bringing sports reporting out of what he called the "toy department" and making it a serious part of American life, reflecting the values and issues of the larger society. Crepeau cites Cosell's newscasts during heavyweight champion Muhammad Ali's struggles with the draft board and the boxing establishment; he was one of the few to defend Ali in public. Although Cosell liked to portray himself as a critic and something of a cynic, it was obvious if you listened to his twice-daily radio commentaries that he had a deep love of sports. "What was amazing," Crepeau says, "was that in these live broadcast commentaries, Cosell worked without a script and without a clock and came in right on time without an error every time."

Crepeau also mentions Cosell's penchant for using big words, even when he became a fixture on *Monday Night Football*. "He seemed to flaunt his education. This was not an endearing quality, and his ego made him unbearable at times. More often than not, he misused words, but then most people didn't know and probably didn't care."

Getting an Education

Many of the finest broadcasters learned their skills at the broadcast journalism and communications programs of such schools as Syracuse University's S. I. Newhouse School of Public Communications in upstate New York. It is important that the curriculum you choose provides not only journalism basics, but also the management skills necessary for various positions in television.

Many television writers and sportscasters share the opinion that journalism school provides an excellent educational base for this business. Ray Didinger's major in journalism at Temple University has contributed to his success in newspaper, magazine, and television work. During his undergraduate years, he wrote for the university's *Temple News*, while also stringing (freelancing) for the *Philadelphia Inquirer*. After graduation, he worked at the now defunct *Philadelphia Bulletin*, learning the newspaper business as a clerk, and then joined a small suburban paper.

Didinger's first major newspaper job at the *Daily Times* did not meet his financial dreams. "I certainly didn't make much money at the *Times*, which paid me $100.25 a week. I was so embarrassed by how little I was making, when my father asked me how much I was paid, I said, 'A hundred and a quarter,' so that he would think it was a hundred and twenty-five dollars—it sounded better!"

Like most veteran journalists, Didinger says the more practical experience you get—whether it is at the student newspaper, the student radio station, or as an intern in print or broadcast media—the more quickly you will learn about the business. "If I had to do it over again," he says, "I'd sure do it the same way."

Some have become veteran television writers without a degree. Richard Johnson is an example. Although he has been in and out of college, he has been writing for more than three decades, the last thirteen years in television. "I continually flipped between broadcasting and college, until radio finally won," Johnson says. "When I returned to school at age twenty-six, I majored in political science. By then, having decided to move into news, I needed all the liberal arts, history, and political science I could find."

As a journalist, you have to know a little about nearly everything. Johnson warns that "all those courses you're sleeping through now will come back to haunt you when some editor assumes you actually know about the three branches of the federal government. If you don't, you're branded as a child idiot and given assignments reflecting that brand."

Stephanie Sawyer, who interned in the Philadelphia area at WCAU-TV, graduated from the communications program at Marymount University in Arlington, Virginia. Her program included journalism and broadcasting courses and required an internship for graduation, which Sawyer considers vital. "The university has many connections in broadcasting," she says, "which help students gain valuable experience and make excellent contacts in the business."

Internship Opportunities

Writing and broadcasting internships generally seem to be plentiful in television for both college students and graduates. At NFL Films in Mount Laurel, New Jersey, six interns are hired each year to work in various departments (e.g., public relations, research archives, production). Those interns work hard and become involved in television productions, such as NFL game footage and promotional films, while learning the business.

The summer before she graduated, Stephanie Sawyer (no relation to well-known network personality Diane Sawyer) was the only woman among five television interns at WCAU-TV. While assisting the sportscasters and producers, she learned "how to prepare for press conferences and sportscasts, but most of my work was evaluating the televised game films to recommend unusual or spectacular plays that might later make it to the sports newscast.

"The major educational value of my internship," she adds, "was in the station control room, learning the direction and production of whole news shows and the decision process for placement of stories." The station interns are not paid, but earn college credits for their summer work. "A few interns who are interested in trying for careers in television apply for positions and may be hired by the station," Sawyer says. "I wanted to try my hand at children's television, so I opted for another internship with ABC in Washington instead.

"I enthusiastically recommend students interested in sports production to apply for internships like mine," she concludes. "It's not like you can't start a career without an internship, but the on-the-job experience is invaluable."

The Internet website called TV Jobs provides potential television writers with listings of available positions throughout the industry. Its Internet address is http://www.tvjobs.com. The following list, provided courtesy of TV Jobs, provides a sampling of television stations that advertise for and welcome applications from high-potential writing candidates for various positions. Note that sportswriting positions are not available at all stations.

Television Stations

AETV (PBS) Arkansas Educational Television

KGTV (ABC), San Diego

KNSD-TV (NBC), San Diego

KQED-TV (PBS), San Francisco

KRON-TV (NBC), San Francisco

WETA-TV (PBS), Washington

WLRN-TV (PBS), Miami

WNDU-TV (NBC), South Bend, Ind.

WMAR-TV (ABC), Baltimore

WGBY-TV (PBS), Springfield, Mass.

WWLP-TV (NBC), Springfield, Mass.

KPLR-TV (WB), St. Louis

WNBC-TV (NBC), New York

WTVH-TV (CBS), Syracuse

UNCTV (PBS), University of North Carolina, Research Triangle Park

WHP-TV (CBS)/ WLYH-TV (UPN), Harrisburg, Pa.

WNEP-TV (ABC), Moosic, Pa.

KVUE-TV (ABC), Austin, Tex.

WFAA-TV (ABC), Dallas

KTXA-TV (UPN), Dallas

WHRO-TV (PBS), Norfolk, Va.

WDBJ-TV (CBS), Roanoke, Va.

KCPQ-TV (FOX), Tacoma, Wash.

KSTW-TV (UPN), Tacoma, Wash.

Cable Stations

Blue Ridge Cable, Stroudsburg, Pa.

Media One, Elmhurst, Ill.

Waccamaw Cable Advertising/GSM Productions, Myrtle Beach, SC

Broadcasting Groups

Hearst Broadcasting, Washington, D.C.

Miscellaneous

Nickelodeon Studios, Orlando

Audio, Radio & Television Services (ARTS), College of DuPage, Glen Ellyn, Ill.
City Arts—Visual and Performing Arts, New York

Custom Creations Inc., Hoboken, N.J.

Radio and Television News Directors Foundation, Washington, D.C.

Showtime Summer Internship Program

Worldnet, United States Information Agency, Washington, D.C.

That First Job

Although in recent years there have been more applicants than television journalism positions, there is constant movement in the business and jobs regularly become available. The research of Vernon Stone, University of Missouri journalism professor emeritus and author of *Let's Talk Pay in Television and Radio News,* shows that about 44,000 people were working in news at commercial television and radio stations in the 1990s. The average newsperson typically holds the same position only three to four years, so openings occur often. Each year, hundreds of positions open up for entry-level television applicants, according to Stone.

No matter where you apply in this business, it is important to be aggressive and confident. The way Harry Donahue got his first job as a play-by-play announcer many years ago is an excellent example of what preparation, aggressiveness, and confidence can do for someone hungry to enter the business.

When the short-lived United States Football League (USFL) was born, Philadelphia Stars owner Myles Tannenbaum said he would like to have legendary broadcaster Bill Campbell call the games. But Campbell was announcing games at another station, so he was not available.

To apply for the job, Donahue spoke to the Stars' owner, who said, "I listen to you every morning (on KYW radio), but have you ever done play-by-play?" Donahue answered, "No, I haven't, but now I'm in a position in my career where I'd never entertain doing a job that I didn't think I could handle. I wouldn't embarrass myself, that's the most important thing. I wouldn't put you in the position of being embarrassed. You're going to have to trust me on this."

Tannenbaum seemed to like that answer and hired Donahue pending an audition with Bill Neal, the Stars' producer. Donahue learned that Neal was leaning toward Tom Lamaine, then a television weatherman, to do the games. "All I wanted was a fair chance," Donahue recalls.

Neal explained that for Donahue's audition he would choose a tape of a "well-known" football game and Donahue would call the play-by-play by watching on a monitor. Without being able to prepare, Donahue worried that he would make mistakes, in an audition that would make or break his attempt to enter sports broadcasting, but he had to go along. Since it was February, Donahue thought, "Maybe he'll give me the 1983 Super Bowl between Washington and Miami," which had been played recently. For practice, he reviewed the tape of the Super Bowl on his VCR, charting the plays and making out a depth chart of the rosters.

On the day of audition, Neal put him in a room with a monitor and a VCR and announced that Donahue would be calling the plays from the taped Super Bowl game of two weeks before. "I almost screamed; I couldn't believe it!" Donahue laughs. "It was like studying for a test by looking at last year's exam and then the teacher giving you that same exam. Neal couldn't believe it. I just ripped it—a network-quality audition." After the Stars' management heard the audition, Donahue was called two days later and told the job was his.

From his maiden voyage into play-by-play broadcasting, Donahue learned that "if you prepare and act on your hunches, you'll be astonished sometimes how well things can work out for you." Surprisingly, after he started broadcasting the Stars' games, Mike Fetchko, then of Temple University and now executive director of the Major League Baseball Players Alumni, also liked his play-by-play and offered him the job of broadcasting Temple football, to which Donahue agreed. His career took off from there with broadcasting college football and basketball games. The Temple job led to his becoming the voice of the Atlantic 10 Conference on Sports-Channel. Now, this ex-seminarian can be seen and heard on the tube everywhere you look.

Coming Up with the Cash

Although this chapter began by warning you that the television sportswriting field is not a common way for young writers to fatten their wallets, one cannot deny there is plenty of money to be made for those who work hard as they climb the ladder.

Major Markets

Major television markets are where the big money is for sportswriters because, at a typical major network, $80,000 is the *low* end of the salary range for a correspondent. Those kind of salaries come with significant risks, however, in this high-pressure, ratings-driven business. After being hired, you may be tossed into deep water to see how well you swim with your writing and reporting. If the news or sports director likes what he or she sees, you may be offered a life preserver in the form of a contract offer.

Job security is not guaranteed, however. Those who improve may get rich, but those who become too complacent and satisfied with their work—thinking they have made it—may quickly find themselves in the unemployment line. That is the reality of television.

In the pressurized, competitive environment of the networks, the writers who can write *and* deliver extremely well are the people who are rewarded with the largest salaries. If you are good enough to move from print media to major-market television (and very few are that good), it can mean a rather dramatic jump in salary. Sports anchors at the networks and largest major-market stations typically earn six figures, ranging from approximately $90,000 to $500,000 per year. It is not uncommon for a top-notch network television writer to double or triple his or her print media income after a few years in television.

Smaller Markets

In the smaller markets, things are not nearly so financially satisfying for anchors. Vernon Stone's recent research shows that the median television salary for sports anchors was $38,100. Allowing for the fact that this figure reflects hundreds of very small stations, salaries are not competitive.

While some stations in the five largest markets (New York, Chicago, Los Angeles, Philadelphia, and San Francisco) pay their top news anchors close to or more than $1 million a year, reporters in the sixty smallest television markets make as little as $16,000!

In smaller markets, companies usually only sign a writer to a standard contract trial period of thirteen weeks, after which it may or may not be renewed. As Stone's research indicates, "Smaller-market television reporters are close to the poverty level, and the findings indicate we should not look for any major improvements in broadcast journalism salaries as measured against the cost of living through the end of the century."

Sports anchors, with rare exceptions, are the lowest-paid members of television anchor teams. Their income seems to grow in the largest markets, but not in the smaller ones.

Stone estimates that by 2000 reporters will average eight to nine times as much at the top as at the bottom of the pay scale.

As Stone projects from his comprehensive surveys based on the expected growth of the Consumer Price Index, the median television station salary for sports anchors (by Nielsen market size) is as follows:

Largest 25 Markets: $111,831

Markets 26–50: $64,600

Markets 51–100: $44,146

Markets 101–150: $31,930

Smallest 60 Markets: $25,790

All stations: $38,100

Freelancing

Freelancing in television is different from freelancing for the print media. Newspapers and magazines, for example, buy sports articles and stories from writers and reporters by the piece or by the assignment. At a television station or network, freelancers work and are paid by the hour, day, or week. They work on a contract basis, which may commit them to work for a specific period of time or to an assigned story with an hourly rate. Usually, they are not entitled to more than rudimentary benefits, with no medical or life insurance. But many freelancers work this way throughout their career and earn a good income without the security that full-time, permanent in-house employees enjoy.

Although his workload is unpredictable, Richard Johnson's freelance television assignments are plentiful during vacation time and employee turnovers and when television stations occasionally cut their staffs too deeply. Impressive freelancers are often extended the opportunity to become full-time employees.

Freelance income is determined by union scale in many markets, as contracted by organizations such as the writers' guilds and the National Association of Broadcast Employees and Technicians (NABET), which control the rates for their industry. The top freelance rate for experienced television writers is $240 per day; the low end is about $175 per day. Some companies make up for the lack of benefits by paying writers a "benefits penalty," such as $50 per day extra, in lieu of health insurance, pension, and other benefits. "As a freelancer, lack of security is important to consider as you assess your potential future," Johnson advises.

The Top Ten Newsroom Questions

In closing this chapter, we thought you would enjoy Linda Ellerbee's column in the *Oregonian*'s "New TV Journalist Parade," in which she compiled the following humorous list of questions that a writer can expect in the television newsroom:

1. All the assignment editor wants to know: How fast can you get it shot?

2. All the producer wants to know: How short can you make it?

3. All the photographer wants to know: Do I have to set up lights?

4. All the editor wants to know: Where are the cutaways?

5. All the reporter wants to know: Can I sell it to the networks?

6. All the anchor wants to know: If it's a long lead-in, will I get to read it?

7. All the news director wants to know: Will we get sued?

8. All the general manager wants to know: Will it cost us a sponsor?

9. All the newspaper television critic wants to know: Can I make fun of it?

10. All the viewer wants to know: Isn't that reporter doing her hair differently?

Although we didn't focus on it heavily, item 10 reminds us of a good piece of advice to follow if you end up on camera someday: even if your research is flawless and your report is fascinating, keep a comb handy!

12 Photojournalism in Sports

I think I have the best seat in the house and the best job in the world as a freelance television sports camera operator.

Timothy S. McCarty
Freelance television videographer

Most sportswriters, editors, and sports information directors toil from the confines of a well-furnished office setting, with all the comforts required to do the job. Even the reporter on the beat has an "office away from the office," which is often a comfortably furnished press box protected from the elements and served by waitresses bringing around hot or cold drinks throughout the game. Writers also have the luxury of using the press lounge in many stadiums and arenas to mingle, eat, and relax before and after their work begins.

Then there is the photojournalist's office. It can be on the "frozen tundra" of Lambeau Field in Green Bay, with subzero temperatures and windchill factors or in 110-degree heat at a golf tournament or baseball game. The photojournalist's workplace often includes nothing more than floor space at an indoor arena, where he or she must sit and follow the action through the viewfinder, never getting up until halftime. He or she may need to jockey for space on the sidelines at a football or outdoor event, often with several hundred fellow photographers battling for the best angle for an award-winning picture.

Sports photographers are the "Goodyear tires" of any newspaper, meaning they must be prepared to perform in torrential rain, snowstorms, and subzero weather. There is very little glamour attached to sports photography, but the rewards and satisfaction are immense when the film is developed and the pictures or videotape produced. There is no greater thrill for the sports photographer than being "the one" who captures the defining moment of the key play that decides a contest.

The very best rise high above the competition. In that regard, photojournalism is very similar to sportswriting—the thrill of the byline on an excellent story, and the pride of a photographer's credit line on the front-page shot that everyone is talking about the day after the game.

As you might have guessed, the biggest difference between photography and sportswriting is also very obvious—there is very little writing in photojournalism. Then why is photojournalism included here? What does photojournalism have to do with writing? Photography is photography, isn't it? Anyone can take photos and sell them, can't they? Anyone can be a sports photographer, can't they? Quite the contrary.

What's Worth a Thousand Words?

As you speak to the professionals, the real photojournalists, you get a quick lesson in the depth and complexities of the business. It is not just about lenses, tripods, apertures, and depth of field. It's about telling a story through or with pictures. We cannot emphasize enough the part about telling the story, because some of the best stories ever told have been done exclusively in pictures. The photojournalist simply does with pictures what a reporter does with words. Success is measured in the same way: the impact you have on the viewer/reader and how clearly and concisely the story has been told. Written text must complement and clearly define the visual images. The average sports fan is often fascinated by the skillful still picture and video camera work they see in all forms of sports communications, but few newspaper or magazine readers or television fans who are captured by a photo or a film realize all that went into its production behind the scenes and on game day.

A good photojournalist does not have to love or even like the sports he or she is shooting. But a good knowledge of the game, its strategies, and its players is vital. Even if you are not a sports fan, you must know enough about the strategy of the sport to know when and where to expect the big play. For example, in a football game, you must be aware that, if it is third and ten, the Dallas Cowboys will call a pass play. And you should also know the team well enough to anticipate the who, what, and where of the potential game-deciding play. When you are on the field with fifty other photographers, anticipating, knowing *the* spot, and *you're the one* that captures the peak moment of the key play, you rise high above the competition. You have to know the sport well enough to understand the flow of the game. You do not have to like the sport. Sometimes it's better not to be a big fan, because when you love a sport too much, there is a tendency to get emotionally involved in watching it rather than preparing to shoot it perfectly.

Capturing the Essence and Drama of Sports

The photojournalist must be able to formulate *and write* cohesive ideas, no matter which of the many sports media is involved. David Bergman, sports photographer for the *Miami Herald,* states, "If there are two finalists competing for a photojournalism job and only one can write his or her own stories, guess who will get the job? Well-thought-out captions must be submitted for every picture shot for the editor who may be unaware of the story line."

Michael Mercanti is executive photo editor at the *Philadelphia Daily News* and knows the importance of clear writing. "It's true that a college graduate can become a photographer without writing ability, but the bigger question is can you get by on the ability just to shoot good pictures?" To a certain extent, the answer is yes, but according to Mercanti, "Eventually you'll be embarrassed enough that you'll want to learn writing. Becoming a journalist first puts you way ahead of your competition. Also, you must write captions that clearly define and set up the photo. We take that very seriously and it's an important talent we look for in the major newspaper markets."

Most photographers and photo editors interviewed for this chapter repeatedly made the same point. They lose interest in a prospective hire very quickly if it is apparent that he or she cannot write good captions.

How the Experts Got Started

Michael Mercanti maintains that if you have the skills and love to live behind the lens, a career in photojournalism can begin in many different ways and result in a fulfilling, rewarding profession. After two years of college and a brief sojourn into the computer field, Mercanti turned his passion for photography into freelance work for a local weekly newspaper, while taking five photography courses at a community college to enhance his skills.

"I made only $8 on each print they bought but the work was creatively fulfilling, and I decided then that photojournalism would be my profession," Mercanti recalls. After compiling a strong portfolio, he worked full time at a small daily newspaper, the *Atlantic City Press,* where he learned all the facets of photojournalism, including how to shoot features, sports, and news.

Mercanti's first position in a major market came in 1981 at the short-lived *Philadelphia Journal* for its last six months. Although it was a well-read, sports-oriented tabloid, it ceased publication in December 1981, followed shortly by the demise of the *Evening Bulletin.* As a result, everyone in the business was scrambling for jobs. Mercanti started to freelance for the *Philadelphia Daily News.* Three months later, a photographer position opened, and he was hired as full time. He has been there ever since.

In David Bergman's experience, the best photographers are the ones who always seem to get lucky. "Doesn't it seem that the same people always 'get lucky' over and over?" he asks. His favorite expression is "Luck is when preparation meets opportunity," meaning that the best photographers are the ones who are prepared.

When asked his definition of a "good" photo, Bergman explains that it must evoke an emotion in the person looking at it. "It almost doesn't matter which emotion," he says. "As long as it makes you laugh, get angry, or feel sadness, it's a good one. When I show someone an action photo, I love to hear him or her say, 'Ouch!' If that happens, I know it's a 'good' photo."

"I always had a camera as a kid," Bergman remembers, "but I didn't know the difference between a shutter speed and an aperture." During his sophomore year at the University of Miami, he volunteered to take pictures for the school newspaper, the *Miami Hurricane*. With a lot of encouragement from the staff, he soon became the assistant photo editor, then the photo editor. "Before I knew it," he admits, "I'd sold my drum set and started buying more camera equipment."

Some veterans enjoyed photography at a young age and learned the trade with the eagerness of a pro as they grew older. Others, like Mercanti, seem to have fallen into it. "I'm a visual person," Mercanti notes. "There are visual people and there are linear people, and I express myself in visual ways and am very comfortable in a visual world. I've always liked art history and things that affect me visually. I can read a line and be touched by it, but a photo does something different to me. It excites me to do in a photo what someone else does with text. That really is a talent, and I don't know where it comes from. My brother is in the arts as a sculptor, and my sister also is very visual. Oddly, our father is a management analyst, an accountant; but for some reason his three children are very successful artistic people. So, photography found me, and I love every minute of my work."

Photojournalism skills are like riding a bicycle—you do not lose the basic instincts or talent even if you go on to other pursuits, as did Dave Coskey, vice president of marketing and operations for the Philadelphia 76ers. Because of his love of photography from high school, he first began working in the sports information department at Villanova University as a student photographer. During that period, he also worked as a stringer for the Associated Press (AP) in photography. Even now, when an emergency arises, he has been known to open his automobile trunk, grab his equipment, and start shooting. He is still a photographer at heart.

Education Basics

Professional photojournalists agree that a great place to learn from the bottom up is at the high school paper, where many award-winning professionals were first introduced to most sports. There you learn how to shoot baseball, football, basketball, field hockey, and other sports. It is also important to enjoy and learn from the work of other professionals you meet at local games.

Climbing the career ladder requires the traditional route of learning your craft and getting constant practice to become very proficient. You can earn an impressive degree in photojournalism from a number of schools, such as Ohio University and the University of Missouri. But many editors and experts advise that a full four-year program in photojournalism is too much and perhaps unnecessary. They would rather look at a candidate with writing talent and a degree in journalism who can think analytically, than at someone who is exclusively a photojournalist. Most of the hundreds of university journalism programs include a full complement of photojournalism courses that many employers prefer.

Timothy S. McCarty, a professional sports videographer (television photojournalist) based in Cleveland, graduated with a bachelor's degree in telecommunications (TV, radio, and film) from Kent State University in Ohio. With a minor in English, advertising, and photography, he developed writing skills that helped him in the television business. This background gave him a unique ability to understand conceptually both of the basic elements of television's production process: editorial content and the technical tools (cameras, editing equipment, etc.). He believes, "A thorough understanding of both areas makes for a better professional."

Although he was able to enter the fast track in this profession by parlaying a love of photography and basic writing skills with hard work, Michael Mercanti does not think you can become successful today with only technical knowledge. He now knows that you must have a college journalism/English education that includes significant photojournalism courses if you expect to be one of the better photojournalists in the business. He advises aspiring photojournalists to obtain a complete journalism education because of its obvious long-term value and the great potential it provides. This type of curriculum also equips you to develop and write a sports feature story or breaking news story, if needed. Magazine editors and newspaper sports editors in the smaller markets appreciate well-rounded photojournalists who give them that option. At small publications, it is much less expensive to have one multitalented professional to do an illustrated feature or series than to send both a sports reporter and a photographer on an assignment.

In his junior year, David Bergman became a photojournalism major at the University of Miami (the major is called Photocommunications as part of the School of Communications). He agrees that for those hoping to become career photojournalists, a degree in journalism, communications, or photocommunications is important. "You must be a journalist first and a photographer second," he observes. "Anyone can learn how to properly expose a piece of film; but only a journalist can communicate a story, whether through pictures or words. Of course, actual photography classes are necessary. By studying the masters, you'll see what the profession is all about. Even in this age of digital cameras and film scanning, before you can properly expose the film you must know what the image should look like when it's finished."

Getting Your Talent Noticed

Whether you are a high school or college student or an inexperienced, forty-year-old accountant who loves photography, there are opportunities in any small town and big city to become a sports photographer. David Bergman suggests that, "the most practical and realistic way to learn about the business is to meet professionals. Most photographers need assistants and you may be able to help, whether by carrying heavy equipment or filing negatives in the office. At the same time," he says, "you should shoot, shoot, and shoot some more. As you build your portfolio, research opportunities for internships."

Fine photography must gain the experts' attention. Great photos cannot help but get noticed. When an award-winning action photo by a freelancer or a cameraperson at a suburban newspaper is published, photo editors at nearby major metropolitan papers see and remember it. Photo editors know the best photographers in their areas and keep a watchful eye for applicants at their newspaper or magazine. Remember that you never know who is looking at your work.

Some photo editors take the time to compliment, via phone or note, the work of an up-and-coming photojournalist at another publication. Your work, good or mediocre, is on display. No matter where you work, assume that each photo is an audition for a major sports magazine or newspaper sports section. An outstanding photo can be an entry into the big time, just as a poor picture can make you a forgettable applicant.

Another way to sell talent and potential is the photo contest, in which newcomers can compete against the major metropolitan staff. Monthly contests are also held by many state press associations and frequently are won by a freelancer or a little-known amateur. To gain maximum exposure, enter your best photos each month in the sports category of these contests.

The Wire Services

The wire services, such as Associated Press (AP), Knight Ridder, Scripps Howard, and Bloomberg News are always on the lookout for good sports photographers. If you display better-than-average talent, they may initially hire you on a freelance basis for a specific assignment. Wire services also hire staffers to process film before making them full-time photojournalists. Later, they may be assigned to a few innings or a quarter of a game until the photo editor has sufficient confidence in their abilities to want them on the field for the whole game.

The sidelines at the University of Miami football games is where David Bergman began to meet some of the veteran photographers from the *Miami Herald,* AP, and United Press International (UPI). "One day, the UPI photo chief asked if I might be interested in doing some stringing. I jumped at the chance; my first work outside of college. It was a great learning experience; on-the-job training to complement my education."

Seizing Opportunities

Dave Coskey has been involved in a variety of sports journalism pursuits from photo internships, to sports information, to professional public relations, to administration of an NBA team. He offers this advice: "Make opportunities to talk to photojournalists on the sidelines of high school and college games. Find out about the business from them, how they learned to shoot, and what tips they have for different photo opportunities. Most professionals are very helpful, especially if they sense that you're really serious about wanting to know."

Often questions can lead to an unforeseen opportunity. From his UPI experience and an impressive portfolio, David Bergman gained the confidence to attempt the step up to AP. Each morning, he called the bureau chief to see if he had anything for him, with little success. Finally, after six weeks, he was offered an assignment in Key Largo, sixty miles south of Miami. Maybe none of the staffers wanted to bother with the trip, and he got it by default. "But, I didn't care," he recalls," I was just happy for the opportunity."

The story was about an "aquanaut," who was finally coming up after living underwater for three months. "I worked every angle I could think of," Bergman says. "When I returned to the office, they edited a frame and transmitted it on the wire. I didn't think too much of it." The next day, to his surprise, his picture ran in *USA Today*. "I bought ten copies!" he says. "The AP chief also called and gave me an assignment to shoot Don Shula, the *Miami Dolphins* head coach."

After a year of steady work for AP, management at the *Miami Herald* saw Bergman's work on the wires and liked it. They wanted him to work in one of their regional "Neighbors" offices twice a week, and he happily obliged. He covered local features, buildings going up, and "pet of the week" types of assignments for about six months until he was transferred downtown. A year later, he was hired as part-time staff, and two years later as a full-timer. The rest, as they say, is sports photojournalism history.

The Impact of Modern Equipment

"It's very important to be comfortable with computers," David Bergman observes, "and technology in general. Technology is certainly changing the business. My philosophy is to embrace the technology and not fight it. I'd rather be on the cutting edge, helping to shape the equipment of the future, instead of just reacting to what equipment developers decide."

The intrinsic, fundamental skills of photojournalism are particularly apparent today, with the advent of auto-focus lenses and superior equipment. Ten years ago, you had to have a great feel for the mechanics of the cameras to get great shots of a crucial play that were sharp and tightly framed. Now, everybody can do that. The action focus is better because the camera does it. For peak action, you just have to be positioned for the best angle, and the cameras will capture it. But the really thoughtful, ideal images are what's in the mind of the photographer. Anticipation and decisions about camera location and subject matter are what separates the best photographs from the common ones. Photo editors may examine 500 images to find ten that are superlative.

During a typical pro football game, a cameraman will shoot ten to twenty rolls of 36-exposure film. Only five to eight frames of those may find their way into a large newspaper sports section. Most of the film is used in anticipation of shots. For example, when a punt is about to occur on a fourth down, one of the normal shooting tricks is "running" behind the punter for the clearest angle on a possible block. Every punt, you have to run fifteen or twenty yards to get behind the punter, get focused, and then shoot frames of him kicking because one of those frames may end up with a blocked kick. You lose lots of film on just the punts, knowing you will never use it.

For the record, budding photographers should know that darkroom skills are no longer a requirement for the sports professional on staff at a major newspaper. The trend of modern technology is toward digital photography, minimizing the need for film developing. Film is still used, but it is scanned and processed digitally. It is helpful for photographers to have some knowledge of this technology, which can be acquired in college photojournalism courses.

Film vs. Video Photography

Despite the differences in the production and visual aspects of film and video, the film photographer and the video cameraperson (videographer) both perform their skills at athletic contests, documenting the live event. To be effective, both need to be familiar with the technical aspects of the sport and its players, and both require field access to get the shots. Videographer McCarty thinks the rewards are also similar. "In live television, I still get a thrill out of putting my personal stamp on a game," he said. "During any broadcast, the director talking into my headset is not telling me what to shoot. He can't; there's simply no time. In every game, there are numerous occasions when I shoot without being directed, which adds production value to the final product that the director didn't expect. That is a thrill for me. As the videographer, I'm expected to know my assignments before the game and provide the camera work without the director having to ask."

The biggest difference between film and video photography is that video shot for broadcast is copyrighted by Major League Baseball, the NBA, and so on. "The television cameraperson does not own the rights to the 'pictures, descriptions or accounts of the game,'" explains McCarty. "Still photographers, on the other hand, do own the copyright to their photos and can sell rights to their use."

McCarty estimates that as an independent contractor he has videographed approximately 2,500 live sports broadcasts. "I think I have the best seat in the house," he said, " and the best job in the world as a freelance television sports cameraman." To date, he's shot three Super Bowls; four World Series; four U.S. Open golf tournaments; and two Ryder Cups, including Valderrama, for a variety of national and international broadcast networks.

Aspiring videographers should note that in sports television and production, most of the technical and engineering positions (e.g., camera operators, videotape people, audio technicians, directors, and producers) are independent contractors (freelancers), not permanent employees. "Positions for staff camerapeople on network television are dwindling because they require high overhead for the network to maintain," explains McCarty, who runs his own production company (Commando Productions). "Like many businesses, it's now a matter of outsourcing labor."

Heavy travel is another fact of life for television camerapeople. According to McCarty, "For some sports freelancers, 180 days away from home in planes, hotels, and cars is normal." If you hate to travel, freelancing in this field may not be for you.

Although Ray Didinger of NFL Films was a sportswriter/columnist for most of his career, he thoroughly enjoys his recent move to the exciting world of film and video. "When it all fits together, the pictures, the interviews, and the music, it can be very powerful, very great," he said. He recently wrote and produced an NFL Films Emmy Award–winning film that his company produced for the TNT cable network called Football America. It won the television Emmy in the "Best Sports Special" category. Didinger said that it "was very gratifying, a tremendous satisfaction to see it after its final assembly on the screen."

Favorite Sports to Shoot

In the opinion of some experts, basketball is the easiest of the major sports for the average photographer to shoot. With a minimum of experience and talent, you can get high-quality photographs. To some, football, hockey, and baseball provide fewer opportunities for good action photos.

Typically, photojournalists favor the challenge of an exciting football game. Football can provide a series of battles for the best position and the best shot. You either capture that moment and win the battle, or miss and see the winner's pictures in a rival publication. The best photographers in the business estimate that there are probably ten to fifteen crucial plays in the course of a good football game, and you know at the end of it whether you have one, five, ten, or all fifteen.

David Bergman enjoys shooting football because of its frequent movement, unlike baseball which has much less "peak action." In football, you must anticipate what is about to happen so you can be ideally positioned in the right place. "For example," he remarks, "if you know one team has a good defense and the other team likes to run the ball, you may want to shoot on the sideline behind the line of scrimmage to get the quarterback getting sacked or the running back getting hit for a loss. Of course, if they complete a pass downfield you'll be out of the picture. You can't always be right, but you can increase your odds by knowing the game."

Photographers of baseball must have a special talent to be quality shooters. Anyone, it seems, can focus on second base and get the play that develops there. Anyone can focus on the batter and get the swing. But to get superlative baseball shots, you have to be expert enough to anticipate the action that is about to happen.

This expertise is what usually separates the best camerapeople from their peers. Michael Mercanti credits one of his competing colleagues at the *Philadelphia Inquirer*, Jerry Lodriguss, with that innate skill: "He used to speak of the zen of football, the zen of the sports. Even though I wouldn't call it that, he's right that a lot of sports photographers have it in their heads. They have the talent, the dexterity, and the knowledge of when to shoot. It's almost as if there's a mind game going on between the photographer and the action that will eventually occur before him or her. It's true that the outstanding photographers are in a different world. Every time you open their newspapers, you see that they nail it consistently."

Sometimes, the photojournalist becomes the news. Perhaps the most recent example of this was when Eugene Amos, Minnesota Timberwolves videographer, filmed NBA basketball action from the sideline. When we asked experienced cameramen about their feelings concerning the infamous 1997 incident in which Dennis Rodman of the Chicago Bulls kicked Amos in the groin after diving out of bounds for a loose ball, we heard "a real cameraman's confession" from Tim McCarty. "If Rodman kicks me in 'that area,' you can bet a bottle of hair color I would hold out for more than the $200,000 Amos allegedly took from him as a settlement. As a professional sports camera operator, I don't know which got me more upset, Mr. Rodman's misguided thinking that money, fame, and his self-proclaimed, 'Bad As I Wanna Be' image entitles him to feel he's immune to common decency; or the cameraman he kicked settling for the pittance Rodman tossed his way so quickly like a glorified handout.

"Hey, Dennis," McCarty adds, "don't kick the messenger! We're the guys showing off your latest tattoo and hair color combo to the rest of the civilized world. Had I been on the receiving end of Dennis's Converse All-Star, I would have simply asked Mr. Rodman for a public apology. If he's incapable of admitting in public he lost his cool in the heat of the moment, then I would threaten him, his employer the Bulls, and the NBA with the indignity of a public hearing until The Worm squirms enough and offers an apology in front of the same number of people who witnessed the kick itself. If Mr. Rodman still insists his image is more important than decency, well, then sorry pal, my damaged pride is worth much more than $200,000. At least when I donate my settlement, after legal fees and taxes, to a worthy charity, I'll have a clean conscience."

A Photojournalism Icon

Charles M. Conlon was the foremost baseball photographer of his or any time, immortalizing the sport's greatest players. It was he who captured the tough and friendly visage of Babe Ruth we have seen so often. "Ruth was easy to picture," Conlon wrote, "and yet sometimes very hard. Most batters have a certain arc through which they swing, and you can set yourself for them. But you couldn't rely on the Babe swinging according to Hoyle. Most of the pictures we took of Ruth turned out to be excellent rear views."

Conlon's memories bring back a gentler, simpler sports era. "I have seen baseball change, though not so much. I have seen the player type change. From wooden stands to steel and concrete stadiums; from crowds of 5,000 to jams of 77,000; from the days when Matty [Christy Mathewson] got $7,000 to the days when Ruth got $80,000—well, it's been fun and it's been thrilling."

Salaries

Full-time opportunities in this business most often become available in new, start-up publications or through internships, as opposed to with established companies. The new media in sports also present growing, unique opportunities for the photojournalist, as explained in Chapter 14. Staff photojournalists' salaries, of course, vary by location, circulation size, and experience.

Timothy McCarty says that "freelance salary rates between still photographers and videographers are similar in structure. An experienced videographer can earn the television standard rate of between $250 and $350 per ten-hour day, plus expenses." Rates for freelance professionals are somewhat higher than those of permanent staff personnel because they seldom receive any benefits, such as medical coverage. Rates vary depending on whether the job is for a local station or for a major network, the latter usually paying higher rates because they require union affiliation. Unions and professional guilds maintain staff photographer salary standards that vary among cities similar to those for newspaper guilds (see Chapter 2 for salary information for professional photojournalists and reporters at newspapers and wire services that are members of The Newspaper Guild).

In areas without union or guild salary contracts, it is up to management and the individual photojournalist to negotiate a satisfactory arrangement. Often, classifications and salaries are a function of the experience and the photographer's skill in camera techniques, advanced lighting, and editing. Newspaper photographer salaries usually range from lower levels of $600 to $800 weekly to veterans earning between $800 and $1,300 weekly.

Freelancing

Freelance photojournalism is a full-time career for many professionals. For others, it is a way to earn extra income and to have their work seen in a variety of markets by potential employers. Then there is the plight of the young person trying to enter the field using freelancing, not so much to make money, but to impress photo editors. In any case, freelance photojournalism is the best approach for showing your talent to photo editors. Sports photographers who make their living as freelancers have built up relationships over time with the major sports magazines, newspapers, and agencies, and they receive assignment calls on a regular basis.

David Bergman's advice is that because each newspaper is different, the best way to secure freelance work from a newspaper or magazine is "to request an appointment to display your portfolio. Look and act as professional as possible; be willing to shoot anything. Be persistent, but not a pest, and you may get some work eventually." Also, local newspapers often receive calls from out-of-town publications and agencies looking for freelancers. "If you are in their good graces and they trust your work, you may get a recommendation," Bergman adds.

To grow as a freelancer, you should ask high school coaches for access to the sidelines and offer to give them reprints of shots they like. In that way, you can hone your talent and become involved in that school's program. Although it will not be a staff job at a paper, it could help you develop your eye, experience enjoyment, and earn freelance fees as well. The key is to master the craft, and eventually the markets will come. Soon you can take your next batch of photos to the local weekly newspaper and, if they are good enough, a photo editor may want to use them.

Freelancers are important to newspapers and magazines because they attend events and go to locations that staff photographers cannot cover. Not too many freelancers become wealthy at photography, but if they are proficient and work hard, they can gradually increase their skills and the number of clients they serve. In order to stay in business, most good sports freelancers must also work at general news assignments.

Normally newspapers pay freelancers by the job or assignment instead of by the photo, except at the very small papers. Typically, a frequently used photographer is paid between $75 and $125 for a job; $50 to $75 if they are used only occasionally. Like any service industry, two people can do the same job and charge very different fees. Simple public relations photo shoots may pay as low as $150, whereas a Nike ad may pay as much as $5,000 a day.

Memorable Sports Shots

All photojournalists have favorite photos of which they are proudest. The picture the great Charles Conlon took of Ty Cobb stealing third at the old Hilltop ballgrounds of the New York Yankees is rated one of the greatest baseball action photographs in the history of the game.

Philadelphia fans loved the Charlie Hustle game that Pete Rose played every day of his career, especially when he performed in a Philadelphia Phillies uniform. The most memorable example of his energy was the enduring photo taken by Norman Lono during the 1980 World Series. Lono, a staff photographer for the *Philadelphia Daily News,* was stationed with twenty other photographers in the camera box beside the home dugout. All of them had the same camera lenses; all anticipated the same kind of plays. The Phillies were ahead in the bottom of the ninth inning, one out, with this crucial game on the line.

All of a sudden, a foul fly ball dropped directly toward the dugout. Lono was the only one with a wide-angle-lens camera around his neck and therefore the only one who could shoot Rose in the opponents' dugout catching the ball for an out that Phillies catcher Bob Boone bobbled. The play was right in front of Lono but what really made the picture outstanding was that he had anticipated something like that and had the lens ready to shoot it. "There's no feeling so helpless as having the wrong lens, knowing that you can't use your camera, and just watching that ball fall in front of you," Michael Mercanti says. Because of that one play, many photographers now "wear" a seldom-used, wide-angle lens just in case.

Although he finds it difficult to take interesting baseball photos, David Bergman considers a shot he took at the 1997 World Series one of his most exciting. It was a storybook finish to a season in which his local team, the Florida Marlins, won it all. He got a picture of Craig Counsel crossing the plate for the winning run in the bottom of the eleventh inning of Game 7 in Miami. "What I love about it is that in the background, you can see about 100 fans on their feet, hands in the air, screaming as loud as they can," Bergman smiles. "This was a moment like I've never experienced; 65,000 fans in that stadium screaming like there was no tomorrow. Every time I look at that picture, I remember being there. For the rest of my life, I can say I saw that game and documented it on film."

The picture he took was enlarged to fill almost the entire front page of the *Miami Herald* the next morning. Its impact helped to sell an additional 70,000 copies. "It was a great feeling to know I'd nailed it," he says.

13 Writing About Sports Business

Sports business writing is a good way to get into sports journalism, because there are not many writers doing it. A lot of reporters just like to go cover the games and take their free meal. That is fine; it is a nice life. But if you develop a sports business story that is done well, it will be picked up and published in papers all over the country—and even the world.

Scott Newman
Sports business writer, Bloomberg Wire Services

Will the top sports story of the year be the Chicago Bulls winning another NBA championship or another power hitter's pursuit of Mark McGwire's single-season home run record? Or will it be that NBC secured the right to televise the Olympic Games through 2008, or the wide-ranging impact of the NFL's new $17.6 billion television contracts with Fox, CBS, ABC, and ESPN?

We will remember the late 1990s as a time when sports and business became equally important to the sports fan. We now see that sports is an important subject in the news and business sections of publications, and business is an integral part of the newspaper sports section of the paper.

When we were younger, many of us received our sports news by reading about how the games were played, the exploits of our athletic heroes, and the results of competitions in box scores. But, in recent years, we have been deluged with as much information on team franchises, player contracts, and sports legal issues as on the game itself. Modern fans know that sports is not only fun, it is *big business*. "Sports and business are now one," confirms Andrew Brandt, sports attorney/agent for Woolf Associates, a sports management and marketing firm.

Bill Carter, television/business writer for the *New York Times* writes many stories on the business of the media and television. He says that real sports fans are now much more sophisticated about these subjects, and they know how their teams are affected. "Because television money is now fueling so much of sports business, there are many issues I can explore and write about," he said. "I'm a sports fan, so it gives me an excuse for doing what I like. I can become much more a part of the whole sports scene. Since I like watching sports events, it's a way for me to stay connected to the sports industry by reporting on its television and business aspects."

Some writers, such as Jeffrey Pollack, former editor of *The Sports Business Daily,* see sports as an entertainment industry. "Whenever I see an athlete like Dennis Rodman sign a deal to star in a major motion picture, that is exciting," Pollack says. "Some of the most interesting stories are when we see athletes on television talk shows or appearing on sitcoms. We watch those as well."

To others, sports business writing is about reducing a complicated subject to an easy read for sports fans. Scott Newman, sports business writer for Bloomberg Wire Services, explains, "If you can understand the subject, you can make the complex business story fun for readers. For example, although many newspaper readers do not have a tremendous amount of business knowledge, they'll enjoy the story we write about how CBS may turn a profit of $100 million at the Winter Olympics. Our story has to be interesting by explaining that although the network pays $300 million for the advertising rights, they turn a nice profit by selling television advertising."

A growing number of sports journalists find that the unique field of sports business writing is as rewarding as reporting on the games themselves. Although there are many similarities between this profession and conventional sportswriting, the focus and subjects differ. This new profession has spawned radio programs, Internet websites, business and cultural newspaper sections, and university curricula dedicated entirely to the business of sports.

The World of Sports Business Writing

When you look outside the white lines of a sports field, you see and read a plethora of stories, facts, and statistics about players, owners, and businesspeople, which many fans also crave. Readers' interest levels have risen greatly with the prominence of the economic aspects of salaries, stadiums, television, and so on that proliferate throughout the sports world. Those who make a living writing about sports business find their information in the most unlikely places. Here is a sampling of subjects:

- *The business of television.* Modern, mature sports fans understand that "if they're going to root for a team, they have to pay attention to the economics of their franchise," says Bill Carter, "because how much money it's taking in via television and other business dealings helps determine who their team can employ. There are certain teams that obviously can't keep their players, because they do not make enough money."

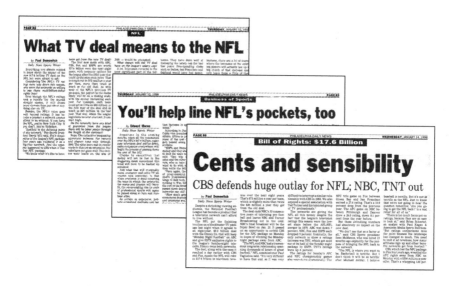

- *Athlete criminal behavior and immorality.* Although this subject does not sound like business, it is. The police blotters of small and large communities are fertile fields of sports information. There you can learn about the off-the-field activities of the Sprewells, the Barkleys, and the Irvins.

- *Sponsorships.* We now seem to have an appetite for all of the contract negotiations that franchises, athletes, and coaches have with sports companies to market their product. Readers and businesspeople need to know who is wearing what product name or logo on their shorts and jackets and which sneaker company has signed a licensing deal with what college to wear its shoes on the field next season.

- *Personal services contracts.* Which professional coach or athlete has signed a long-term contract with which bank and for what services?

- *Player affiliations.* Which of our favorite pro players, coaches, and even many college teams are in the stables of which sneaker companies?

- *Name recognition sponsorships.* It has become very important to banks, computer firms, and other companies to buy the rights to have their corporate names adorn major playing arenas and stadiums, as well as broad categories of consumer products. Did you know that Compaq computer signed a sponsorship deal with the NCAA and is now known as the "Official Computer of the NCAA Championships"? It only cost the company a little more than $10 million for the privilege.

- *Agent activity.* Many fans now read as much about the activities of and advice from these player representatives—good and bad—as about the athletes they represent.

- *Broadcast and print media.* Learn about the players' broadcasting careers and the books and columns they "write." Read about the latest colossal television contracts for professional sports and Olympic events.

- *Websites.* Fans can now read the life stories of Michael Jordan and golf phenom Tiger Woods on CBS SportsLine (http://cbs.sportsline.com/) and hundreds of others on their own special Internet websites. You can even "chat" with the stars and buy clothing and souvenirs bearing their names and numbers with just a click of your PC mouse.

- *Stadiums and arenas.* Details about attendance figures, no-shows, and economic statistics abound focusing on sales of tickets, corporate suites, and luxury boxes.

- *Salaries.* Information on player incomes from personal contracts and endorsements is readily available to interested fans.

- *Business transactions and takeovers.* If high finance is your bag, you can research and write about such sports subjects as takeover bids and franchise transfers.

- *Free agency and player rights.* There are sensationally larger salaries resulting from antitrust cases and collective bargaining. Who would have imagined ten years ago that the most discussed aspect of pro sports—specifically the NBA and NFL—would be something as boring and complicated as salary?

This extensive range of ever-changing subjects to be reported on is only a sampling of topics to pique your interest.

The Hunt for Stories

Sports business story lines such as those listed in the previous section come from a variety of sources, depending on the publication. Some, like the ones in *The Sports Business Daily,* are taken from the news wires, television, newspapers, and the Internet. Many other publications ferret out material by investigating tips from people in the business, examining public records, and sometimes conducting secretive interviews.

Scott Newman's ideas come from many places, but wire services, business contacts, including sports franchise owners, are helpful starting points for him. "It helps us because when you go to the people who have the power—the general managers, the presidents, the owners—that is where the business stories come from, not the players," Newman reminds us. "Sometimes, I'll just look around the business and sports world to find a story. For example, I found that there were a lot of college basketball coaches getting raises last year, mostly because they were having job discussions with other schools that needed coaches. It piqued my interest, and I looked into it. I found out how many millions of dollars colleges were shelling out to coaches they already had under contract for lesser salaries."

The Skills You'll Need to Succeed

Employment opportunities for sports business writers are not often found in the Sunday newspaper want ads alongside those for computer engineers. This one appeared on the Internet and suggests the typical skills required for this career field:

> Sports business writer: Ability to write under deadline pressure and during early morning hours a must. One year writing PR a minimum. Must understand the business side of the sports industry, have entrepreneurial instincts and be Internet savvy. Must have car and be a team player. If you are just a sports fan, please do not apply. Salary: commensurate w/experience.

As with most of the professions we address in this book, sports business also demands that newcomers exhibit a talent for writing. Kellee "Sparky" Harris, owner of MarketSpark, explains that if you cannot communicate well in writing or speaking, you are at a major disadvantage. As is the case in other sports journalism fields, the sports business climate is constantly changing. According to Harris, "You have to think on your feet and be able to communicate clearly."

Although he agrees that writing and communication skills are vital, Andrew Brandt offers this approach to becoming a sports business writer: "Read everything possible about sports business, and by that I mean collective bargaining agreements of the four major sports leagues, contracts and salary caps, free agency, and franchise relocation. You have to look hard for all the literature that is available, but to be able to write about it, you have to be knowledgeable about it." However, he is not necessarily referring to practical experience beyond the conventional sports pages but more to reading the business section as a source of knowledge, to become familiar with terminology and current events in the field.

Writing sports business for wire services differs from standard reporting and investigative reporting. Scott Newman says that "in writing investigative stories for television, I would spend a month or two on a project, but not here. We are just at the incubation period of the sports wire, and I'm not able to take a month for a story." If you write for a wire service, you have to be quick and accurate in telling your story.

Brandt suggests a labor relations background could be helpful. With ProServ, he helped represent Michael Jordan, Patrick Ewing, Boomer Esiason, and many other top NFL and NBA players and has also worked as a general manager of the Barcelona Dragons of the World League of American Football (now called NFL Europe).

In comparing the different writing styles used for sports television or business and for normal sportswriting, Bill Carter says, "I think the approach is totally different. I'm writing for the financial world and page one readers. Reporters covering the games know instinctively that their audience understands what they are writing about. Instead of that, I'm writing for the general audience, so I have to make sure I explain exactly what is going on. I can't automatically say 'Michael Jordan' and assume they'll know who it is, because that is also the name of the CEO of CBS."

Becoming Knowledgeable

Sports business writers tend to have varied educational backgrounds. Jeffrey Pollack is a graduate of Northwestern University with a bachelor's degree in journalism. Most daily business publications require writers to have degrees in communications, journalism, or liberal arts in addition to some familiarity with business.

Bill Carter graduated from the University of Notre Dame with a bachelor's degree in English. After receiving a master's degree in journalism from Pennsylvania State University, he was hired by the *Baltimore Sun* newspaper to work on the copy desk, which he did for a while. For several years after that, he was assistant foreign editor at the *Sun*, but switched to writing about television sports in the late 1970s and continued in that role for over ten years. He was hired by the *New York Times* as its chief television writer. Many of his stories concern the business of the media and television.

"Anyone who wants to be a writer should focus on getting the broadest possible education," said Carter, "and later narrowing their sights to specific areas. It does not make much sense to me to only pay attention to sports or to business. You need to have as broad a range as possible, because that gives you more flexibility. I wasn't a journalism major, I was an English major.

"Frankly, for me getting a master's degree in journalism was strictly a way to make business contacts," he adds. "I didn't do it to learn anything. You learn journalism by doing it. If you're interested in any kind of sports business career, learn all kinds of economic background, which is much more important than, for example, taking specialized courses in sports marketing."

One of Pollack's recent interns, Josh Zeide, majored in philosophy and African-American studies at Emory University in Atlanta and is currently studying at Georgia State University School of Law.

Another pro who exemplifies the variety of skills and opportunities you can master in this business is Brandt, who does considerable sports business writing for his website and for Woolf Associates. His firm represents such personalities as Tom Glavine of the Atlanta Braves, David Wells of the New York Yankees, and Grant Fuhr of the St. Louis Blues. Brandt describes himself as a sports attorney/agent, with responsibilities that include representing athletes, negotiating contracts, and marketing clients to sponsors. He graduated from Stanford University and earned his law degree at Georgetown University. He recommends adding law courses to your academic curriculum.

A question you may be pondering now is, "Do I go to law school, business school, or a college that offers sports management?"

"I'd never tell anyone not to go law school because it is such a big discipline," Brandt says. "But if you're interested in a sports-related career, the only curriculum choice of your whole three years in law school is the one-time class, Sports Law. Unfortunately, there is no magic formula to getting into sports business writing. Learn what you can and try to gain experience in whatever way possible." Sports management programs offer many different options applicable to sports, such as facility management, marketing, and others beyond the legal side. Business school offers other disciplines, but only one or two classes will be devoted to sports.

Scott Newman majored in journalism at Northeastern University in Boston, but now that he has made sports business his career, he wishes he had majored in business. A writer interested in this field would do well to become comfortable with many subjects. Newman, for example, admits, "I'm a sportswriter who does not listen to sports talk radio. Instead, I turn to the other news sections, such as business, before sports."

Internships

Internships are available in a variety of sports businesses to let you get involved and learn the ropes. However, Andrew Brandt advises newcomers to avoid focusing on the glamorous side of the field, such as representing athletes, at this stage because that is just a small part of the sports business. Better starting points and internship targets include the following:

- Minor league franchises
- Major league organizations
- Unions for the major sports
- Sports syndicates

Look past the obvious in terms of sports business careers and find where you can best employ your writing skills.

Expect to be working at all sorts of tasks while you learn the business: ticket sales, public relations (PR), facilities, leases, arena management, and so on. "When there is a job to do, just raise your hand and jump in," suggests Brandt, "whether it is in selling tickets or marketing surveys."

Experts claim the best thing to do is just jump in with both feet, because that helps you get noticed in many different areas. You may fancy a job with the New York Yankees, but although it would be a great experience, Brandt says if he were looking for someone to hire, "it would be someone who worked for a minor league baseball team, because those organizations are so small that you would have learned to do everything: contracts, merchandising, sponsorship and licensing, PR, and ticket sales and budgeting. Conversely, with the Yankees, your job might be as simple as helping the assistant ticket manager with sales and group seating, proofreading copy for a new radio commercial, or hyping an upcoming home stand."

Jay Beberman hires interns for training and productive writing on an average of two or three each summer. They are usually journalism majors with a knowledge of sports. Now and then a talented intern is rewarded with a full-time position on graduation.

Jeffrey Pollack bemoans the fact that more students do not make themselves available to publications like his. "We would make good use of those who are qualified," he insists, "but not many present themselves for work." It is possible that this is because his company does not seem to actively advertise these internships, which we also found commonplace in the newspaper business.

Josh Zeide, a recent intern at *The Sports Business Daily*, gives good advice for other would-be interns to follow: "I learned of internship possibilities through due diligence in pursuit of my goal of representing athletes. I found that once you decide what you want, once you go for it, things begin to fall in place. I turned over many stones, and although lots had nothing under them, some led to opportunities."

From his experience, Zeide claims most interns receive no salary because of the transitory nature of the job and the fact that its chief purpose is to give students opportunities to learn and gain hands-on experience. "Certain schools do give credits for internships," he concedes, "but I never went that route. In hindsight, maybe I should have focused on getting some credit. Like many interns, I did odd jobs such as bartending at night for income."

We think all interns deserve to be paid more than just the valuable experience they receive. Many professional organizations do pay a decent wage to interns, who often need to pick up odd jobs to make ends meet. Most interns work quite hard to impress their employers and, whether or not they receive school credits for that work, companies should not take advantage.

Zeide has had internships on and off for about four years with organizations such as the Atlanta Committee for the Olympic Games (ACOG), after which he was hired full time. At ACOG, he negotiated with entertainers, persuading them to come to Atlanta and work without pay for the Olympics. He also interned with the Atlanta Thunder tennis team, the U.S. Olympic Committee, and the Atlanta Sports Council. His ultimate goal is to succeed not as a journalist, but as a sports agent, helping clients pursue professional sports careers.

One of the most practical pieces of advice a young writer can carry into an internship or entry-level position in the sports business field is Zeide's thought that "although the work may be tedious and mindless, there are high-powered people with whom you are interacting and a vast amount of information with which you come in contact."

On the Job

The Sports Business Daily is the first daily trade publication dedicated to the business of sports. Nearly 20,000 subscribers receive essential sports industry news on their terminals while it is still fresh, enabling them to make more informed business decisions. These subscribers include leading sports, entertainment, financial, and media executives, many of whom are referred to in the business as "infopreneurs." Writers compile and write unusual sports stories on such subjects as the following:

- Sponsorships

- Endorsements

- Labor relations

- Licensing

- Team ownership

- Stadiums

- Marketing

- Advertising

- League operations

- Broadcasting

- College sports

- Public policy

The Sports Business Daily is a subsidiary of Street & Smith's Sports Group, which also publishes a weekly print magazine about sports business called *The Sports Business Journal.* Jeffrey Pollack, former editor of *The Sports Business Daily,* managed a full-time staff of four writers, an assistant editor, a media relations manager, and an editor-in-chief. He explained that the major qualification for becoming a successful sports business writer on his staff was writing and communication skills. "We do not do a lot of original investigative reporting, so our writers are not trained journalists for the most part. They're bright, young, eager people who want to get into the business of sports, not necessarily as journalists."

He calls *The Sports Business Daily* a "cover the coverage" publication, which means the staff examine what other media outlets are printing or broadcasting about the business of sports and filter it, summarize it, and condense it for subscribers. "We look at seventy-five major markets, daily newspapers, every day," Pollack says. "We tape about twenty-four hours of television coverage every day, and we search for the most salient pieces of sports business news."

While hundreds of thousands of readers might cross paths with something authored by newspaper and magazine sportswriters, publications such as *The Sports Business Daily* reach close to 20,000. Their readers are mostly managers of professional sports leagues, television network executives, player representation firms, and corporate sponsors. Pollack's background, too, is unlike that of the typical sports journalist in that he previously worked for six years as a communications consultant for corporations, handling crisis management, political management, and image consultation. "A couple of our clients were in sports," he remembers, "but it was about identifying, recognizing, and attempting to solve communication challenges within the sports industry."

Pollack believes that sports runs much deeper than some businesses. "It is really an entertainment business," he said. "As such, it requires a daily trade publication, just as Hollywood has *Variety* and *Hollywood Reporter.*"

Show Us the Money!

It is not surprising that some managers in the business are very uncommunicative about what they pay writers. It seems apparent that income for many is only around $22,000 in what is probably one of the highest per-capita income cities, New York.

Unlike the more conventional sports media, however, sports business writing seems to run the gamut of salary levels. Some of our experts spoke with satisfaction about the incomes they are earning in this relatively new journalistic endeavor, with examples of annual raises that can average between 10 percent and 15 percent per year at some companies—a nice increase for anyone. We are told that you can make a fine salary in the range of $90,000 to $120,000, particularly if you are doing investigative business writing at a network level. On the other hand, the percentage of people who make six figures as newspaper sports reporters in this field is negligible.

Scott Newman says his company "pays well," describing it as one of the few he knows that is a true "meritocracy." He continues, "What has happened at many newspapers is that writers are unionized and not rewarded for breaking stories. Our company does reward us, because when we get our stories placed, they make it a point to praise us, which often translates into higher paychecks." This incentive system seems to pay off because writers want to do better than the competition.

Assignments

Writers in sports business writing should have a love of journalism, sports, and economics. Josh Zeide found his reporting work interesting, especially the investigative projects as opposed to the strictly journalistic pieces. His research focused on the Internet, magazines, television, radio, and in whatever else he could dabble. "Writing about sports business takes a definite understanding of the complex relationships between corporations and society," he says. "It also takes a sound grasp of the sports world and the intricacies involved in business so you can present the two worlds as one."

Zeide describes two enjoyable projects: tabulating the number and length of the television commercials that ran throughout the

NBA Finals and the NHL Stanley Cup Finals. "Although the process was tedious," he concedes, "the compiled information was powerful. When finished and separated into companies and their subsidiaries, you were able to see the influence of certain corporations on the minds of the sports audience. It told us that General Motors ran ten spots totaling three minutes across their many different car lines (Oldsmobile, Buick, and Cadillac) in both halves of an NBA game. If viewers didn't know all the lines the parent corporation owned, it would be hard to know who was pouring the most money into and benefiting the most from sports."

Scott Newman's sports business writing assignments require much of his work to be far from the playing fields. "When I went to the World Series," he recalls, "I went around with the undercover cops in Miami catching ticket scalpers." Another was at the 1998 Winter Olympics in Nagano, Japan, where he did research for a story on Japan's heavy spending for the games. "They were the most costly in Olympic history, estimated at close to $12 billion," Newman notes. "While Americans complain about their property taxes going up a hundred dollars, each household in the prefecture of Nagano is going to incur a much more substantial (about a $30,000) debt. How they'll pay this back, they haven't decided yet. But I think a lot of the Japanese people will see higher taxes coming."

Such stories as these are read by American sports fans in various media, which obtain the Newman stories via his company's wire service. Bloomberg's service is installed in approximately 900 newspapers around the world and its client list includes the New York Times Wire Service. "What I'm trying to do is obviously serve our clients," Newman says, "but more important I'm trying to get stories in papers. I have to do things differently than anybody else."

Bill Carter recently broke an interesting story about "how the recent NFL television deals are probably going to be instrumental in changing the economics of the television networks' relationship to the stations. They're trying to get the stations to pay for much of their costs. That could lead to a big breakthrough in how networks deal with stations. It is an anachronistic system where the networks still pay the stations to carry programs, which seems kind of ridiculous because they also get commercial time. If they succeed in getting considerations for football, I think you will see more and more of this in the future for all of television, so it is sort of a watershed moment."

Where the Pros Started

Scott Newman was a sportswriter covering television sports news until he discovered the excitement of sports business reporting. Previously, he had worked in investigative writing for six years, with WPXI-TV in Pittsburgh and KGO-TV in San Francisco after covering sports for newspapers. He went from writing about Tommy Lasorda and the Los Angeles Dodgers to breaking stories about multimillion-dollar insurance and HMO scams.

For those unfamiliar with wire services such as Bloomberg, Knight Ridder, and Associated Press, these organizations sell their news-gathering and writing services to business and financial newspapers, magazines, and other publications via terminals rented and installed in customers' offices. Newman was hired to enhance Bloomberg marketability by organizing its sports wire to interest client brokers and traders who subscribed for business news. His job entails mostly sports business writing and some hard news-reporting. The financial world's readers are also very interested in sports business, which now is a component of the terminal services.

Jay Beberman is Bloomberg's sports editor, and he has twelve sportswriters in Princeton, New Jersey, and six in the London office. Although most do not focus on the business side of sports, these writers must have a good knowledge of sports and be accomplished journalists, as Newman is. When he was in college, he worked at the *Boston Globe* covering sports but soon became dissatisfied with the problem of covering today's pampered, uncooperative athletes. But he found that he liked breaking sports news stories. After working as a sportswriter for the *Pittsburgh Press* (which went out of business), he decided to try television.

Newman recalled management's goal when he was first approached by WPXI. "They said, 'We'd like you to come over and head up this investigative unit and break a lot of stories,'" he recalls. "I became good at it by sending my stuff out to producers at *Dateline* and *20/20* television shows. I walked into the business, learning as I went along. I did a story that resulted from a tip we had that the box office of the Pittsburgh Pirates' baseball team was scalping All

Star tickets. I convinced the station to give me $1,000 for the research. It took me a couple days to learn the lingo, but I watched this taking place, and then I was able to buy two seats behind home plate for 500 bucks apiece. And the rest made great news.

"I first became interested in investigative reporting," he continues, "when I uncovered improper payments to athletes at the University of Pittsburgh. I had fun doing it, but it becomes a tough act, because the coaches and the players get tired of seeing you and you of seeing them. They do what they can to make your job difficult. Unfortunately, today too many reporters just do not chase news or break stories; they hide them. You can't keep getting beaten down day after day." Hence his move into the field of sports business writing.

As Bloomberg's senior writer on a sports staff of twelve, Newman focuses on business enterprise and investigative stories. Typical of the pieces he's worked on was one about John Spano who tried to buy the NHL's New York Islanders. "Spano said he was worth $250 million, but it was determined that he only had $1.4 million to make the purchase," Newman explains. "I wrote another story on how CBS entertains its top clients; for example, paying $25,000 to wine and dine executives on its most expensive sports junket ever. That is the type of story we do."

"There was a time," says Bill Carter, "when I thought it would be nice to write for a publication such as *Sports Illustrated*, because I always admired their writing style. But interestingly, after a while of writing about television, I realized that on the sports beat, as much as you might like the sport, they tend to become somewhat repetitive."

Advice to the Up-and-Coming

According to Scott Newman, "Sports business writing is a good way to get into sports journalism, because there are not many writers doing it. My advice to young journalists interested in sports business is to start in general news reporting to get your feet wet. Some may say that is a boring job because you might start out doing reports on town meetings, but such research teaches you where and how to look for and find holes in conventional stories and get to the hidden elements of real issues."

14 New Media Sportswriting

*If you live in Riyadh, Saudi Arabia, you can listen to a
New York Giants football game and then use your PC to
call up the New York newspapers and read the
sportswriter's analysis of the game or access the Dallas
papers to hear what they say about the same game.*

Kevin Monaghan
Director of business development, NBC Sports

Are you Web savvy and sports smart, as well as a good writer? If
so, the world of new media may be waiting at your doorstep.
The 1996 Summer Olympics in Atlanta marked the first time a
major athletic event received "on-line" coverage in the homes and
offices of Internet subscribers. For weeks, computer users were able
to watch and interactively participate at the worldwide Games. This
exciting new medium employed the creative talents of a new breed
of sports journalists and photojournalists, although what we enjoyed
on our terminals was the same audio and video we were used to on
our radios and televisions.

NBC, the first to present the Olympics via this newest form of
media, originally presumed that its veteran sports broadcasters and
analysts would easily do all of the writing required for this medium.
Not so! Most of them had not written much in recent years, and

274

some may never have been more than good-looking television faces. Suddenly, they were expected to write the sports and news in actual prose for the text-happy Web. Instead of constantly talking spontaneously at an audience, they now had to develop special material. Most could not do it. But their shortcomings gave rise to a new breed of writer; one capable of meeting the demands of this new order of interactive audiences—new media sportswriters.

The writers anticipated the types of questions we would ask about the Olympics via computer. They developed unique graphics and concocted sports quizzes and challenges to stimulate us and keep us on-line, away from the competing broadcast media. The Information Superhighway became the potential birthplace of thousands of new cyberjournalists.

This chapter focuses on what sportswriters of new media need to know: the character and technology of the Web, its peculiar language and disciplines, and what distinguishes it from writing for the print media. We will learn why the sports journalist needs to add HTML (Hyper Text Markup Language) to his or her professional portfolio. HTML codes create the computer dialect that generates the World Wide Web. It explains to your Web browser what is text, where the links go, where to put pictures, and everything else about the pages of the sports story, release, or advertisement that will appear on the computer screens of millions of sports fans.

Many experts say that, as the wave of the future (and a reality of the present), computers and the Internet are forever changing the news publishing business. While the scope of that change is debatable, it's obvious that millions of Americans are and will be gaining much of their sports news electronically and on-line in a variety of ways. Students and experienced sports communicators must come to grips with this reality and become skilled in its ways, or they may find themselves on an off-ramp of the Information Superhighway rather than part of the traffic flow.

Defining New Media

Ask cyberexperts or teachers of new media journalism to explain "new media" and you may hear a variety of answers. To most, it consists of the following:

- *The Internet* (or the World Wide Web). Media carried on this international communications network includes Web pages, E-mail, mailing lists, and "chat" rooms.

- *Information Superhighway* (cyberspace). Synonymous with communications on the World Wide Web.

- *Multimedia.* Sound, image, and video productions are available on-line or on CD-ROM.

- *On-line newspapers.* Versions of the conventional print media. Some versions are identical to their print news; others provide edited or shortened versions. Many provide news in a format and with content independent of newspapers. Colorful graphics are usually employed with computer hyperlinks (called links) that take readers or subscribers to related stories or websites. *Editor & Publisher* magazine recently listed 1,638 newspapers on the Internet's World Wide Web, and the number keeps growing.

- *News magazines.* Like the on-line newspapers, these provide journalism with a new type of delivery. Some are repeats of popular magazines; others have been created specifically as new media.

- *Websites.* Millions of individuals, companies, teams, and players have created sites on the Web that can be accessed with a simple mouse click; two major ones are Total Sports (see fig. 14.1) and CBS SportsLine. You can easily find Michael Jordan or Tiger Woods, with enough data, history, and insights on each to satisfy even the hungriest fan's appetite. Their sites as well as those of many other sports stars can be found on CBS SportsLine, which is among many sports media companies with similar on-line sports journalism.

Almost all of these are considered journalism because they are the result of news gathering, research, writing, and editing by individuals or news organizations. Most of the larger and widely read new media have significant sports news and commentary, and

Figure 14.1 A typical sports website.

many are devoted to nothing but sports. We will refer to all of this information generically as "new media," but we will focus only on those elements with strong sports content. All of the categories of new media, such as those previously listed, are in constant need of sportswriters, website developers, and editors.

Many observers feel that there is much more hype than reality involved in the world of electronic communications. But when we examine the magnitude of what is out there—being watched by millions of PC and multimedia viewers—we think you will agree that new media is a force to be reckoned with and possibly a career path you will want to set your sights on. Let us define some of the actual publications using sports journalism.

Web publications are often called "e-zines" or "zines" which are short for an electronic magazine you can read on your computer screen courtesy of the Internet. Once it's available on your screen, of course, you can print it out. (You also need a modem on your system and a Web browser [software] to gain access to the Web and its publications.) Many are produced by one person or a small organization for fun or personal enjoyment. Some focus on being offbeat or irreverent for a small audience. Only the more prominent zines seek advertisements or paying subscribers and therefore make a profit with which to pay editors or writers.

We will focus on the larger, profit-making type of sports Web zine, or website that may provide career opportunities for sports journalists.

The Writer's Role

Kevin Monaghan of NBC Sports directs business development for the network as well as new media. "Right now," he says, "new media is a whole new area for journalism, and it draws from all points."

Much of the information that the Internet has processed has been text. The Internet is a writer's medium, because it is much easier to transmit text than it is photos, full-motion videos, or even audio, all of which require more bandwidth. Eventually, modem connection speeds will increase so much that the Internet will be able to support audio as well as it does its text base.

Right now, you cannot obtain video of competitions or games, because it takes so long for it to download. To see a video clip of Emmett Smith running for a touchdown, it might take you several minutes to download the clip, and it will appear jerky. But soon video will flow freely onto our screens. "The beauty of the Internet," says Monaghan, "is that you can have anything you want, anytime you want it."

With so many niches in sports, if you are a slow-pitch softball fanatic, there is probably an area on the Internet where you can reference all the information you can digest. Some writer is paid to make it available. There is an E-mail list called the "Phillies list," and fans interact with each other, including Curt Schilling, who was the National League strikeout leader in 1997 and is an avid sports fan. Columnists, reporters, and fans like Schilling communicate with each other regularly.

New Media, New Techniques

Some on-line publications are geared only toward Web users, and as we will see, new media writing is somewhat different from writing for the school paper or the sports pages of the local daily. Some publishers, however, create electronic versions of the same material you read in hard-copy publications. If you read many of both, the differences will be obvious.

Not much has been written about Web writing styles, but that is the subject of a *Writer's Digest* article (October 1997), in which Lisa and Jonathan Price explain:

> You must write tighter for Web zines than you do for print publications because each chunk of your article appears in a rectangle about the size of a 4 × 6 index card. The poor resolution and tight space mean people do not like to read any more than they have on screen. When you create a paragraph that works well on paper, you will probably have to cut it in half for it to work on the Web. You will need to write in shorter chunks, too, and use more subheads.

Experienced editors who must trim written words to fit available space and broadcast writers who must fit their reports into small, defined time slots are already familiar with the discipline and problems new media writers face in writing about sports for the Web. The same discipline for tight writing applies to developers of websites and home pages. It is similar to writing what you presume is a compact article of 2,000 words for a newspaper or magazine, only to have an editor tell you it will only work if you trim it to 800 words. What a job—cutting so many of your finely crafted sentences that took days to organize. That is what writing for the Web can be like.

Unlike many on-line newspapers, which publish duplicate or shortened versions of sports stories from their print editions, on-line magazines often provide expanded versions of their print copies. Will Wagner was editor of *Inside Sports* magazine, which also had a complete on-line version by the same name, for which he wrote regular sports commentaries. "A few months ago," he recalls "we did an interview with Troy Aikman (Dallas Cowboys quarterback). The story that was turned in was about 5,500 words, but due to space constraints, the print magazine had space for only 3,500 words, so it was trimmed considerably. When the issue hit the newsstand, we posted the complete interview on the on-line magazine's website for readers who wanted to read the complete piece."

Typical On-line Publications

Whether it is on a zine, an on-line newspaper, or a well-read website, you can be sure there are plenty of jobs for writers. It seems that every week there are new on-line publications, many of which specialize in sports or have a significant sports element. A sampling of types of periodicals containing sports focused sections include:

- *Chicago Tribune.* Named the best on-line newspaper by the Newspaper Association of America (NAA). The paper's website was singled out by the NAA (July 22, 1997) for its "keen editorial judgment and an eye to the exploratory habits of on-line readers."

- *InterZine Productions.* A new media studio specializing in the development and distribution of original sports information and entertainment via the Internet and CD-ROM. InterZine was developed to support "info-preneurs" developing unique on-line content. InterZine produces *iGOLF, iRACE, iSKI, SOL* (Snowboarding On-line), *Golfcourse.com,* and *GolfAmerica.*

- *Los Angeles Times.com* (@latimes.com). An on-line version of the newspaper. A sign of these cyberspace times is that its editor's title is "Editorial Director, New Media."

- *@NY Newsletter.* An interactive Web zine/newsletter E-mailed to 18,000 subscribers with all the news of New York City and environs.

- *Sidewalk.* Microsoft's on-line city guide regularly seeks sports and recreation producers and writers for their numerous metropolitan sites such as San Francisco and Seattle. J. D. Lasica, copy chief of Microsoft's *San Fran-*

cisco Sidewalk, explains that the site's writers develop stories for "on-line media based on user feedback, local events, and seasonal activities. The stories are not printed in hard copy. Writers for *Sidewalk* cities all over the country, including sportswriters, must have a solid background in journalism, familiarity with the Internet, keen understanding of a topic area, and an ability to juggle many things at a time."

The following is a cross section of sports-oriented electronic or new media publications:

- *The Sports Business Daily*

- *ESPN Sportszone*

- *PGAtour.com*

- *CNN Auto Racing*

- *Nascar.com*

- *Winston Cup Online*

- *RacingZone*

- *NBC Online*

- *CBS Sportsline*

- *Total Sports*

- *Interactive Journal of the Wall Street Journal*

- *Sportspages* website

Another type of website gaining popularity is that which provides different types of journalists with up-to-date and complete information to help in their writing. One such site is our own, Sportswriting (www.sportswriting.com); another is Sportspages (www.sportspages.com). Both can be accessed by sports fans without charge. Like other such sites that provide comprehensive reference data, the latter site, owned by ABC Radio sportscaster Richard Johnson, charges a small fee for access to full service by sportswriting professionals.

New Media Schools

It is unlikely that you will find a college undergraduate program featuring cybersports journalism or Information Superhighway sports communications. Maybe next year. For the time being, practitioners of this specialized writing field have been and are being educated in more conventional curricula, although not always in English or journalism. Many journalism schools are preparing for or actually teaching courses in new media. Their curricula development efforts are varied, with only a few satisfied that they are the ideal. Some concentrate on the technical aspects (software, graphics, etc.) and others combine traditional journalism with technical considerations.

One of the early pioneers is Columbia University, which has a concentration in new media that emphasizes student projects on-line with some design element (basic HTML and Photoshop software). Increasingly, however, this business and the curriculum that evolves is a composite of design and journalism. Just as it is vital for a newspaper editor to know production, it is essential that on-line journalists understand some of the technical aspects of the field so that they know what can be done.

One expert in new media sports, Mike Emmett, has a bachelor's degree in journalism from Marshall University in Huntington, West Virginia. He is now the managing editor for Total Sports on-line publications. His company provides live sports sites for publications that want their own on-line sports section, such as the *Wall Street Journal*'s site, titled the *Interactive Journal*. While at Marshall, Emmett worked on the student paper and was its managing editor in his senior year. He was the first sports editor on the Web, when he worked with the earliest of the on-line news and sports servers, the *Nando Times*, at www.nando.net.

Tom Watson, coeditor of on-line publication *@NY*, began his formal journalism career at Columbia University writing sports columns about soccer, football, basketball, and baseball for the *Daily Spectator*. High school and college student newspapers seem to be a very common way for sports professionals to get a definitive taste of journalism.

Interns, Interns, Everywhere

Despite the youthfulness of this profession, new media writing businesses have emulated some of the more successful approaches of their print brethren. One is the idea of internships, which we know are beneficial to the employer in terms of receiving productive work for little or no cost, and to the student who receives invaluable training and future contacts, sometimes with a little income. One Web publishing firm, InterZine Productions, invites journalism and marketing majors with enthusiasm for sports to apply for their regular internships.

"There are tons of internships available, some of which pay and some don't," Tom Watson says. He confesses that his publication does not currently pay, "unless you contribute a bylined story. Then it is a whopping $50. But I think the on-line medium has made it easier to break into the field at a fairly high level. And of course, you can always start your own publication nowadays, which is a huge plus."

Mike Emmett reports that Total Sports does not have internships. But he estimates that on-line publications that do pay about $10 to $12 an hour. His alternative to internships for interested writers is to gain entry into the business by first building your own website. There are free hosting services for those interested in such a start and most schools and Internet Service Providers (ISPs) supply some sort of Web space to students. "After you have your own website," he says, "find sports editors and news producers to offer your writing services to for nothing, to prove your skills. Some editors may be willing, and if you get a gig like that, you can build upon it. Someday, you can command a rate such as $200 for a twenty-inch piece."

New Media Job Hunting

"The media possibilities for sports journalists have just exploded," said Kevin Monaghan of NBC Sports. In a survey by Steve Outing discussed in the "Cyberincome" section later in this chapter, 73 percent of the 140 news sites that responded reported adding staff in 1997; almost half of those added five or more employees, indicating that this field is ripe for newcomers.

As one would expect, the Web is the best place to look for employment in new media journalism. There are a number of websites with on-line news mailing lists that advertise for editorial opportunities, such as the following:

- www.planetary.com

- www.siliconalleyjobs.com

- www.newslink.org/joblink.html

- J-Jobs website

As you might expect, professional jobs for new media have new titles and descriptions. Shown below are the types of writing skills that the major new media publications recently advertised in the J-Jobs website and posted to on-line newspapers (we have changed some names to protect the innocent):

> Sports producer: The Bugle.com is looking for a sports producer to help us refocus our sports areas. Successful candidates will have a sports journalism background, strong technical aptitude and a solid sense of Web storytelling. This is not a reporter position, nor is it a webmaster position, although preference will be given to candidates with Web experience, multimedia and scripting skills. HTML skills are a must. We're looking for flexible, enthusiastic, high-energy, forward-thinkers. This position involves night and weekend work.

Typical of the training required for this profession were these requirements specified in an ad for a sports editor placed on the Discussion List for Journalism Education (journet-l@american.edu) by *Student Net*, a national Web publication for college students located in Cambridge, Massachusetts:

> *Student Net* seeks an energetic, obsessed sports editor to help build and maintain a top-notch, national-quality sports section for the company's website (http://www.student.net). The ideal candidate has strong writing and editing skills, can generate story ideas, establish a network of freelance writers, and possesses enough computer and HTML experience to know what works and what does not on the Web. The editor will assign both daily

roundup stories and longer, more conceptual feature articles that will help non-athletes enjoy the world of sports. Experience covering college sports is a must. If you can watch more than one TV during March Madness just to keep up with the games, follow the college bowl games like a diehard fan, and can explain Title IX's intricacies, then this is the job for you.

J-Jobs website is typical of the many journalism-oriented "help wanted" sites all over the Internet. It is a digest of journalism jobs and internships that have been posted elsewhere on the Internet and is therefore ideal for writers exploring this field to either anticipate new media educational requirements or find a position. J-Jobs can be accessed at websites at the University of California at Berkeley Graduate School of Journalism and at Louisiana Tech University. The Web addresses are http://www.journalism.berkeley.edu/resources/jobs/ and http://eb.journ.latech.edu/jobs/jobs_home.html.

New Media Professional Titles

We are used to conventional journalism titles such as sports editor, columnist, beat writer, advertising copywriter, all of which are referred to in other chapters. But here are some new ones to get used to, because they will probably be with us for a long time:

- Sports producer
- On-line content manager
- Director of on-line strategy
- Electronic editor

The latter position, although it could remind you of a computer software title or a science fiction character, is a bona fide job with responsibilities for creating original content, packaging articles and listings for the Web, and coordinating with freelancers. (Many more new media job titles and their average salaries are listed in the "Cyberincome" section later in this chapter.)

Guides for New Media

If you are planning to try your hand at applying for one of these jobs but do not have the actual experience in cyberjournalism, there are instruction books which may help. For example, Mary McGuire has written *The Internet Handbook for Writers, Researchers and Journalists.* It includes all the basics for beginners, as well as a section on developing search strategies and using resources beyond the Web. There is also a chapter for journalists on writing HTML language and designing Web pages. The appendix includes AP's policy on using Internet resources in news stories.

For those writing for Internet publications, Gary Gach has written *Writers.Net (Every Writer's Essential Guide to Online Resources and Opportunities)*. This Internet primer for writers includes basic terminology, a guided tour and an essay that puts the Net in perspective for both new and seasoned "Internauts." He also discusses the new worlds of electronic publishing, interactive and collaboratory writing, Net censorship, and cyberjournalism.

"Getting information from the Internet can be like trying to get a glass of water off an open fire hydrant," Gach warns, "but with *Writers.Net*, writers now have a handbook to help them control the unlimited resources that make up the Internet."

Qualifications

Applicants for these jobs should be careful to think in terms of the technology when applying. For example, if you are a recent journalism graduate, you will get the attention of Mike Emmett, if your resume is *on-line* and you also have your own website with impressive sports writing examples. If you send an editor such as Emmett a hard copy of your resume when applying for a position in his new media publication, the message you will have sent is a negative one concerning your knowledge and understanding of the Internet. The preferred means of communication for this work is E-mail, rather than phones, faxes, or letters.

Many on-line editors want their writers to have a journalism degree, and of course, know sports well. Emmett says, "I do not have time to teach them things like the fact that Marshall University is in the Mid-American Conference (MAC) or how to figure out a batting average."

Where Do New Media Careers Begin?

While this industry is still in its formative stages, there are not many sports journalists who dreamed of being a new media writer from their childhood. Maybe one day they will, but for now those with any experience have come up through the print media ranks.

Tom Watson is the managing coeditor of one of the most popular New York on-line publications. It is called @NY and is a daily on-line publication for New Yorkers containing a variety of news, features, and columns, including sports. Watson gained his interest in newspapers from his father, a production foreman for the Gannett chain. He was also a big sports fan, especially of the '69 Mets, "the defining moment" of Watson's childhood. His mother, an English teacher, taught him how to write a lead and become a decent writer, even in grade school.

His father helped Watson land a stringer's job with Gannett in the sports department, for $14.50 per six-hour night, taking scores on the phone. As a part-time reporter, he won an Associated Press award for a column on a high school wrestler who died in a match and how his teammates dealt with it. After graduation, he took a job as news reporter for the *Riverdale Press*, a 15,000 circulation weekly in the northwest Bronx at $200 per week.

Watson soon became assistant editor, deputy editor, and, finally, executive editor of the *Riverdale Press,* which has won many state and national writing awards; he won a Pulitzer Prize for editing in 1998. In February 1989, another event occurred which he calls a "career galvanizer."

"A terrorist working for the Ayatollah Khomeini [according to the FBI] firebombed the *Riverdale Press* offices because of an editorial we carried on Salman Rushdie's right to publish. It happened on our production day, but we got the paper out anyway, covered our own story even while making international news, and never missed an issue. For that we received the Society of Professional Journalists (SPJ) First Amendment Award."

Watson began to write freelance for the *New York Times* and then discovered the Internet. He still freelances for the *New York Times on the Web.* As Timothy Maloy's article about @NY in *Writer's Digest* explains, "Watson's transition from print journalist to 'new media scribe' has brought him from the ranks of newswriters laboring in the trenches to having a publication all his own." This new media editor says he "was drawn to new media journalism by the fact that suddenly, I owned the printing press." Watson left the *Press* in June 1996, freelancing to pay the bills. He and

Jason Chervokas founded *@NY* in 1995 and have been building it ever since.

Mike Emmett began his career as a newspaper reporter and did a lot of sports freelancing for various wire services and publications. He moved on-line full time in the early 1990s.

Cyberincome

"Wide ranging" would be the best adjective to describe new media income, especially for on-line news and on-line newspapers. In its relative infancy, journalist salaries are far from being standardized.

It seems typical throughout many parts of this growing industry that profitability has not yet been proven, and therefore on-line publications are hesitant to hire and pay experienced sports journalists. We found that hiring young graduates was based primarily on economics and secondarily on computer literacy and Web savviness. On the other hand, new media provides great opportunities for newcomers interested in becoming cybersportswriters.

The new media industry has yet to establish industrywide standards as the newspaper guilds and unions have. In a January 1998 column titled "How Much Should You Pay Your New Media Staff" (underwritten by *Editor & Publisher* magazine), Steve Outing summarizes responses to his survey (returned by 140 sites) on the subject:

> There is a topic on many publishing executives' minds. What do you pay employees in a newly created field where there is not a lot of information to go on about what your competitors are doing? (And probably not a lot of revenue coming in to pay high salaries.) Certainly, the results of this modest survey are far from scientific, but I suspect that you may find them useful nevertheless. At some union papers, the new media operation is covered by the same union as the print editorial staff, so salaries are identical for on-line and print employees.

His survey salaries equated generally with those given in Chapters 3 and 4 and agreed with our other research. The actual results were as follows and should be indicative of what is out there, financially:

Average Annual Starting Rate for Recent College Graduate

	Total	U.S./Canada	Europe
Less than $20,000	15%	9%	23%
$20,000–$23,999	17%	18%	9%
$24,000–$25,999	21%	27%	0%
$26,000–$29,999	15%	19%	9%
$30,000–$31,999	18%	20%	14%
More than $32,000	14%	8%	46%

Average Annual Starting Salary for Recent Graduates Working at Print Publication Sites

	Fewer than 100,000 circulation	100,000–300,000 circulation	More than 300,000 circulation
Less than $20,000	21%	11%	4%
$20,000–$23,999	27%	8%	21%
$24,000–$25,999	18%	19%	21%
$26,000–$29,999	12%	19%	21%
$30,000–$31,999	12%	25%	13%
More than $32,000	12%	17%	21%

Outing found the typical on-line news starting annual salary to be about $25,000 ($31,000 in Europe). He says that "new media managers are earning salaries comparable to their print counterparts." At the lower staff levels of newspaper new media departments, there is not much money to go around. Those with journalism training and experience can command salaries equivalent to that received by print reporters and editors. But there is also a range of jobs involving only HTML coding and site maintenance that pay less. The following survey research shows the variety of job titles in new media as well as salary ranges.

	Percentage of sites paying		
Position	**Less than $35,000**	**$35,000– $55,000**	**More than $55,000**
Vice president	0%	8%	92%
President/CEO/GM/publisher	11%	11%	78%
New media manager/director	13%	24%	63%
Other manager	13%	42%	45%
Editor-in-chief/on-line editor	24%	32%	44%
Programmer/coder	37%	38%	26%
Webmaster	31%	45%	24%
Marketing	23%	57%	20%
Advertising sales	33%	54%	15%
Other sales	71%	14%	14%
Technical support	42%	46%	12%
Other editor	40%	48%	11%
Freelancer/stringer	74%	20%	7%
Writer/reporter	46%	48%	6%
Artist/designer/photographer	44%	50%	6%
Other content developer	64%	33%	3%
Clerical support	84%	16%	0%
Researcher/librarian	89%	11%	0%
Customer service	90%	10%	0%
Intern	100%	0%	0%

(In addition to writing a regular column called "Stop the Presses" for *Editor & Publisher*, Outing is president of Planetary News, an interactive media research and consulting company in Boulder, Colorado.)

Freelancing in Cyberspace

One writer quips that some of the Net publications pay about as well as college newspapers—nothing (or close to it). The best-paid work seems to be in the on-line version of a major publication.

As in the print media, freelancing in the new media is fraught with peril and challenge. There seem to be more opportunities, what with all the lists you can subscribe to that accept writings in all genres, including sports. Too many of the lists that accept and "publish" fiction and nonfiction, however, do not pay the writers a cent. That is also true of print media, in which compensation for freelance articles is sometimes via free copies of the publication or only the "thrill" of seeing your work published. But it is very typical on the Internet that publishers want your hard work for no pay, tempting writers with the idea that when it is "published" on-line, it becomes part of your clip portfolio that you can display to more bona fide print or on-line media. That may be true in a few cases, but genuine publishers are savvy to the concept of unpaid articles and are unimpressed with them for the good reason that those who publish them will publish anything. Furthermore, this demeans the entire freelancing concept of writers selling the product of their knowledge and skill for the enjoyment of readers.

Tom Watson continues to earn extra income by freelancing to reputable Internet zines, such as *Wired,* and print publications, including *Yahoo Internet Life,* which carries some of his sports pieces. He also writes for the Center for New Media at Columbia University and is an adjunct professor at the university.

Major Web zines offer different levels of pay to freelancers. Microsoft's electronic publication, *Slate,* pays $1 per word or more for a variety of article subjects, including sports. *Women's Wire* pays $300 for 500- to 700-word articles on subjects like sports and fitness. This zine targets "well-educated, well-to-do women" and likes writers "who can write cheeky, punchy, fast—with attitude."

Mike Emmett's company (Total Sports) also develops websites, such as the site for Grant Hill of the NBA's Detroit Pistons. "He had a special need," Emmett explains. "Grant wanted us to produce a story on a shooting coach who helped him with his shot last summer. The coach goes by the nickname 'The Shot Doctor.' He lives in New Jersey and I have a stringer up there. So, I called Don Hunt and gave him the assignment. Don has written several books and worked for papers around Philly. He made $200 for one twenty-inch piece."

Note that when most zines pay for an assignment, they are buying nonexclusive and other rights to your work that enable them to use it whenever and wherever they wish.

Advice from Experts

"Visit any Web zine you are thinking of writing for and study it just as you would read through back issues of a print magazine before submitting," advise Lisa and Jonathan Price in their article, "Web Writing."

Tom Watson's comments on journalism and publishing in this media offer sound ground rules for all writers:

1. Write short and punchy for the Web; on-line readers don't like to scroll too much.

2. Think visually.

3. Be open and available to your readers; answer E-mail and snail mail promptly.

4. Get yourself out of the way of the story. Tell the story and serve your readers, not yourself. They will trust you and you can then build a relationship.

5. Do not overwrite.

6. Do not switch jobs every six months. That is the most disturbing trend among young journalists today.

7. Play it straight and check all your facts.

Tangled Tales from the Web

Many of this new breed of journalists got their start from being frequent contributors to the on-line postings on the Web, much of which is devoted solely to sports. Kevin Monaghan remembers finding a new media sportswriter as a diamond in the rough. He describes how Sue Leopold, a Phillies fan from Lafayette College, in Easton Pennsylvania, was discovered as a writer by NBC staff members because of her constant writing of insightful postings about the Philadelphia Phillies' baseball team. "Out of a clear blue sky, they hired her to write a column about baseball for our on-line area because we were very impressed with her," Monaghan says.

In a similar storybook start, NBC found a young writer, David Fischer of Brown University, from his sports posts, for its NBC On-line. "One of his first assignments was selecting 'Athlete of the Day' at the Olympics and writing a daily story for the NBC website," Monaghan explains. Heady stuff for a 22-year old computer sports geek–turned–NBC cybersportswriter.

Tom Watson traveled to Buffalo last year to interview the former Bill's quarterback Jim Kelly for *Yahoo Internet Life* magazine. The story line was to be about the two of them surfing the Net. The story eventually made the cover of the magazine, but almost threatened to be a disaster! They could not get a viable Net connection and Watson, supposedly an expert in surfing, was thoroughly embarrassed. "But we ended up playing catch with the football in Kelly's living room," he laughs. The episode wasn't a total loss because the quarterback paid him a "Good hands, Tom" compliment for his receiving skills.

Mike Emmett (Total Sports) has had his embarrassments, too. At Media Day before the Memorial Tournament in Muirfield, Ohio in the early 1980s, all sportswriters and photographers were invited to play nine holes before the tournament. As Emmett was getting ready to tee off, Jack Nicklaus showed up with a video camera to record the golfers and his playing partner, sports columnist Kaye Kessler, a good friend of Nicklaus. Emmett, who admits to normally being a pretty good golfer, says, "Jack was joking with us as I started to swing, and my first shot went dead smack into the woods. I picked up my tee and said, 'Well, that is enough for today.' Although I skipped the first hole, I still managed to shoot well that day. That night, they showed the video of all our miscues, including mine, at the dinner.

"Later, Nicklaus came over to our table to invite Kessler to play another nine holes, adding, 'You can come along, too, Mike.' But I was afraid I'd choke again and answered, 'Jack, I wouldn't have the nerve to carry your golf bag for nine holes let alone play golf with you!'" Today, Emmett regrets not joining the golfing great, but at the time prevention against possible further embarrassment seemed more important.

Growing Pains in the Industry

Just as other media grappled with questions of journalistic ethics at one time or other during their formative stages, so too do the new media. A major current concern for writers as they consider this profession is the practice of some advertisers to try to affect the content of the on-line media they sponsor. On-line publications depend on advertiser revenue for their existence, and advertisers are assuming a significant role in determining what is written. Print magazines and other periodicals have fought in this ethical "no-man's land" with advertisers for a long time, and now fledgling on-line publishers are experiencing the same pressures. Before you leap into a position in which you may be forced to compromise your journalistic principles, thoroughly research and query publishers to determine their integrity.

The Future

Kevin Monaghan cites an example of the simultaneity of interactive new media, when NBC recently televised a Chicago Bulls–Detroit Pistons basketball game, using a new type of courtside sky-cam that traveled back and forth along the sidelines almost at the players' level. "It was very jarring to viewers," reports Monaghan, "because we probably had not tested it fully. But the point is that we immediately received thousands of E-mail messages from around the country from fans telling us they didn't like it and why."

The Internet offers countless new media opportunities that did not exist five years ago. Currently, print media sportswriters produce their story and sometimes also a radio report, which is easy to do over the Internet now. Soon, they will also do a video report, so on-line viewers can find additional information and links to other data about the game or the team. Many viewers who do not have time to read the print story will enjoy the Net posting done with the reporter's own television camera, which can be the size of a cell phone. That is the sports journalist's completely interactive new media. If you write a controversial column, no longer will you wait a day or two for fan reactions; you will have them microseconds after your report hits cyberspace.

Do not expect the high-tech influence of computers, the Internet, and multimedia to slow very much in the near future. You have to stay abreast of advances, because as you are reading this, hundreds or thousands of infopreneurs out there are attempting to improve the system and create a new market.

An example of this constant change is the influence of multimedia technology on the careers of well-established, professional sportswriters. Currently, to be successful in a major market, you have to be a good sportswriter and unafraid of controversy. Soon, it will be important to be comfortable and effective in multimedia arts. Journalists are and will be required more and more to appear on radio and television. "As the bandwidth on the Internet increases," predicts Monaghan, "reporters will have to communicate via text, audio, radio, and video. Writers will carry make-up kits and combs. They'll have to dress better and become multimedia conscious in everything they do."

15 Freelance Sportswriting

Freelancers are people who have intimate relations with their mailboxes, because that's where their paychecks arrive at painfully erratic intervals.

Tom Mangan
Copy editor, *Journal Star* (Peoria, Illinois)

A freelance sportswriter writes works of nonfiction and fiction in the form of books, magazine articles, or stories for print, electronic, new, or broadcast media. Freelance sportswriting applies mostly to newspapers, print magazines, on-line magazines, radio and television news and features, advertising, marketing, and public relations.

As freelancers, writers are usually self-employed, and many also hold down full-time jobs apart from their writing pursuits. Experienced writers and authors recommend that unless your freelance writing becomes financially stable, it's best to get or keep a day job. Sportswriters operate as freelancers in two essential ways:

- Selling their writing to publications at agreed prices

- Working "for hire" for a company or individual to write, edit, photograph, and so forth for an hourly (or weekly) rate

Freelancing can be enjoyable and fulfilling, as it is to thousands of moonlighters, homemakers, retirees, financially independent journalists, and some newspaper and magazine writers who have made it a full-time career.

Why Companies Use Freelancers

Print and broadcast sports media hire freelancers to supplement their coverage of events or to cut their costs. It is often less expensive to buy material from freelancers than to pay salaries (plus benefits) to staff writers. Less established freelancers can be had for low rates because they may be underemployed; they also receive no benefits, which keeps overhead down. Freelancers are only needed on a short-term basis, for example, to cover a local game or investigate and write a one-of-a-kind story, which is also called "stringing." Some freelancers have only one story that an editor wants. If you aren't an insider (receiving assignments from an editor), your ideas will have to come from your creativity and/or the connections you may have in the business.

Who Are the Successful Freelance Writers?

John Rawlings, editor of *The Sporting News,* buys a lot of freelance work from established writers. He says "It's a tough market, but it's like anything else—you've got to be talented and you've got to know what the publication you're pitching a story to wants. Obviously, we're in a position where most of the freelance writers we use have a lot of experience and have demonstrated their skills, but we take flyers on young people all the time."

It's important for new freelancers to remember that editors can't tolerate writers who pitch ideas or stories that prove they haven't read the publication. According to Rawlings, "You'd be shocked at how many people pitch a story to us, and they obviously don't read our magazine. My time is no more valuable than anyone else's, but I do resent people who want to take up my time when they don't have any idea what my product is. Some writers call to push a swimming story or a soccer story. If you look at *The Sporting News* at all, you know that's not what we're about."

Tom Mangan says, "You can tell who the newcomers are; they're the ones with the ribs showing." Budding freelancers should remember these words while considering whether to enter the field. Those who think that freelancing is a glamorous, financially fulfilling career should be forewarned that it isn't, except to the following groups:

- A small number of sportswriters who have attained prominence in their sport or field and can therefore live comfortably on their full-time vocation, writing successful sports books or regularly taking on rewarding freelance assignments for major publications.

- Full-time newspaper sportswriters who regularly "moonlight" as part-time freelancers or stringers. Most freelance sportswriting for publications is by authorities in the field. For example, the reporter who works full time as the NBA beat writer for a major newspaper may be asked by a magazine such as *Street & Smith's Basketball* to provide specific insights or feature stories about a team or player, because she or he has access and better knowledge than "outsiders" or can get the story required.

  The corollary to this is that companies buying freelancers' work take the risk their hires will save the best or juiciest bits of information for the newspaper, magazine, or other publication that pays them a full-time salary. Those who practice such unethical behavior, obviously, have short freelance careers.

- Writers from other professions—teachers, salesmen, television producers, commentators, public relations (PR) people—who don't need to rely on freelancing as their sole (or most important) source of income.

Why Become a Freelance Sportswriter?

Freelance sportswriting can be an effective and enjoyable way to expose your writing talents and sports knowledge to the world, and maybe to make some considerable income. In authoring this book, we are freelancing, even though we each have independent careers. We can attest to the idea that freelancing can be a gratifying pursuit.

Howard Unger, a freelancer who has written for print and on-line publications in and around New York, says, "I prefer freelancing because it is, as its name infers, free. A writer is free to choose who to write for, when to write, and, most importantly, what to write about. A 500-word story can fetch me anywhere from $100 at a small e-zine to $1,000 at the large magazines."

In many earlier chapters, we have emphasized the importance of "clips" for various types of sportswriting. Clips, or copies of your published work, are an editor's or publisher's introduction to you. Freelancing is one way to get published so that you have clips to present to other potential employers. Now, the smart writers will ask, "How do I obtain clips before my first work is published?"

Well, the answer is that you take every opportunity to write that comes up. Volunteer to write for as many publications as possible, and gradually your clip file will grow as a proud display of your talent. Write for the following, whether or not they pay for your work:

- *Community newspapers.* Local dailies and weeklies welcome well-crafted articles and stories about local athletes and sports events. Even an opinionated Letter to the Editor can be an impressive clip.

- *High school and college newspapers.* Join as a staff member or volunteer to write about what you know or can learn.

- *High school and college broadcasting.* Volunteer to write, broadcast, or do camera work at sports events and record your efforts on video- or audiotape for future employers.

You may choose to create a website to show off your abilities or provide well-written input to other on-line media, so that new media employers can judge your capabilities.

Learning to Be a Freelancer

When you write as a freelancer, one good feature is that you are your own master. Also, few editors will decline your talents or stories because your education is deficient. You can sell well-written sports material no matter what your background. Having established that theory, let's look at reality.

Without a formal education (English, journalism, liberal arts, etc.) similar to those for all of the journalism professions discussed in earlier chapters, you may not have the knowledge or skill necessary to communicate effectively with readers. Therefore, few freelancers can expect to do well without standard journalism training. Howard Unger prepared for his journalism career by double-majoring in literature/rhetoric and political science at the State University of New York at Binghamton. The coauthors of this book are freelancers and majored in liberal arts and English. Both have freelanced for many publications—Kevin for *The Sporting News* and the *College Basketball Yearbook*, among others.

Checklist for Freelance Success

Sportswriters starting to freelance or those already earning income for their work can benefit from a well-ordered approach. To operate a successful writing business, you should practice all of the following steps as you prepare to write for publication.

- ☐ Have the right equipment for your tasks (a laptop, tape recorder, etc.).

- ☐ Establish an interesting idea, story line, or article.

- ☐ Target one or more publications for your article or book.

- ☐ Know your publication and its audience. Read back issues and obtain writer's guidelines.

- ☐ Identify the correct name and address of the editor who will be most interested in your query idea.

- ☐ Contact sports editors by phone, aggressively offering your services for hire.

- ☐ Determine a deadline you can meet. Don't agree to unrealistic deadlines.

- ☐ Extensively research the subject.

- ☐ Consider possible photos/illustrations/art work.

❑ Determine the scope and value of the job and the minimum pay you will accept.

❑ Estimate the expenses necessary (travel/phone/materials, etc.).

❑ Identify and communicate any contract stipulations you expect.

❑ Write a strong, informative query letter.

❑ Estimate the piece's word count or agree to the editor's specification(s).

❑ Be conscious of schedules of visiting sports teams, whose home-town newspapers may not be staffing an event.

❑ On agreeing to cover a game or story, verify the publicaton's filing process (i.e., computer parameters, deadline, and confirmation number).

❑ Set up a system to keep your accounts in order.

Where Ideas Come From

The key to freelancing success is finding interesting subjects that will grab an editor's attention. Young sports fans don't come across special stories about personalities such as Michael Jordan or Monica Seles that can be sold to the media. The common question of new writers is, "Where can I find ideas?" The answer is they're everywhere for a creative mind. Once you've settled on an interesting idea, research it and write the story. Edit it carefully and show it to another writer for input. Polish it and personally deliver it to a local newspaper or publication. Here are some suggestions for finding an idea you can develop into something special:

- Go to a ball game and report on something unusual either on or off the field (the team mascot, concession sales, ticket scalping, fan-related angles).

- Speak to an athlete about

  —rare happenings during a game

  —a human-interest story about a teammate or competitor

—injuries and their concerns about getting hurt or treatment of athletes by team doctors or trainers

—his or her favorite coach

—what sitting on the bench is like

—conversations in the huddle, during time-outs, on the mound, and so on

—how he or she is supported by family or friends

- See a sports movie. Write an interesting review about how it relates to local sports, or how "real" the acting and plot were.

- Write a feature on a local reporter.

- Cover local sports-related guest speakers at area banquets or civic functions.

- Research your library or Internet for

—anniversaries of historic Olympic contests or regional events, relating them to current local sports

—record-breaking feats that have stood the test of time

—what sports teams were great in your area twenty-five or fifty years ago (Are there stars around for you to interview?)

—"where are they now" features

- Interview someone who attended a historical sports happening, and write an account of his or her impressions.

- Read the papers for sports personalities with interesting off-the-field hobbies and contact them for details.

- Speculate on the future of a local sport, team, or athlete.

- Write a funny story on a particular facet of a game or sport.

- List the best and worst games, plays, uniforms, team logos, mascots, and so on.

- Write a day-in-the-life account of a player, coach, cheerleader, or referee.

- Survey a number of people on various subjects, such as "How to save/improve/support the local team."

Well, you get the idea about ideas. As a freelancer, don't worry about others stealing your idea; if you query an editor on one and then get to work writing it, there's little risk of theft. Ideas can be sold, but it's unusual. If you have an idea that could be a breakthrough story, talk to an editor. Some of the larger publications may show interest in a great story idea, offer a few hundred dollars for it and then let a staffer write it. But that's so unusual that you're better off writing the story and selling it yourself.

Writing on Spec or on Assignment

When editors become interested in a story or article proposed in a query from an unfamiliar freelancer, the response is usually, "Okay, develop it for us on spec (speculation)." That means they may like the idea, but don't know how well you'll develop it and don't want to commit themselves to it. But they *are* interested, which is reason for optimism.

Herman Holtz, a veteran freelancer and author of more than sixty books, says that "the major problem in writing freelance for periodicals and book publishers is doing it all on spec, as most do, at least when they are starting out. The trick, if there is one, is to graduate as soon as possible from working on spec."

The place to graduate to is working "on assignment," which means that the editor knows you are dependable and you'll deliver what he or she can publish, on deadline. Freelancers with such reputations can often skip the routine of query letters; calling or E-mailing editors with an idea instead. Editors frequently rely on trusted freelancers to the extent that they call the writer to place him or her on assignment with a story line they've already selected.

The next step up for a successful freelancer is to be put on contract by an editor. In this arrangement, employed by many of the sports magazines, a writer agrees on a rate per story or period of time. The writer researches and writes a prescribed number of reports or stories, receiving fees as he or she produces. This, of course, removes much of the risk from both parties and gives the freelancer something of a guarantee of steady work and income. The corresponding risk for the writer is that the connection can be broken if the editor changes jobs to work for a publication that doesn't accept freelancer material.

Many of the magazine editors we spoke to have a stable of free-lancers, some of whom write ten or twelve stories a year for a specific publication and others who write one or two. Often the latter group may be working on more than one assignment at a time. Jon Hendershott, associate editor for *Track and Field News*, says, "The basic requirement for writing for us is deep, insightful knowledge of the sport being written about and its athletes. Less than 10 percent of each issue is freelanced, with *T&F News* paying $150 for a short, one-page feature story."

"You need not be a newspaper beat writer or sports expert to come up with thoughtful articles," says Michael Perry, author of the *Handbook for Freelance Writing*. Perry, who has written hundreds of articles, but few involving sports, recently wrote an article about the truck drivers who transport the equipment and cargo for the Chicago Bears, for a trucking magazine called *Road King*. You just need to be creative.

Finding Markets

Freelance sportswriters who are interested in making serious income must consider which publications provide information on markets and what each market pays. The following publications discuss the marketplace or have a "Markets" section, which frequently includes sports markets:

- *Writer's Market* (annual)
- *Inklings: Inkspot's Newsletter for Writers on the Net* (www.inkspot.com/inklings)
- *New Writer's Magazine*
- *Writer's Digest* magazine
- *The Writer* magazine

Most of these resources address both magazine markets and book markets, providing publishers' requirements for various genres, including sports.

Most freelancers agree that the most valuable resource is the comprehensive *Writer's Market*, which is published each year. The current version has 1,114 pages, in which are detailed "4,200 places to sell what you write." Included are instructions on getting published and the business of writing, as well as the following market sections we recommend for sports journalists:

- Book publishers, including Canadian and International

- Book producers (companies that assemble books—and employ writers, editors, designers, and illustrators—for publishers)

- Consumer magazines, including over fifty pages of consumer sports magazines

- Trade, technical, and professional journals, including sports trade magazines

- Contests and awards (e.g., tennis writing)

- Resources (publications, organizations, websites, etc.)

There are still other ways to find a market for your article or book. Howard Unger is an experienced writer in print and on-line publications, including stories on the New York Mets' baseball team for the *Village Voice* newspaper. He says that he finds the markets that produce such assignments mostly by E-mail. Many freelancers use this method to communicate their ideas to editors with good success. We recommend that when starting out, the best way to send queries is via postal mail, with self-addressed envelopes (SASES) included, except for those magazines that *Writer's Market* specifies "E-mail queries welcome."

Penetrating the Magazine Markets

Freelancers market their work by first targeting the magazines most likely to have an interest in it. Research magazines in the annual *Writer's Market*. Write a strong, informative query letter to the attention of a specific editor whose name you can find at the front of the magazine. If you can't find anyone who sounds right, call the magazine to ask for the appropriate name.

Unless you write in the class of George Plimpton or Roy Blunt, Jr., you're not likely to market articles to the major sports magazines like *Sports Illustrated,* some of which buy very few freelance articles. But even the majors may be interested if you have special knowledge their staff writers can't learn and you can propose an idea, provide proof of your conclusions, and name sources who will go on the record.

There is, however, a ripe marketplace for knowledgeable sportswriters in sports magazines of all sizes and circulations. Chapter 6 explains that many such magazines carry mostly freelance articles, usually by the best in the business. *Writer's Market* lists approximately 200 magazines in its section on consumer sports, ranging alphabetically from *Bowhunter* magazine to *Wrestling,* for which freelance stories, articles, and photos are accepted. Each listing explains what it takes to get published, how much the magazine pays, tips on acceptable story lines, and details on who to contact. A sampling of sports publications indicates that most receive more than half of their material from freelance writers (up to 90 percent to 100 percent for some). Pay ranges from a low of $100 (for the smaller publications) to a high of $2,500 (*Skiing*). Other typically higher paying periodicals are *Runner's World,* with a maximum of $2,000, and *Field and Stream,* with $1,500.

Note that although most *Writer's Market* sports publications are listed under "Consumer Sports," it's wise to check other sections too, because some sports-oriented magazines are listed elsewhere. We found *Sports Illustrated for Kids* under "Consumer/Juvenile."

One of the larger sports magazine publishers, Century Publishing Co., told us that, like most of the sports magazines we researched, their stable of sports publications accept considerable freelance input, but doesn't accept unsolicited manuscripts. This publisher prints and distributes *Basketball Digest, Baseball Digest, Auto Racing Digest, Bowling Digest, Football Digest, Hockey Digest, Soccer Digest,* and *Home Gym and Fitness* magazines. They advise that "if you're interested in writing for one of our digests, send them a resume, some writing samples, and a brief description of what sort of articles you would be willing to write (i.e., college, NBA, previews, profiles, interviews, historical pieces, story ideas, or items about your local sports environment)."

Remember that publishing houses give advertised freelancing fees as estimates of what they may pay and are subject to negotiation. Rates vary with the experience and reputation of the writer, length of the piece, and of course the importance of the subject.

Contracting for Magazine Articles

Writing sports articles for magazines involves both a search for the right publication and contractual considerations. The following are some terms you should understand:

- *First serial rights.* When you sell an article to a magazine for first serial rights, which is what most magazines will require, the magazine has the right to be the first publication to publish it. Once they have, you have the rights to sell it anywhere else for what is then referred to as reprint rights or second serial rights.

- *All rights.* This means that you give the publication the right to do whatever they wish with the article (e.g., publish it many times or sell it to someone else).

- *Electronic rights.* The publication can publish your piece in electronic media. Writers should avoid giving up this right without recompense, because it could mean that the article will also be published on the Internet as often as the buyer wishes.

- *Work for hire.* Essentially, you have no rights concerning your work because you have been paid a salary to develop it, after which it becomes the property of the payer. This is not a good deal for a writer, unless the money is more important to you than your ability to claim the work as your own.

Where's the Money?

Magazine writer income varies tremendously. One of the biggest frustrations with freelance writing is the seemingly low financial return for the tremendous amount of time invested in a story.

Freelancer income is sporadic and low when you calculate all of your labor. Mark Kram explains, "I just spent six weeks developing a story on a part-time basis for $3,000. If I had done it on more of a full-time schedule—in three weeks—the $3,000 after taxes would net $2,200. For three weeks' work? That's ridiculous."

John Rawlings admits that fees "depend on a lot of things, but if we're planning a moderate-length feature, we might pay as little as $500 or as much as $3,000. It just depends on how much we want a particular writer and similar considerations."

Authoring Sports Books

In a book on freelancing, *Writing for Dollars,* author John McCollister advises sportswriters to concentrate on the minor sports rather than the four major ones. His theory is that with the minor sports "you have little or no competition." As an example, he refers to the late Jim Fixx of running fame. McCollister wrote that "Fixx discovered that a lot of people were fascinated with his favorite sport—running; yet even he was not able to predict the phenomenal success of his 1977 classic *The Complete Book of Running.*" After his book sold more than a million hardback copies, Fixx was hailed as the nation's expert in the field. Sales of his articles and columns increased over the next ten years.

Doug Looney, coauthor of *Under the Tarnished Dome,* a model for books on sports investigative reporting that tells the inside story of Notre Dame football, advises that if your book involves major sports celebrities and really takes off, it's possible to realize income on the order of $300,000 to $500,000. But that's very unusual, and it's more likely that writing a sports book will put you in the neighborhood of $50,000—and that's if it is really good. Some books and movies on sports subjects that are good entertainment for sports fans and educational for sports freelancers are:

- Campbell, J. *Hero with a Thousand Faces.* Princeton, NJ: Princeton University Press, 1972.

- ———. *Myths to Live By.* New York: Bantam Books, 1988.

- Coover, Robert. *The Universal Baseball Association, Inc., R. J. Henry Waugh, Prop.* New York: Random House, 1968.

- Gent, P. *North Dallas Forty*. New York: Morrow, 1973.

- Hemingway, E. "The Capital of the World." *The Complete Short Stories of Ernest Hemingway*. New York: Charles Scribner's Sons, 1987.

- Housman, A. E. "To An Athlete Dying Young." *The Collected Poems of A. E. Housman*. New York: Holt, Rinehart Winston, 1987.

- Jenkins, D. *Sports Inside Out: Game Face*. Fort Worth, TX: Texas Christian University Press, 1985.

- Kinsella, W. P. *Shoeless Joe*. Boston: Houghton Mifflin, 1982.

- London, J. *The Abysmal Brute*. New York: Century, 1913.

- London, J. *The Game*. New York: Grosset & Dunlap, 1905.

- Malamud, B. *The Natural*. New York: Avon, 1952.

- Novak, M. *The Joy of Sports*. Lanham, MD: Hamilton Press, 1988.

- Shaw, I. "The Eighty Yard Run." In Vanderwerken, D. and S. Wertz (eds.). *Sport Inside Out*. Fort Worth, TX: Texas Christian University Press, 1985.

- Speed, E. "The Coach Who Didn't Teach Civics." In Vanderwerken, D. and S. Wertz (eds.). *Sport Inside Out*. Fort Worth, TX: Texas Christian University Press, 1985.

- Thayer, E. L. *Casey at the Bat. Sports Poems*. New York: Dell, 1971.

- Wright, J. "Autumn Begins in Martins Ferry, Ohio." In *The Branch Will Not Break*. Middletown, CT: Wesleyan University Press, 1962.

Writer's Market is also one of the best references to research before you decide on a book subject and publisher. In its listing of subjects in which specific publishers are interested, it shows over 150 book publishers interested in books written on the subject of sports.

As with the information listed for periodicals, this book provides information on what each publisher is looking for from authors.

Books for Hire

Sometimes publishers write book contracts with trusted authors on a "for hire" basis. Usually writers are given no advance. Instead, they are paid a fixed fee, which they receive no matter how many copies are sold. Fees vary enormously, and can range from $2,000 to more than $25,000. This is a no-risk proposition for an author, but if the book sells very well, she or he does not share in royalties. Michael Perry explains, "I wrote *Handbook for Freelance Writing* as a 'book for hire.' My experience says that it's best to negotiate a royalty contract rather than a flat-fee contract if you have a choice and think the book will sell. The reality is that you may not be given the option."

We understand that most authors would counsel against a flat-fee contract, but from one standpoint they are safe in that if the book isn't a terrific bestseller, they've made their money with no risk. Conversely, with a royalty contract, if the book is a howling success, the money from royalties will continue to accrue to them with every copy sold.

There are two additional ways of getting your book published:

- *Outright purchase.* Similar to books for hire, the publisher may purchase a completed manuscript from you without preassigning the work.

- *Vanity press or self-publishing.* These are common terms for publishers who publish your book if you pay all expenses. Some authors make money if such books sell well, but our research indicates that you should try all other approaches before this one.

Newspaper Stringers

Freelancing sports articles for newspapers is usually referred to as "stringing," where a part-time reporter is assigned to attend and develop a game-day story about a local team competition.

"Stringer" is a term most often used at smaller papers, mostly because of the pay scale. It should be noted that some stringers with talent eventually become staff reporters.

Stringers may be students, fledgling writers, college newspaper reporters, and others who earn a modest fee for reporting on a part-time basis. Such work is generally low paid and comes under the heading of one-time rights or work for hire, explained earlier. Once the writer is paid for the piece, he or she has no continuing rights to it.

Most stringers work at other jobs and freelance at small newspapers for pocket money and minimal exposure. Typically, smaller newspapers pay $35 to $50 per story; mid-size papers, $75 to $150; and major market papers, $125 to over $200, depending on the length and importance of the story. At small-circulation papers like the *Gaston Gazette* (North Carolina), stringers should have a decent-paying day job. Mark Anderson, the sports editor, says: "We use stringers, and we pay $30 a story, which isn't much."

At larger papers, such part-time contributors are often referred to as freelancers and are usually veteran writers who are glad for the significant and usually regular additional income. Freelancers write about their respective areas of sports expertise for magazines, program publications, and so on, usually when they are not busy with writing assignments for their own papers.

Freelancing by the Hour

Earlier, we discussed freelancing by the hour or week, similar to part-time status. It's also referred to as "independent contracting." Generally speaking, if you work on an hourly, daily, or weekly basis and receive no benefits, you are an independent contractor.

In an unusual bit of candor about her income as a part-time sports reporter for the suburban New York Gannett newspapers, Jane Allison Havsy of Yonkers says, "Honestly, I have no clue what I make. I think it started around $10 an hour plus a night differential, and now it's up to $11.50 or so, but I'm not certain. I guess I never really concerned myself with stuff like that. I just do the work because it's fun and get paid afterward." Isn't that a great attitude for a young journalist?

Putting Out Feelers

Writing a Query Letter

Query letters should be only one page for articles and two pages at most for books. The query must be interesting—or if possible, fascinating. It's tempting to pick up the phone and call an editor, but don't. She or he gets hundreds of queries and may not appreciate your intrusion.

In your first paragraph, pitch your idea and then give a brief resume targeted to the piece and publication. Next, mention what types of articles you've had published and include clips of your best. If you don't have anything published, cite your background or expertise in the area your article involves.

Finally, explain how long you expect the piece to be and how soon you can deliver it.

Book Proposals

A book proposal is essentially an expanded query. After you've written your query letter and gotten a nibble from an editor, the next step is preparing the book proposal, in which the ideas and promises set forth in your query must be expanded, researched, and implemented.

Some experts tell us that you need only a dozen or so pages for it, others want dozens or more pages. Be sure to ask each acquisitions editor what he or she wants. The proposal should contain one or more sample chapters of the actual book; ideally the best you have. Most editors don't want to see the entire manuscript, and will let you know if you haven't included enough.

There are many texts available on the subject of book proposal development, such as *How to Write a Book Proposal* by Michael Larsen (Writer's Digest Books). The one we like best is computerized, *Get Paid to Write Your Book* by David R. Yale (Yale Info Inc., Bayside, NY). It comes on a floppy disk and provides thorough, step-by-step instructions on every facet of the process.

Herman Holtz markets his disk book *How to Write a Book Proposal* in the *Freelance Writer or Independent Consultant*. It also includes a sample proposal that was successful in winning a book contract.

The following outline includes all of the most common elements of a successful book proposal.

I. Introduction

II. Why This Book Is Needed

III. Who Will Buy This Book?

IV. Why This Book Is Unique

V. A Quick Overview

VI. The Competition

    A. Books in Print

    B. Forthcoming Books

    C. Our Conclusion About the Competition and the Potential Marketplace

VII. Advertising and Marketing Possibilities

VIII. Table of Contents

IX. The Outline

X. Chapter Summaries

XI. Resources Needed to Complete This Book

XII. Book Resource Team

XIII. About the Authors

XIV. Sample Chapter

Support for Freelancers

One of the drawbacks of freelancing is that you are unaffiliated, independent, and generally alone, without representation in various business matters such as contractual matters with publishers. The National Writers Union (NWU) can be of great assistance in these cases.

The NWU is the trade union for freelance writers of all genres. With 4,500 members, it advertises that it is "committed to improving the economic and working conditions of freelance writers through the collective strength of our members. We are a modern, innovative union offering grievance resolution, industry campaigns, contract advice, health and dental plans, member education, job banks, networking, social events, and much more."

Three popular websites provide forums for freelancers:

- One has been established by Creative Freelancers as a central connection point for professional writers and others (www.freelancers.com).

- Freelance magazine writers gather at a site called MAG-WRITE, which provides a friendly community of journalists with common interests and problems (magwrite@maelstrom.stjohns.edu).

- National Writer's monthly is an electronic marketing magazine for freelance writers and journalists (Writers@reporters.net).

Advice from Freelancers

Michael Perry advises writers, "Allow yourself extra time to allow your manuscript to 'ripen' somewhat before putting it to bed and mailing it to the publisher."

Newcomers to this business will benefit from the uncompromising candor of Howard Unger, who speaks of his profession in these terms: "Journalism breeds apathy and cynicism. Don't fall prey to these traits at a relatively young age, where youthful idealism should be your trademark. Choosing a field with little respect among middle America, low pay, and long hours is a very hard choice. Journalism, however, cleanses the soul and informs the public. Imagine people reading what you've written, trusting you, arguing with you, listening to you, and believing you. And you? You're forty miles away, sleeping, and don't even remember that article you wrote four days ago."

"There's nothing more important than knocking on doors," says John Rawlings. "You have to be persistent, pleasant, and know when you're making yourself a pain in the butt. You can't take anything personally. If someone is willing to critique your work, never turn that down; learn from it. It also helps if you can find someone who has been in the business a little while, who has some contacts, who can open a door for you."

Most freelance writers, we should point out, aren't instantly successful in this tough business. It's very important, however, to avoid becoming disillusioned by editors' rejections. The best, including all of the writers we've written about, have had many rejections. They've put them aside and moved on to the next story idea and query. They were often successful and their writing style and marketability improved with each submission. Remember, it takes only one "hit" to launch a career.

Bibliography

Aethlon, Journal of Sports Literature. Johnson City, TN: East Tennessee State University Press, published quarterly.

The Associated Press Stylebook and Libel Manual. Reading, MA: Addison-Wesley, 1998.

Bard, Mitchell. "Bob Woodward Gets to the Bottom of Things." *Writer's Digest* (August 1996): 33–35.

Bettmann, Otto L. *The Delights of Reading: Quotes, Notes, and Anecdotes.* Lincoln, MA: David Godine, 1992.

Brohaugh, William. *Write Tight: How to Keep Your Prose Sharp, Focused, and Concise.* Cincinnati, OH: Writer's Digest Books, 1993.

Brooks, Christine M. *Sports Marketing: Competitive Business Strategies for Sport.* New York: Prentice Hall, 1994.

Coover, Robert. *The Universal Baseball Association, Inc., J. Henry Waugh, Prop.* New York: Random House, 1968.

Copy Editor Newsletter. Published quarterly.

Cosida Directory, 1997–1998. Published by the College Sports Information Directors of America.

Cronkite, Walter. *A Reporter's Life.* New York: Alfred Knopf, 1996.

Fixx, James F. *The Complete Book of Running.* New York: Random House, 1977.

Fredette, Jean M., ed. *Writer's Digest Handbook of Magazine Article Writing.* Cincinnati, OH: Writer's Digest Books, 1988.

Gach, Gary. *Writers.Net: Every Writer's Essential Guide to Online Resources and Opportunities.* Rocklin, CA: Prima, 1997.

Gent, Peter. *North Dallas Forty.* New York: William Morrow, 1973.

Green, Marianne Ehrlich. *Internship Success.* Lincolnwood, IL: VGM Careers (NTC/Contemporary), 1997.

Halberstam, David. *The Breaks of the Game.* New York: Alfred Knopf, 1981.

Halberstam, David. *Summer of '49.* New York: William Morrow, 1989.

Helitzer, Melvin. *The Dream Job: $port$ Publicity, Promotion and Public Relations,* 2nd ed. Athens, OH: University Sports, 1996.

Holtz, Herman. "How to Write a Book Proposal" (disk). In *Freelancer Writer or Independent Consultant.* E-mail address: holtz@paltech.com.

Investigative Reporters and Editors, Inc. *The Reporter's Handbook: An Investigator's Guide to Documents and Techniques.* New York: St. Martin's Press, 1983.

Jenkins, D. *Sport Inside Out: Game Face.* Fort Worth, TX: Texas Christian University Press, 1985.

The Journalist's Road to Success. Princeton, NJ: Dow Jones Newspaper Fund, 1996.

Kinsella, W. P. *Shoeless Joe.* Boston: Houghton Mifflin, 1982.

Larsen, Michael. *How to Write a Book Proposal.* Cincinnati, OH: Writer's Digest Books, 1985.

McCollister, John. *Writing for Dollars.* Middle Village, NY: Jonathan David Publishers, Inc., 1995.

Making Money Writing. Cincinnati, OH: Writer's Digest Books, 1997.

Malamud, B. *The Natural.* New York: Avon, 1952.

Neft, David C., Richard M. Cohen, and Rick Korch. *The Football Encyclopedia: The Complete History of Professional NFL Football from 1892 to the Present*. New York: St. Martin's Press, 1991.

Novak, Michael. *The Joy of Sports: End Zones, Bases, Baskets, Balls, and the Consecration of the American Spirit*. New York: Basic Books, 1976.

Outing, Steve. "How Much Should You Pay Your New Media Staff?" *Editor & Publisher* (January 1998).

Perry, Michael. *Handbook of Freelance Writing*. Lincolnwood, IL: NTC/Contemporary, 1997.

Price, Jonathan and Lisa Price. "Web Writing." *Writer's Digest* (October 1997): 45–46.

Stone, Vernon. *Let's Talk Pay in Television and Radio News*. Chicago: Bonus Books, 1998.

Swan, Jennifer, ed. *Sports Style Guide and Reference Manual: The Complete Reference for Sports Editors, Writers, and Broadcasters*. Chicago: Triumph Books, 1996.

Thayer, Ernest Lawrence. *Casey at the Bat*. New York: Dell, 1971.

Writer's Digest. *Writer's Market*. Cincinnati, OH: Writer's Digest Books, published annually.

Yaeger, Don, and Douglas S. Looney. *Under the Tarnished Dome: How Notre Dame Betrayed Its Ideals for Football Glory*. New York: Simon & Schuster, 1993.

Yale, David R. *Get Paid to Write Your Book*. Bayside, NY: Yale Information Inc., 1996.

Appendix

Minority Internships and Other Programs

American Society of Newspaper Editors

Each year the ASNE sponsors regional job fairs throughout the country to help minority college students find internships and entry-level jobs. Contact the ASNE for more information about job fairs in Los Angeles, Chicago, Washington, New York, and other major metropolitan areas.

Minority Journalists Association

The Minority Journalists Association holds conferences in various cities throughout the country each year. Contact these organizations for more information:

Asian American Journalists Association
Contact: 415/346-2051

National Association of Black Journalists
Contact: 301/405-8500

National Association of Hispanic Journalists
Contact: 202/662-7145

Native American Journalists Association
Contact: 612/874-8833

The Associated Press

The Associated Press (AP) operates news bureaus throughout the world and offers internships in cities across the United States. The AP minority intern program is a thirteen-week training program for African-American, Hispanic, Asian, and Native American students currently enrolled in four-year colleges and universities. Candidates must be enrolled as full-time juniors, seniors, or graduate students and must take a test at a site designated by the Associated Press. For more information, contact:

Jack Stokes
The Associated Press
50 Rockefeller Plaza
New York, NY 10020

Dow Jones Newspaper Fund

Each summer the Dow Jones Newspaper Fund selects seventy-two college juniors, seniors, and graduate students to work at daily newspapers throughout the country as copy editors. The students undergo two weeks of editing training and then they are assigned to various newspapers. For more information about this program, write to:

The Dow Jones Newspaper Fund
P.O. Box 300
Princeton, NJ 08543
800/DOWFUND

IRE Minority Conference Scholarships

Investigative Reporters and Editors (IRE) Minority Conference Scholarships are for minority journalists who want to attend IRE's annual conference and computer-assisted reporting conference. For questions concerning applications and other information, write to:

IRE
100 Neff Hall
School of Journalism
University of Missouri
Columbia, MO 65211

National Association of Black Journalists

The National Association of Black Journalists (NABJ) offers internships for minority sophomores and juniors majoring in journalism or planning a journalism career. For more information, contact:

NABJ
Internship Coordinator
3100 Taliaferro Hall
University of Maryland
College Park, MD 20742-7717

Poynter Institute

The Poynter Institute offers a number of programs for college students, primarily in graphics and ethics. For information on these and other programs offered, contact:

The Poynter Institute
801 Third Street South
St. Petersburg, FL 33701

Index